PTSD
LIVING COMFORTABLY NUMB

KEVIN J MERVIN

Published by
Eleusinian Press Ltd
www.eleusinianpress.co.uk

First Edition published 2016
© remains with the author

Printed and bound in Great Britain
by Copytech (UK) Ltd

A catalogue record for this book is available from
The British Library

ISBN 978-1-909494-10-7

This book is dedicated to all that have fought in conflicts only to return home and had their lives turned upside down, either through injury or combat stress related trauma. And to those who bravely paid the ultimate price for the sake of freedom and liberty, which we all take for granted.

Freedom is for those that have served and fought.
For those who inherit should earn it..

CONTENTS

ACKNOWLEDGMENTS

Not only the TA but all soldiers, sailors, marines and airmen, regular and reserve alike, continue to fight conflicts around the globe on their government's behalf. They endure experiences and have to deal with the many mixed emotions from seeing atrocities of war that civilians can never possibly begin to understand. Amongst those that have fought, our entire outlook on life has changed because of war. For some it is too much to handle, regrettably ending in suicide.

TA units pride themselves being available 24/7 throughout all campaigns; organising weekend activities for wives and families, giving them the chance to meet others living with the same anxieties and fears, and answering the many questions raised by families and loved ones during tours. I thank these TA units, and families of TA soldiers called-out, for supporting their loved ones in conflicts around the globe and sending bluey's and parcels. A great boost to any soldier's morale.

Having to struggle with my own mental state of mind I wish to thank the following that have unknowingly helped my return to almost complete sanity: Steve Coogan – Alan Partridge, Jeremy Clarkson and the Top Gear team; Mike Mendoza and TalkSport Radio; Red Dwarf; The Goons show; Pink Floyd and David Tennant.

A strange concoction to thank, I know, yet all have been extremely beneficial towards my personal recovery. Without re-runs on television, DVD and CDs or the dulcet tones of David Tennant in my head weirdly returning my sanity to calmer waters, I would still be struggling with demons and silent screams running riot within my subconscious mind.

PREFACE

Since its birth in 1908 the TA (Territorial Army) and other arms of our reserve forces have regularly been called upon to fight in operations including the Falklands, Bosnia, Iraq and Afghanistan. Not since the Suez crises of 1956 has there been such a large number of TA soldiers mobilised to fight alongside their regular counterpart in any single conflict. TA reserve forces, making up a quarter of the regular army strength, are relied upon by the government not only to fight wars, but also quash civil unrest, maintain homeland defence and assist the emergency services during national and international disasters.

When the conflict ends men and women of our reserve forces return home, discretely dipping below the radar of story-hungry journalists, hoping to return to their civilian lives without fuss or question. Unfortunately fuss, questions and the horror of war refuses to go away; be it due to curious civilians or a soldier's subconscience. Fuelled by trials and tribulations of war, demons simmer in the back of vulnerable and damaged minds. These demons are eager to relinquish a fresh pain of pent-up anger, frustration, anxiety, fear, rejection and hopelessness. Unnoticed by the public, reserve soldiers returning to civvy street become trapped in a storm brewing within their heads, facing an impossible quest for sanity.

Kevin continues his quest – a personal journey embarked upon an unshakeable and somewhat addictive path towards self-destruction, thwarted by a single wish. A wish to quantum leap back to when he disembarked that aeroplane at Birmingham airport 26th April 2003 and start all over again. Only this time put right the bad decisions he made that cost him his home, marriage and family. Decisions, as he explains, made for him by the voices in his head. Voices created not by fighting a bloody war, but being shamelessly dismissed by a troubled government, hated by a biased media and despised by a hostile public for doing so.

He is almost back in control of his life, and on the surface appears normal and relaxed. Underneath his calm exterior, however, the storm in his head continues to rage, reminding him of his true mental state that will taunt him for the rest of his life – living comfortably numb.

INTRODUCTION

When Kevin returned home from Iraq in 2003, he was leaping out of the frying pan into the fire. From the hell of war he re-entered civilian life at its worst. As a casualty evacuated to the UK he discovered his civilian boss had sacked him for being called-out for war and his wife, Helen, was pregnant. Faced with unemployment and little means of supporting his family, Kevin was confident that once recovered from his injury he sustained in Iraq he would soon find work and return to a normal life. But that wasn't to be. Potential employers wouldn't hire him because he was in the TA and those that opposed the invasion renounced him from society because of his involvement in the war, even calling him a murderer and spitting in his face.

Finding full-time employment became an impossible and frustrating task, so he went cap-in-hand to the local job centre for advice and to claim unemployment benefit. He was wasting his time. When mobilised Kevin automatically became a regular soldier for the duration of his tour, and therefore, by default, in full-time employment. After demobilisation he once again became a TA soldier and unbeknown to him, due to a loophole within employment law, made himself intentionally unemployed. The civil servant at the local unemployment benefit office seemingly took great joy in telling him this, rubbing salt into the wound by adding he was not entitled to any social security benefits.

Kevin felt as if he was backed into a corner with nowhere to go. He couldn't find work because no one would hire a TA soldier in fear of a further compulsory call-out, he didn't qualify for unemployment benefit and even his local Member of Parliament turned a cold shoulder when he asked for help. The only remaining prospect was to use his HGV driving licence, ironically earned in the TA, and sign up to various driving agencies.

Unfortunately driving for an agency is never a guaranteed income, so Kevin faced a dilemma: driving for a living would mean having to leave the TA due to the irregular working hours offered, which included weekends. Reluctantly he had no alternative but to leave the TA and take up the offer. But it didn't last. Kevin soon fell victim to the typical driving agency empty promises and work quickly dried up.

Feeling his own country turning against him, Kevin became increasingly paranoid. He mistrusted and hated everyone, thanks to constant anti-war reports television, radio and the print media fed an unsuspecting public about the conflict. Because of his paranoia Kevin begun to suffer terrible flashbacks of the conflict, appearing without warning, triggered by an odour, sound or vision, thrusting his mind back to Iraq. On one occasion, convinced he was back in the war driving under tactical conditions, he switched off all the lights on his articulated lorry, almost ending in a catastrophic pile-up.

Paranoia spread through Kevin's mind like a ferocious cancer; even his wife Helen came under suspicion of having an affair whilst he fought in Iraq, and that her unborn child wasn't his. Returning to a country that hated him, unemployed and not able to find work, Kevin thought his life couldn't get any worse, but it did. Desperate to keep his family together he would try anything. Without thinking of the consequence he sold his car and other valuable possessions to quickly raise desperately needed cash and pay for household bills, a mortgage and even food.

The money raised, however, was nowhere near enough to clear his debts, now spiralling out of control, so he had to sell the family home before a repossession order fell on the doormat. His marriage simply couldn't take any more knock-backs and Helen filed for divorce. He had to accept the loss of his marital home, wife and family, only to end up jobless, homeless and living with the demons screaming in his head. On top of everything else he also lost his father whom sadly died after a long illness.

A MOTHER'S WAR

(WRITTEN BY JUDITH JACQUES)

There were nobody less surprised than me when my eldest son, Kevin, was called-up to go to Iraq. I had a gnawing feeling the day he joined the Territorial Army in 1995 that the fateful day would eventually come, even though it was to be almost eight years later. But as far as I was concerned it was far too soon for me.

It was a lovely day for the time of year and I was going about my normal business in the house. The telephone rang and before I answered it that familiar foreboding swept over me. Call it a mother's intuition. He had teased me so many times about going away to fight, and my reply, as always, was I wouldn't allow it and would write to his colonel excusing him from all dangerous activities. It was an on-going joke, but this time it was for real.

"It's me," he said quietly on the telephone.

The way he said those few words convinced me that it wasn't good news. He wasn't his usual jovial self, he sounded far too serious for the Kevin I knew.

"You know what I'm going to say, don't you?" he continued.

I said nothing, I felt numb and waited for him to carry on.

"It's hit the fan, Mum, I've been called up for Iraq. Our unit has to be at Chilwell on the 28th February, so can you give me a lift? Oh, and I'll drive if you want."

That last cheery adage to his sentence was the Kevin I knew. He liked my car and was always badgering me to sell it to him. I knew he had added that piece of joviality to try and lift the conversation, which actually made me feel worse. Even with the difficulty of making that phone call, he was still thinking of my feelings. I can't remember much more of the conversation; only my usual habit of 'lecturing' as he called it, which he took on board with good heart, but we both knew the underlying seriousness. The call ended and I sat on the sofa, phone still in my hand, trying to make sense of what I had just heard. I have no idea for how long I sat there, but the doorbell made me jump and brought me back to earth.

Oh no, I thought, I don't want visitors now. I want to be alone to think about this and figure out how to deal with it. It was the postman. Without saying anything, or even acknowledging his presence, I hastily signed for a parcel, closed the door and threw it in a corner somewhere. I didn't have time for such unimportant things. I wandered into the kitchen to make myself a coffee, I needed the caffeine and a cigarette to calm down. I was getting agitated with every minor little thing: I didn't want the parcel although I knew it was something I had been waiting for, the kettle was taking far too long to boil and why was there a crack in my favourite mug?

Coffee made, cigarettes and lighter in my pocket, I went out into the garden to sit and contemplate Kevin's imminent war. After numerous mugs of coffee, half a packet of cigarettes and a bucketful of tears mixed with a cartload of anger, I kidded myself I could handle it.

The dreadful day to take Kevin to Chilwell came around far too quickly. I refused to watch the television news programmes or listen to the radio because, as far as I was concerned, Iraq didn't exist, and therefore Kevin couldn't go. I hadn't slept properly since he telephoned with the bad news so I was up very early that morning, if only to give my thoughts a chance to reorganise themselves and take stock of the situation – just like a soldier would do before battle. 'Switch on', Kevin would say.

I was proud of the fact I had managed, somehow, to keep the mixed emotions brewing inside under relative control over the past few weeks and concentrate on the rest of my family. After all I still had two other sons in my life that also needed me on tap. Sons always do, and I had to be there for them too.

I looked at the clock and it was almost 10am. Time I was heading for Kevin's house. I quickly pushed some pictures of his grandparents into my bag that I had been promising him for months – I had a feeling he would need them now – and tried to make the half-hour journey last forever. My mind wouldn't behave itself and kept wandering to seek where I found the strength to cope over the past three long weeks. As soon as I turned into his road and saw his house only a few meters away, that inner strength returned and I felt lifted.

"Thank you, Mum," I said out loud looking at the sky through the sunroof. My mother had been dead for thirty-four years, but I still missed her a lot and needed her more than ever now.

I stopped outside Kevin's house and sat there for a while thinking about my parents. In the past I have watched war documentaries and looked upon them as nothing more than history lessons. But now I had a completely new perspective from a personal point of view. I had a better understanding of how my mum felt when Dad was mobilised in 1940, how my grandma felt about her son going to war, and my great grandma felt when my grandad went to war in 1914. It has been the same since the beginning of time, and what makes me so angry is that none of it needed to happen. But I had no time to dwell on that, it was now my son's time to go to war.

I stayed lighthearted on the journey, until it came to saying goodbye, somehow managing to hold back the tears until I drove outside the camp. I lost all concept of time and cannot tell you how long it was before I stopped the car to allow my mind to wander again. I lit a cigarette and opened the window for some fresh air to help clear my head. My thoughts drifted back to the day Kevin was born. A hot summer's day, nearly thirty-seven years ago, in the local maternity hospital. I looked down at his wrinkly pink face, with the biggest mouth I had ever seen on a newborn; yelling so loud he could be heard at the other end of the corridor outside the wards. I fell totally in love with this tiny bundle of joy and promised to keep him safe throughout his life.

Little did I know, in my immature state of mind as a new mother, that it was a promise I couldn't possibly keep once he reached adulthood. I now know only too well that it was simply a matter of time before he had to choose his own path and learn through making his own mistakes. All I could do then was be there for him, no matter how many miles lay between us. And right now was yet another of those frustrating times. Grim as it was I just had to follow my female ancestors and grin and bear it.

In the ensuing months my television was hardly switched off; I was constantly switching channels between the English and American news trying to glean something positive. I wrote regularly to Kevin, but understood when I didn't receive as many replies as I would have liked. I tried my hardest to continue normal family life, but it was a struggle and I only allowed myself to dwell on thoughts of the danger my son was involved with when I was alone.

His army trade was that of a recovery mechanic, and before he left he told me that on no account would he be in any danger. I believed him, then realised soon after I dropped him off at Chilwell that army recovery mechanics in war operations recover tanks and other vehicles that have either broken down in enemy territory or damaged due to being hit by enemy fire.

CHAPTER 1

TICKET TO BLIGHTY

I was suddenly woken by a loud, ear-piecing scream coming from the young Iraqi child a few beds up from mine. At first I thought I was dreaming, but soon realised I wasn't when the chaos of the ward came into focus. Doctors and nurses raced to his aid, trying their best to administer yet more pain-relieving drugs and calm him down. His injuries were so severe chances of survival were at first doubted, but thankfully it looked like he would pull through and make a complete recovery.

The bandages around his head were constantly soaked in blood, even though his wounds were treated time and time again. None of us liked the idea of any child being in so much pain, and it may seem strange but we all wanted to suffer the pain for him. He simply didn't deserve it. On many occasions we would try to cheer him up by acting a fool at the foot of his bed – pulling faces and pretending to hurt each other – not unlike The Three Stooges.

We managed to raise a few grins and giggles from the boy, but obviously he struggled to understand what we were doing. We even made balloons out of latex surgical gloves and drew silly faces on them. Occasionally he'd raise a smile, which was a priceless sight – and not just for us and the hospital staff, but more importantly his parents and older brother.

Everyone in my ward felt guilty for the boy's injuries. In a way we felt at fault for his wound. When the conflict ended countless civilians continued to die, caught in the crossfire between fighting Islamic tribes, caring not a jot about whom or how many were killed during their pitched battles over supremacy of land – Muslim or otherwise. One of the thousands of casualties happened to be this five-year-old boy.

Thankfully he was rushed to our tented field hospital in the nick of time for treatment.

Many in my ward had a whip-round and managed to collect $53.00 for the boy's parents, which was the equivalent of handing over almost six-months wages. At first the boy's father wouldn't accept it. Pride I expect. So we tried to explain – using clumsy sign language and loud, slowly spoken English – that he must take it, if not for the boy's recovery. Thankfully he understood our concerns and eventually accepted it.

It soon became apparent I was facing a further overnight stay. I checked my watch – it was close to 1030hrs local time, and by 1600hrs I had my own concerns as to when I was to be discharged. I'd run out of cigarettes and could only stretch one small bar of 'red cross' soap so far. The other patients in my ward – or inmates as we called ourselves – already had two visits from doctors and surgeons throughout the day, but I was totally ignored. And all I'd done was break my thumb.

A fellow patient offered me a cigarette, so we made our way outside to the smoking area whilst a nurse searched for a doctor to ask about my discharge. Once outside we headed towards the port-a-loo cabins some 50 metres away. Next to the toilets was our smoking area, which was nothing more than a few Euro pallets piled on top of one another to make a crude bench, with a couple of steel dustbins placed next to them.

As we puffed away on our cigarettes a few doctors and surgeons joined us for a fag break, and not just army personnel. Navy and airforce medical staff from our tri-service field hospital, which is how the British armed forces operate in the 21st Century, also joined us for a quick smoke. I noticed some Iraqi PW (Prisoner of War) amputee patients escorted by a nurse and two armed squaddies so the PW's could use the toilets, or hobble around on crutches for a bit of exercise. Their horrific injuries caused by either being unfortunate to face British soldiers in the heat of battle or by stepping on their own landmines. Some were even beaten and shot by their own officers for simply refusing to fight.

We finished our cigarettes and made our way back to the ward where the duty corporal nurse bore bad news: I was to stay for at least a further two days. I couldn't believe it. As far as I was concerned I was ready to return to my battlegroup. More importantly I had no means of fetching clean clothes or extra kit from my unit, not unless I risked sneaking out without telling anyone. In a way that would mean going AWOL (Absent Without Leave).

But every cloud has a silver lining. The SAT (satellite) phones in the hospital supplied by the army welfare department for patients to telephone loved ones back home never seemed to have any queues, which was a particular problem elsewhere throughout the entire brigade. I had four unused 20-minute phone cards (I never had the chance to use them before my unexpected arrival) so I telephoned my wife that evening to explain why I was in hospital and put her mind at rest. I think she was pleased to hear I was out of the war, and at least knew I was alive and in one piece. Well, almost.

Now on my third day as a hospital patient I was becoming quite established amongst fellow casualties, even allowed to join their escape committee. Stupid idea I know, but we had to think of things to do otherwise we'd have gone mad with boredom. We also planned runs to the EFI (Expeditionary Forces Institute) shop, selling mainly crisps, coke, toilet roll and cigarettes from a rigid ISO container. But there was one small problem. The shop was beyond the perimeter of the hospital and therefore out of bounds to patients. If caught we weren't exactly shot at dawn for desertion; we just had to hand over some of our bounty to the nurses. And thanks to the EFI runs I had a decent wash and shave kit, shower gel, deodorant, and some cigarettes.

By the end of my third day some of the inmates from my ward had recovered enough to be discharged and either return to their battlegroups or back to Blighty for further treatment. A US marine, who had been nominated for a Purple Heart because of his dreadful battlefield injury inflicted by Saddam's ultimate terror weapon – a bite from a camel spider – and a sergeant from the LI (Light Infantry) with a leg in plaster, were first to go.

As soon as one squaddie was discharged, however, another quickly replaced the vacant bed. On this particular occasion an attractive blonde young lady of about twenty-years-old. Through no fault of her own she had us wrapped around her little finger. Well, what do you expect from a bunch of red-blooded squaddies. A scorpion stung the poor girl on her hand, causing it to swell and her temperature to dramatically rise. Thankfully she made a full recovery within a few days. Selfish thought, I know, but we couldn't help wish that her injuries were a bit worse than a scorpion sting, just so she could stay a little longer and make our stay more colourful.

I returned from another visit to the smokers' corner only to find I had visitors from my recovery unit waiting for me: Phil, SSgt (Staff Sergeant) from our CRARRV (Challenger Armoured Recovery & Repair Vehicle); QMS-Green (Quartermaster);

Smudge, our VM (Vehicle Mechanic) reservist, and Stuart, my L/Cpl (Lance Corporal) crewman. They also brought with them my kit, which at first confused me as to why.

"You missed the doctor, Kev," Phil said.

"You're going home, you lucky bastard," Stuart quickly added.

At first his comment didn't register, so Q-Green explained. "We spoke to the surgeon whilst you were having a fag. He said you'd be useless to us with your type of injury so you're going home, tomorrow, leaving at 0830hrs by helicopter for Kuwait, and then a plane home."

"We've booked in your bergen, webbing and rifle at reception. It's now in a container ready for you to collect when you leave," added Phil.

"So this is goodbye, then. Not the way I planned it but – " I didn't know what else to say, apart from shake their hands and wish them all the best. Well, try to with a bloody plastercast on my wrist. "Send my regards to ma'am, won't you?" I asked Phil.

"Trust you to go home early," joked Stuart.

"Hopefully I'll see you again on some TA weekend," I replied. Stuart was in the same battalion as me. "And as for the rest of you – " again, I didn't know what else to say.

"I know," Phil quickly said, somehow understanding my mixed emotions.

I shook his hand again – awkwardly – before they walked out of the ward, and my life for the last time.

"You lucky bastard, Kev," a voice bellowed from my left. It was Trog, a nickname given to drivers from the RLC (Royal Logistics Corps). He'd fallen off the roof of his 4-ton Bedford truck whilst covering it with a cam-net, only to shatter two of his vertebrae.

"I can't believe it. I thought I'd end up doing GD's or something similar. Never expected to be sent home."

Trog sighed. "But what use would you be? You can't use your rifle, write anything down cos' you're right handed, or even wipe the CO's arse."

He was right; I'd be useless. And should the war have sparked up again I couldn't even don my respirator, especially within the nine-seconds our IA (Immediate Action) drill expected us to do before any chemical agent took effect.

The following morning I was once again woken by a commotion a few beds up from me – it was the little boy. His ear-piercing screams throughout the night were becoming a common sound and we'd grown accustomed to them, if it's ever possible to grow accustomed to a child suffering excruciating pain. On this occasion, however, there was nothing the doctors could do. He suddenly stopped thrashing about, only to fall still and silent – he was dead.

I couldn't wait to be discharged. It's bad enough when soldiers die, but an innocent child so young? I simply couldn't bear it. I wanted out of this hospital. A few hours later a young medic arrived to take me to a waiting helicopter charted for the RAF casevac (casualty evacuation) station at Kuwait City airport. I said my goodbyes to the other patients and thanked the staff for looking after me. There were sad faces all around, but of course they were not for me, it was obvious for whom.

One unnerving helicopter ride later I was sitting in another tented field hospital on the boundary of Kuwait City airport waiting for an aeroplane to take me home. The hospital was full of casualties – regular and TA soldiers alike – hanging around to be either sent home or further treatment in Germany and the UK. Some of the injuries were horrific, putting my broken thumb to shame. Young soldiers not much older than their early twenties had parts of their bodies missing, limbs shot to splinters and head wounds weeping blood through bandages.

Others not so lucky lay motionless on stretchers, seemingly kept alive by bleeping machines and saline drips. The smell of burnt flesh crept along the hot tented corridors from casualties that had fallen victim to exploding shells and mortar rounds. One poor lad wheeled past on a stretcher was covered in blood. His face, neck and shoulders chard by horrific burns. This is the reality of what modern weapons can do to flesh and bone when young lads are sent to fight a war, supposedly in the name of liberty, but most definitely on someone else's political behalf. This was the reality of war most definitely kept away from civilian eyes back home.

A Royal Air Force VC10 aeroplane converted to take battlefield casualties waited on the tarmac ready to take us to RAF Akrotiri, Cyprus. It was when we boarded the aeroplane I discovered casualties of war with very different injuries. Unable to physically see them, these casualties suffered from what was once known as shellshock. A more recent acronym would be combat stress or PTSD (Post Traumatic Stress Disorder).

In the First World War such casualties were found wandering around the battlefield unaware of their symptoms, blissfully walking aimlessly into German machine guns or back to their own trenches. Those wandering towards their own lines were often treated as cowards. Regrettably many were charged with cowardice and condemned to death by firing squad. Thankfully civilisation has since learnt the symptoms of shellshock and can treat it, or attempt to. It may take many, many years, if not decades of psychiatric treatment.

During our flight to Cyprus I sat next to a young Lieutenant, not much older than his early twenties. We started to chat about anything and everything, and he seemed okay at first. But when the inevitable happened and we begun to talk about the conflict I noticed he kept repeating his sentences over and over again. I felt increasingly uncomfortable with this and was relieved when he suddenly changed the subject by asking if I wanted a cup of coffee. Before I could answer him he jumped out of his seat and quickly returned with two coffees. He settled down and sweetened his drink with sachets of sugar; I noticed he emptied at least half-a-dozen into his small plastic cup.

"Like your coffee sweet?" I said half jokingly.

He stared at his cup for a few unnerving minutes, passed it to me, then jumped out of his seat only to return with two more coffees.

"Want a coffee? I'm having one," he asked, holding two cups.

"You already have one, sir, look." I pointed at his other cup sitting on my table.

Totally ignoring me he sat down placing his fresh cup of coffee on his tilt-over table and stared at it again before emptying more sachets of sugar into it.

He took a sip. "Oh, this is too sweet."

A nurse sitting further down the plane noticed the Lieutenant's unusual behaviour and thankfully intervened. "Why don't you come with me, sir, and I'll get you a fresh one."

"Yes, good idea, nurse. Do you want one, corporal?" he asked again, rising from his seat.

Before I could answer the nurse took away our unwanted coffees and folded the table before escorting the lieutenant to the rear of the aeroplane. That was the last I saw of him. Five minutes later the nurse returned to explain why he was acting out of character.

He was an Infantry Officer and whilst in Basrah witnessed some Iraqi civilians, including women and children, blown to pieces in front of him with small arms fire, RPG's (Rocket Propelled Grenades) and mortars by retreating Fedayeen militiamen. The civilians were deliberately fired upon by militia to slow down the Lieutenant's advancing section and cause as much confusion as possible whilst they made their escape. The quick thinking Lieutenant realised what was happening and ordered his men to clear a safe path by drawing enemy fire away from the fleeing civilians; at the same time as an advance to quash and win the firefight as quickly as possible, saving as many civilian lives as possible. Unfortunately some died in the crossfire.

He'd witnessed blood and guts before this incident, but on this particular occasion it was too much for him to handle, convincing himself he was to blame for the civilian deaths. Of course he wasn't to blame, and everyone knew this, but as far as he was concerned he was at fault. His behaviour became erratic and impulsive, which could have easily put himself and his platoon in danger on any future engagements.

The Lieutenant's symptoms were immediately recognised and he was quickly casualty evacuated to the field hospital in Shaibah. The conclusion was that he was unfit for duty and required immediate treatment in Germany. One casualty, putting aside the guys with physical injuries, I will never forget.

Landing at Akrotiri we were split into two groups – one boarding a flight to Germany whilst the rest of us boarded a converted civilian Boeing 757 to Birmingham International Airport. There wasn't even time to sneak in a quick cigarette. As soon as the plane came to a halt we were ushered to our next awaiting flight. The stretcher cases were first to disembark, quickly followed by the walking wounded. When I say walking, it was more of a hop, stagger and crawl descending the portable steps.

One casualty with both eyes bandaged couldn't see anything. In true squaddie humour we took the opportunity to play a little prank by guiding him down the steps and once on the tarmac directed him back towards the runway. The poor guy continued to walk on his own, nervously at first, but quickly gained confidence on the flat surface. He must have walked about 50 metres before he heard us giggling like naughty schoolboys and realised it was a prank.

Saturday 26th April 0600hrs BST (British Summer Time). Five hours after leaving Cyprus I was back in good ole' Blighty, greeted by a typical early morning mist, wearing only my light desert DPM (Disruptive Pattern Markings) trousers, desert boots and a faded olive green teeshirt. Not exactly the best clothes to wear on a cold April morning in England.

We were taken to a hanger at one end of the airport, carefully chosen for our own safety; kept away from prying civilian eyes, including journalists, reporters and anti-war activists seething for our blood. A gang of activists were waiting outside the airport entrance shouting slogans and waving banners, eagerly wanting to jump on us – not giving a jot that we were casualties of a conflict to oust a tyrant. They must have done their homework to know we used Birmingham airport for casualty evacuees needing further treatment.

Inside the hanger we were greeted by a Colonel whom fed us instructions whilst our luggage was searched by the snowdrops (RAF Police) for any war trophies we might have picked up during our tour. Of course, being good boys, none of us did. On a table were telephones and a fax machine, should we have wanted to tell anyone of our sudden arrival home. We all declined the offer, opting instead to surprise our wives and girlfriends, thinking if we turned up on our doorsteps unannounced it would be more fun. The Colonel even offered each of us £25 cash to help with any unexpected purchases during our journey home. This gesture wasn't declined.

Taxis were also arranged to take us home, paid for by the army – or the taxpayer – depending on how you look at it. Some of the casualties were travelling as far south as Devon or as far north as Newcastle-upon-Tyne. After a bit of form filling-in and promises to report to our units on the Monday morning I was soon jumping in a taxi, heading south on the M6 motorway.

A light fog lingered over Birmingham but it didn't hinder the taxi driver too much as he hit warp-factor 10. At first he didn't say anything, which didn't help matters because I soon drifted away with my thoughts and started to relive my war.

Looking out of the windscreen, instead of seeing the motorway speeding past I was sitting in my Foden recovery vehicle heading north on Route-6 towards Basrah. The grass embankment along the motorway was suddenly replaced by a 3-metre sand berm, and the trucks and cars travelling on the opposite carriageway became convoys of military vehicles.

I had a strange feeling that what I was seeing wasn't real, but I didn't care. I was in no rush to return to reality. For some reason I felt more at ease sitting back in my Foden, dodging mortar splats and shell craters on the roads of Iraq.

"Mate, are you okay?" the driver asked.

Route-6 suddenly became the M6 and I found myself sitting inside the taxi.

"What? Yeah fine, why?"

"I've been chatting to you for the past five minutes and you just ignored me," he said in his broad Birmingham accent.

"I never realised, sorry, mate."

"Hey, don't worry about it, I'm not going to ask any awkward questions or anything like that."

In fact he never asked any questions, which I appreciated. Instead we caught up on sporting events, football, that sort of thing. Before I knew it we were parked outside the front of my house.

CHAPTER 2

WELCOME HOME

I looked at the silver birch in the corner of my front garden, standing proud like a beacon welcoming me home. Out of the corner of my eye a squaddie wearing civilian clothes caught my attention as he struggled with his bergen and bits of kit on my driveway. My mind was playing tricks again. I was actually watching myself when I left home to start my pre-deployment training at Chilwell. A flashback, maybe? But why could I see someone else's kit on the path next to the taxi?

"Mate, we're here," the driver said, lifting it from the boot of his taxi.

I came back to reality and climbed out of the taxi looking up and down the street as if to remind myself I am actually home and not dreaming. I then noticed the bedroom curtains were closed. Good, my wife and daughter were still in bed.

Walking up my driveway seemed to take an age. Reaching the doorstep I was greeted with a half-chewed mouse left behind by Digby, our black and white cat. It was if he knew I was arriving and left it as some kind of welcome home present.

Careful not to tread on the remains, I was about to ring the doorbell but found myself frozen to the spot. I couldn't do it. For some unknown reason it didn't seem right.

"Are you okay, mate?" the driver asked, struggling with my heavy bergen up the driveway.

"Yeah fine, it seems weird, that's all."

I finally managed to pluck up enough courage to ring my doorbell, but there was no need as the front door burst open.

Helen, with her long blonde hair in a tangled mess and wearing a pink cotton dressing gown, let out a screech. "Kev! What are you doing home?"

I stood in front of her looking not unlike a weary tramp, totally speechless.

"I'll be off now, mate, good luck and welcome home," the taxi driver said.

"Oh right, okay, mate, thanks for bringing me home."

I offered him a £10 tip, which he surprisingly refused, and made his way back to Birmingham so to pick up his next weary squaddie fare.

Helen couldn't contain herself any longer and literally jumped into my arms. Well, arm. "You're home, you're home, I can't believe you're home!" she yelled, wrapping her arms tight around my neck and kissing my head and face over and over again, like some demented woodpecker.

"Hey, calm down, luv."

"No way! I'm never going to let you go, ever!" She started to cry, and I don't mind admitting I shed a tear or three. "So you're back for good. You're not here for a quick visit, then going back?" she nervously asked.

"No, I'm not going back. This bloody plastercast has seen to that."

Helen loosened her vice-like grip and looked at my arm. "Oh my god!" she shrieked as she raised both hands over her mouth, "is it badly hurt?"

I let out a snigger. "Don't you remember, I explained what happened when I phoned you from the hospital. Anyway, it's not as bad as it looks."

After the welcome tears and hugs, Helen helped drag my kit into the hallway where I quickly noticed a young lady racing down the stairs dressed in her 'Barbie' pyjamas.

"Daddy, you're home, you're home!" she shouted.

Of course, it was my four-year-old daughter, Rachel, jumping from the last two steps and launching herself into the air, crash-landing on my chest.

"Hey, slow down," I said trying to calm her. But it was no use. I had no choice but let her do what she had to do, and that was shower me with sloppy kisses and hugs.

When we all settled down I walked into the living room and plonked Rachel on the settee. As if I'd never been away, I calmly switched on the television and we both watched *Playhouse Disney* whilst Helen cooked me the egg and chips I'd been dreaming of for months. I was determined to return to a normal life as soon as possible, and even attempted to grow ignorant to the fact I'd ever been to war. Watching television with my daughter cuddled up by my side added to that illusion.

Catching a glimpse of my plastercast, however, kicked my ignorance into touch, quickly reminding me of the fact I had been fighting in a war, only to be torn away and arrive back home a few hours later. The transition between the two didn't seem real let alone healthy. It was simply too quick to adjust between the extremes.

Wearing a huge smile Helen walked in from the kitchen with a plate of egg and chips, but I couldn't finish the meal. My eyes were definitely bigger than my stomach.

"Sorry, I can't finish this, luv, you've cooked far to much for me."

Helen looked a bit confused. "But you usually eat it all."

"Yeah, I know, but you have to realise I've been on ration-packs for the past few months and my stomach has shrunk a tad. Besides, it was too bloody hot to eat."

Helen struggled to give me half a smile, as if to say she was trying her hardest to understand. "Look, let me take this plate into the kitchen and then I'll explain."

I walked into the kitchen with my unfinished meal, placed it on the table and headed back to the living room. Passing the mirror in the hallway I caught my reflection and found myself looking at a stranger – a scruffy, dirty looking tramp with a two-day old stubble. What the fuck am I doing here? I questioned myself. I must have stared at the mirror for a couple of minutes before my daughter tugged on my trousers. She immediately brought back memories of a little boy Stuart and I met in a small village near Al Amarah, north of Basrah. His family were shot in the back of the head by the Fedayeen militia, only for their corpses to fall into shallow graves they were forced to dig themselves.

"You're not leaving me again are you, Daddy?" Rachel asked looking up at me with her huge blue innocent eyes.

I looked down and smiled at this beautiful child with long blonde hair, living in her safe and secure home, none the wiser as to what Daddy had been doing 3,000 miles away in a war-torn country. She returned a warm, comforting smile that only a child could give. As if to tell you that everything will be okay. My thoughts suddenly returned to the time when I gave a bar of rat-pack (ration pack) chocolate to a little Iraqi girl not much older than Rachel. She smiled at me in much the same way and looked deep into my eyes as if to ask, "will everything be okay?" I only wished it could have been, for her and her family.

"C'mon darling, let's watch *Bear in the Big Blue House*. I think it's just started."

I must have drifted off to sleep. When I woke the television was switched off and the house was empty. I went into the kitchen to make a cup of tea and noticed Helen had scribbled a few lines on a notepad: 'Popped out for some bits and pieces. Took Rachel with me to give you some peace and quiet for a few hours.'

Taking advantage of the quiet I made a brew and thought I'd phone mother to tell her I'm home safe and in one piece. After the initial hyped emotional outbursts only a mother can expel I promised I'd visit on Sunday and put her mind at rest. I was about to replace the handset into its cradle, but instead of a telephone I was now holding a Garmin GPS (Global Positioning System) handset.

I was suddenly taken back to the time I had to program my GPS set with all the co-ordinates Stuart and I were given for our battlegroup advancement prior to going over the border into Iraq. I remember trying to learn how to use the bloody thing because we never received any written or verbal instructions. Stuart once lost his temper with it and came close to blowing it to pieces with a full 30-round magazine due to sheer frustration.

I rubbed my face in an attempt to erase this unwanted thought, stubbornly thinking to myself it were nothing more than my mind unwinding from the untamed memories of war. Out of the corner of my eye I noticed a leaflet being pushed through the letterbox. I picked it up and without reading it placed it on the hallway pine table. My flashback prompted me to find out what was going on in Iraq, so I switched on the television and watched the American Fox News channel for updates on what had been happening since my return home. I chose Fox News because the coverage was far better than any British news channel, albeit extremely patriotic.

The British news coverage, in particular the BBC, I found to be sympathetic toward Saddam's regime and amazingly anti-British forces. It was as if the BBC were sucking up to the anti-war 'paint your arse blue and howl at the moon brigade' tree huggers, purely because they appeared to be winning the public vote. A vote powered and manipulated by a biased anti-UK forces media, which instead of reporting what was actually happening injected their own ill-founded and sub-educated point of view with hope of winning the support of the British public. On the whole it worked.

Out of the blue the doorbell sprang into life. I didn't think it would take long before I had visitors. I half expected Helen to have worked her way through the phonebook, telling everyone I was home whilst I slept. When I opened the front door, still wearing my scruffy desert combats, I found myself face to face with a middle-aged woman proudly wearing a bright red rosette on her lapel. Holding a clipboard close to her chest I could see the smile on her face gradually disappear as she looked up and down my dusty and tired looking combats.

"Morning," she said, quickly regaining a smile. I didn't reply. "May I presume we can rely on your vote?"

I frowned at her question. "What vote?"

"Your vote, for the Labour Party, can we rely on it?"

I was totally bemused at her request. "I haven't a clue what you're talking about, luv."

"The local elections, surely you know about them." She took another look at my combats. I could almost hear the cogs whirring around in her head as she pieced together the clues as to why I wouldn't know anything about the local elections and why I was dressed in dirty combats. "Forgive me for asking, but can I guess that you are in the army?"

"Yes, well done, you guessed right," I sarcastically replied. Quickly adding, "I came home earlier this morning."

"Came home? Oh, been on manoeuvres?"

"Something like that. In Iraq."

"Oh my god, I'm terribly sorry. I would think the elections are the last thing on your mind. Are you okay?" she asked, passing me a leaflet.

"Yes, why d'you ask?"

I opened the door a little wider to grab the leaflet, bringing my plastercast hand into view.

"Oh my god!" she shrieked again, not unlike Helen's reaction when she first noticed it, then dropped her clipboard in the process. Leaflets littered the lawn as she covered the horrified look on her face.

"It's not as bad as you think. I've only broken my thumb," I said giving her a hand to pick up the mess. "Listen, luv, I only got back this morning and I'm – "

"No problem, I expect you need to rest," she interrupted, quickly walking back down the driveway, eager to get away.

I shook my head and gave a little chuckle. Dithering old cow, I thought to myself.

Closing the door I noticed an untidy pile of letters on the hallway table, which I didn't really take notice of before, even when I threw the unwanted leaflet on it earlier. One of the letters, however, grabbed my attention because it had my employer's company emblem franked on the envelope. I picked it up, noticing it had already been opened, and removed the letter. As I read its contents my eyes grew bigger and bigger with disbelief – I'd been sacked.

I read it again, only this time took note of the finer details such as the date, which was around the time I completed the second part of my pre-deployment training at Grantham. The letter continued to say that I had taken too much time off work without giving any adequate reason for my absence.

This pathetic excuse for my termination was lame to say the least. I knew I had explained the situation of my impending call-out prior to departure for Chilwell, and my boss knew I was in the TA before he employed me. He was also aware of the political climate at the time, and the possibility of TA soldiers, including me, being called-out for Iraq was extremely likely.

When the inevitable happened, I remember standing in front of him explaining that I'd been told, unofficially, I was about to be called-out and it was only a matter of weeks before I received my drafting orders. I even asked him if I could take my remaining holiday entitlement to make last-minute arrangements before I was mobilised. And if I received my drafting orders during my holiday I would not be coming back to work until the end of my tour, which could have been anything up to nine months.

My boss agreed with my requests and gave the impression of being sympathetic toward my situation, and he told me he'd see me when I returned home from my tour. So what was the problem? Why did he change his mind and decide to sack me? So many questions ran through my mind, but at that precise moment there was very little I could do about them until Monday morning.

I replaced the letter back in the envelope and threw it on the table. Anger and frustration slowly boiled up inside me. Why or even how could any employer sack an employee for being in the TA, let alone called-out to fight a war, is beyond me. In an attempt to feel a little better I planned to get out of my dirty combats and enjoy a hot bath, a shave and a ceramic flushing toilet.

I started to walk up the stairs when the doorbell rang again, only this time it was my daughter playing around. I opened the door and Rachel immediately hugged my legs as we stood in the doorway, hanging on as tight as she could, almost knocking me off balance.

"Leave Daddy alone," Helen said, struggling with bags of shopping from the boot of her car, "go and put *Playhouse Disney* on the telly, I'll be with you in a mo."

Rachel willingly obeyed and raced past to put her favourite programme on.

"I want a word with you, Helen," I said in a concerned manner.

Helen looked a little worried. "Why, what's up?"

Reaching for the last remaining bags of shopping from the boot of her car I was about to mention I'd found the letter from my employer, but my attention was diverted to a passer-by walking along the pavement opposite. A young lad, no more than maybe eighteen-years-old, wearing scruffy tracksuit bottoms and an England football team tee-shirt, looked directly at me in disgust and muttered something that sounded like 'murderer.'

"What d'ya say, youth?" I shouted.

He put his head down and carried on walking, but when he perceived to be a safe distance away from me he shouted, "You fucking murderer!" then broke into a sprint.

"I'd better tell you what's been happening whilst you were away," Helen said, overhearing the youth.

She put away the shopping whilst telling me about the news reports on television, what the national newspapers had printed and how certain left-wing politicians interpreted the war. I was gobsmacked. All the stories she told me came across as being biased towards Saddam Hussein and totally against the liberation of Iraq.

I now understood why that young lad called me a murderer. It was how the media portrayed the British army – print, television and radio alike. Even pop stars had jumped on the anti-war bandwagon, grabbing every possible opportunity to appear on radio and television only to spread their disillusioned bullshit and anti-war propaganda about the conflict. Or was it to exploit the airtime by promoting their latest book, national tour or album? Whichever, they constantly termed the liberation as an invasion. If it were an invasion that would mean the coalition forces entered Iraq uninvited, not forgetting the total of 22 countries involved to oust Saddam Hussein.

We were very much invited by the people who wanted us there – the oppressed Iraqis for a start – let alone, believe it or not, most of Saddam's 1,000,000 conscripted soldiers. They were only too pleased to be finally freed from a regime that treated them no better than a captive circus performing bear. Not forgetting Saudi Arabia, Turkey, Israel, Jordan, Egypt, the Kurds, and even Syria were pleased the coalition toppled Saddam.

As for Kuwait, they were over the moon with gratitude and couldn't do enough to assist; finally free of their terrifying and unpredictable dangerous neighbour. The only people who didn't invite us were Saddam Hussein and his notorious evil dictatorship. Oh, and not forgetting the pro-Saddam sympathisers such as the BBC, a confused Labour party, Piers Morgan, George Galloway and the 'tree huggers' of the western world.

"There's something else I need to tell you," Helen added.

I didn't like the sound of that, but as I just found out I'd lost my job and my own country seemed to be against me, what could make matters worse?

"I'm pregnant."

The look on my face said it all – total shock – and I forgot to ask her about the 'Dear John' letter from my employer.

"Aren't you going to say anything?"

What could I say? I never expected Helen to say she was pregnant.

"Well, are you pleased?" she nervously asked.

"Er, yes, I think, but how, when?" I had so many questions, but didn't know where to begin.

Helen had a miscarriage in early January 2003, about eight weeks before I was called-out, and although we tried for another baby I never thought she'd fall pregnant again so quickly. Amazingly, she did.

"Does anyone know?" I asked.

"Yes, Mum."

"Are you okay about it? You know, after what happened."

"I am if you are."

"Yes, of course I am. I just can't believe it. We'll have to take each day as it comes though, just in case, you know, what happened before. Now come here and give me a hug."

On the surface I appeared elated; we'd always wanted another child. But after her miscarriage the thought of falling pregnant so soon afterwards was far from my mind. I knew we'd try again sometime, but never thought she'd fall pregnant before I went to war. I suppose, thinking back, I'm glad she did. The thought of trying for a baby after being pumped full of 'God knows what' drugs to help counteract the effects of biological and chemical agents meant the threat of having a deformed child was suspiciously on the cards. And I for one didn't want to bring into this world a baby that relied upon others throughout its life. It just wouldn't be fair on the poor child.

I loosened my hug from around her waist. "We need to sit down and talk about this, but it's difficult when there's a four-year-old running around the house diverting our attention. Besides, I need to talk to you later about that letter from my boss."

"Oh, you read it then."

"Yes, I noticed it on the table."

"What are you going to do?"

"Like I said, we'll talk about it later, when there's no distractions. Put the kettle on, I'm dying for a cuppa," I added, attempting to change the subject. The last thing I wanted to do on my first day home was talk about my job.

I needed to get my head around all this news – good, bad and the bloody outrageous – but first I desperately needed to get out of my dirty combats and take a bath. Washing away the desert – physically and metaphorically – and getting into some clean civilian clothes may clear my head, or so I thought.

As soon as I had a bath, which took longer than usual because of my bloody plastercast, instead of changing into my jeans and shirt, I lay naked on the bed for a bit of a kip. Twelve hours later I woke with Helen fast asleep next to me. It was nearly one o'clock in the morning and I was now wide-awake. There was no way I was going to get back to sleep so I dressed, went down stairs and switched on the television, curious to catch up with the day's events in Iraq. But instead of flicking on to a news channel I came across a discussion programme about the conflict.

A panel of military experts, including a poet, a socialist MP and an anti-war activist, agonisingly spewed their credence about the war, emphasising how British soldiers indiscriminately killed women and children as they pillaged through Iraqi villages. The MP in particular added insult to injury by blaming Tony Blair – his boss – for turning a blind eye to such atrocities. I couldn't believe my ears. How could these morons sit there and spread this bullshit, and why doesn't anyone back home understand we actually liberated a nation from these evil atrocities, I asked myself.

After three-and-a-half minutes of listening to their huge wisdom, knowledge and experience of the conflict, and that the British forces were indiscriminately killing innocent civilians, I couldn't take any more. I had to switch to another channel or the television was about to take a flying lesson through the living room window. I was now watching one of the 24-hour news channels. I can't remember which one because I was engrossed in the images before me. An embedded war correspondent reported events as they unfolded, unwittingly finding himself in the middle of a firefight on the outskirts of Basrah.

Crouching down in the turret of a AFV (Armoured Fighting Vehicle) Warrior troop carrier, his chosen words about the engagement were most likely exaggerated, but that may have been due to fear and lack of combat experience, perhaps lack of awareness as to what was actually happening. But as far as he was concerned he was being personally picked upon and shot at by the Fedayeen militia. These images were the first I'd seen of the conflict since returning home, but something was wrong; they appeared totally different to what I'd experienced.

That was the problem – they were just images captured behind a camera and beamed 3,000 miles to a television in the comfort of my living room. I couldn't see what was happening beyond the lens of the camera or hear anything further than the range of the microphone. I couldn't smell burning oil or feel the adrenaline surge through my veins. What I could see, however, were my memories suddenly appearing in my mind's eye: stench of the desert, warmth of the night air, frantic shouting of orders, and the screaming of soldiers and civilians in terrific pain shot by small arms or blown to pieces by artillery fire.

Suddenly there was a huge explosion.

"Kev, get the fuck down! Take cover, take cover!" a voice cried.

I was confused as to where the voice came from, but instinctively hit the deck, lying flat on the floor with my hands clasped tightly over my head, waiting hopelessly for the next explosion. We were under ballistic attack – scud missiles. Another explosion shook the ground, and this time it was much, much louder.

"Where the fuck did that hit?" I shouted. No one answered.

"*Gas, Gas, Gas!*" another voice bellowed.

"Shit! Where's my respirator?" still no one answered.

With my eyes tightly shut and holding my breath I subconsciously counted nine-seconds I had before the deadly chemical agent took effect should I fail to don my respirator in time, which we learnt to do as part of our 'Immediate Action' (IA) drill. I desperately felt around for it, frantically searching every inch of ground with my fingertips. 7...8...9... Shit! 10...11...12... Where is it, where the fuck is it? I screamed in my head. 13...14...15... I began to panic, desperate to take a breath.

The effort of trying to find my respirator and the thought of being gassed made me feel dizzy. My lungs were fit to bursting as I felt my heart pump harder and harder, desperate to feed my body with much needed oxygen. I dare not take even the slightest of breath or open my eyes just a little, although the temptation was overwhelming. Doing so would quickly seal my fate, and I didn't fancy dying a long agonising death. Thirty seconds passed and still no sign of my respirator. Panic finally got the better of me as sweat poured from my forehead.

"Where's my respirator?" I shouted, still with my eyes tightly closed, "Where is it?" Shit, I'd foolishly taken a breath, but astonishingly I felt okay.

I was now confused as to why my throat and lungs weren't burning, or why I couldn't smell a distinct odour of almonds – an indication of a particular common chemical agent. With my eyes still tightly shut I took advantage of the clear lung-full of air, prayed I got away with it, and held my breath again as I continued to fingertip search the ground for my respirator.

"Why are you shouting?" Helen asked, standing next to me.

I stopped my frantic search and dared to slowly open my eyes, totally confused as to why I heard Helen's voice. I found myself on my knees staring at the television watching a news clip of the time we came under constant scud missile attack. On one occasion we repeated the IA drill fifteen times within only a few hours.

"I could hear you shouting at someone. Are you okay?"

"Yeah, I'm fine, go back to bed, I'll be up in a bit," I replied, still feeling confused.

But I wasn't fine. Somewhat dazed, it took me a moment or two to realise I was actually back in England, safe and well, sitting in my living room. I had to admit, I felt scared. Scared I was losing my sanity.

I couldn't bear to watch any more news reports so I switched off the television and went back to bed, managing only to grab a few hours sleep. Flashbacks continued to play havoc with my thoughts throughout the night, raising many irrational questions: was I responsible for killing innocent civilians? Am I a war criminal? Maybe

I was part of a grand-plan that went catastrophically wrong and I'm to be used as a scapegoat, shelved for when the shit hits the fan. Am I the one to blame to allow Tony Blair and George W, Bush to walk away untarnished? Stupid questions, I know, but I couldn't get them out of my head.

Was my subconscience simply winding down, desperately searching for a way to cope with the sudden influx of thoughts and flashbacks it had never experienced before? Maybe all soldiers go through the same feelings and mixed emotions when they return home from a war. I suppose I could have a chat with the MO (Medical Officer) at Chilwell, but would he listen? Or maybe I should make an appointment with my own civvy doctor, but what could he do, and would he be interested? Or would he be like the rest of the civilian world and turn his back on me? A thousand questions went through my mind, repeating themselves over and over, to the point of almost screaming at me. I was unaware at the time, but my thoughts and flashbacks were beginning to take control of my life and gradually turn me into a nervous wreck.

CHAPTER 3

ARMCHAIR WARRIORS

My daughter came running into the bedroom, and when she wakes so does everyone else. "Get up, Daddy, it's time to get up!"

Yep, that was my early morning alarm call, shouting two inches away from my left ear.

Helen was already up. In fact she'd been up for hours, washing my kit and preparing an 'English breakfast' including black pudding, bacon and fried bread. Something I'm not really used to, but then again I had lost time to make up for (not to mention weight) so I wasn't about to turn it down. After breakfast I wanted to make myself useful rather than mope around doing nothing, so I attempted to do a little vacuuming.

Within a few minutes I was quickly taken off that task because I couldn't control the up-right vacuum cleaner with my left hand and kept bashing into furniture. Instead, Helen ordered me to rest, banning me from any further housework, so I watched a film on television before boredom, once again, set in.

"For God's sake, go out for a walk or something, you're getting under my feet!" Helen snapped.

I willingly obeyed, deciding to take the short walk into town and withdraw a few quid from the hole-in-the-wall cash machine. Walking through the housing estate I couldn't help but notice something wasn't quite right. A feeling I was no longer welcome in my hometown, let alone the UK. Passers by stared at me, and I don't think they were admiring my tan.

I put these strange feelings down to paranoia and gave myself a kick up the arse for thinking such stupid thoughts. I walked over to the cash machine fitted in the wall of the local shop when a young lad, not much older than his early twenties, came out of the shop. We knew each other, if only to say good morning or engage in a bit of small talk at the local pub, but that was it. I raised a smile to acknowledge I'd seen him but he walked straight past, seemingly in total disgust.

"Hey, Gary, how ya doing, mate?" I asked, trying to grab his attention.

He stopped dead in his tracks, turned around and walked straight up to me. "What do you expect me to say to a fucking murderer?" he shouted. Then, quite unexpectedly, spat in my face before casually walking off, proudly wearing his England football shirt.

My first reaction was to rip his lungs out, but I was too shocked to move. After all, he was supposed to be a mate, so why would he tag me as a murderer? I couldn't help but feel renounced, dirty, and most of all confused. I wanted to go home, lock the front door and shut out the world.

Walking back, I felt as if more and more people were staring at me, their eyes burrowing into the back of my skull, totally disgusted with me – a child-killing, murderous thug. They hated me, and I was beginning to hate them. I needed an ally, someone on my side, but they were all in Iraq. So the only other person I could think of was my mother. After all, I planned to see her, and the visit would take me out of town.

The twenty-minute drive on the dual carriageway once again teased my memories of Route-6 in Iraq, less the carnage spewed up and down the entire length of the highway, of course. A further memory jostled to the forefront of my mind, to the time my mother took me to Chilwell for pre-deployment training. When we parked in the car park at the RTMC (Reinforcements Training & Mobilisation Centre) her face said it all: don't go! She wasn't in the best of moods at the time, so I hoped I'd manage to raise a smile on her face when I see her open the front door.

Sure enough, as soon as she opened the door her arms wrapped around my neck. I have never felt a hug so tight before or since. We settled down and talked about anything and everything, other than my exploits of the conflict. The only stories I did tell were the good and funny times, although they were soon exhausted due to the fact there weren't that many to tell.

I'd quickly change the subject in an attempt to stop her from asking a million questions to each anecdote by asking how everyone was, and what they'd been up to since my departure. However, Mother being Mother, she would sneak in the odd question, desperate to know the ins and outs of what I'd been up to. But I simply couldn't tell her the horror stories.

Visiting Mother put a much needed smile on my face, but I still felt I needed to see an ally whom I could share my real thoughts, but who? Yes, of course, my brother-in-law, Darren, and he only lived just around the corner. He was in the TA for thirteen-years, but, along with many others, ordered to hand in his kit due to government cutbacks. Although he had never been called out on any operations, at least he would understand my predicament and be a friendly face.

When I knocked on his door a 6ft 2-inches, 17-stone bruiser with blonde crew-cut hair, wearing a huge menacing smile quickly answered it. "Heard you were back, come in, mate. Wanna cuppa?"

"I could do with something a little stronger."

"Well, tell you what, I'm off down the club this evening. Wanna come for a few pints?" he asked, referring to the local working-men's club.

"Sounds good, and it will have to be only a few. Anymore than that I'll be sliding under the table cos' I've been dry for the past few months!"

Darren let out a chuckle as he filled the kettle. "So you don't fancy a drop of whisky in ya tea, then."

"No way, tempting as it is, I need to be teased gently back into the taste of alcohol."

"Couldn't you drink out there?" he asked.

"Chance would be a fine thing."

I explained about the total ban of alcohol because of being in a Muslim country. Seemed weird considering we were kicking ten colours of shit out of it. But rules are rules and laws of the land had to be respected. When we came across abandoned Iraqi shelters and shell scrapes, however, bottles of whiskey and vodka were abundant, along with piles of girlie magazines. Inevitably, Saddam's iron fist turned a blind eye towards his local militia and soldiers.

We chatted for a couple of hours, mainly about the conflict and my exploits, and Darren updated me with stories and gossip whilst I was away, including the news of Helen discovering she was pregnant. Visiting Darren was a tonic I badly needed, if only to see a friendly face. But as soon as I said my goodbyes and stepped out onto the pavement I felt as if hating eyes were once again burrowing into the back of my head, instantly triggering my paranoia.

I gave myself another mental kick up the arse for thinking such stupid thoughts. After all, by eight o'clock this evening I'll be drinking with the locals, and then I'll see how stupid I've been, I told myself.

I was looking forward to going out for a pint or three with Darren, and Helen thought it would do me the world of good, even though it was only the local working men's club. By seven o'clock, however, my conscience decided to tell me I wasn't ready, and I became increasingly nervous at the thought of mixing with them – the public.

"Are you going to get changed?" Helen asked.

I continued to stare out of the living room window, contemplating the thought of drinking with civilians.

"Oi, did you hear me, deafy?"

"I don't know," I eventually replied, still staring out of the window.

Helen put down her baby clothes catalogue to give me a hug. "Are you okay? You seem distant."

Distant would be one way to describe how I felt. Going nuts would be a better description. So many weird thoughts continued to race through my head, and I simply didn't know where to start to sort them out. I expected to arrive back from Iraq and pick up from where I left off. Instead I found that the world continued to turn whilst I stood still within a void, fighting a bloody war. During which I lost my job, Helen was pregnant, and to top it all I faced a hostile public.

Sod it, I thought, why shouldn't I go out. "I've made up my mind, I'm going."

"Good, cos' you'll enjoy talking to your friends about Iraq and what you got up to," Helen replied, still holding me tight.

Talking about Iraq was one topic I intended to avoid, I had managed to do so far with Helen, and I certainly didn't want to talk to civilians about it. I changed into my smart casuals and splashed on a bit of after-shave. Soon afterwards Darren picked me up and we drove the short distance to the club, parking right outside the entrance.

"Before we go in, are you sure about this?" Darren asked, as if he knew what I was feeling.

"Yes mate, I have to, for my own sanity if anything else."

Darren returned a smile, as if to say 'I'm with you all the way, mate.'

The bar and lounge were full of the usual locals drinking their favourite tipple and engaged in conversation. I half expected a pianist to suddenly stop playing in mid tune, then everyone to fall silent and stare at me, not unlike a scene out of some old Western. But no, that didn't happen. Instead I was totally ignored.

"You having your usual?" Darren asked.

"Yeah please, mate," I replied, looking around feeling a little nervous.

"It's okay Kev, relax," Darren urged, placing a hand on my shoulder to show his support.

Easier said than done. I lit a cigarette and eagerly waited for my drink. After a few minutes Darren eventually handed over my first pint of bitter. I hadn't tasted it for what seemed decades. I slowly lifted the glass to my lips and took a couple of sips. My mouth now primed and ready, I slowly gulped down the first half.

"How's that?" Darren asked, smiling.

"Nectar, pure bloody nectar," I replied, licking the foam from my top lip.

The second half went down as quick as the first, and I was ready for another. I grabbed my wallet from my jeans, but instead of pulling out a black leather one I usually carried, I forgot I still had my green DPM nylon one I used in Iraq, which looked a tad out of place in an English bar.

"What's that?" Darren asked, pointing at it.

"Oh this, I used it in Iraq. I needed something to carry my PW (Prisoner of War) card and my Med (Medical) card, things like that. It was more appropriate to carry around rather than a black leather civvy wallet."

I wanted to place it back in my pocket and out of sight as soon as possible, if only to avoid further questioning, but instead of taking out a £5 note I took out an Iraqi 250-Dinar banknote.

"Shit, I forgot I had these," I muttered under my breath.

"Is that Iraqi money?" Darren asked, quickly spotting it.

"Yeah, we bought them from the locals. I bought this one from a kid for five-dollars."

"How much is it worth, then?" he asked, taking it from my hand to have a closer look, noticing Saddam Hussein's ugly mug on one side.

"About nine pence. I was ripped off," I answered.

"Too right, you were."

"I didn't mind. After all, what's five-dollars worth to us Brits. You'll be struggling to buy a pint with it. To most Iraqis it's worth about two weeks wages, so I thought what the hell, the kid needs it more than me."

I went on to tell Darren the story behind this particular 250-Dinar banknote and the little Iraqi boy.

It was only a few days into the conflict and we'd already witnessed everything a war could throw at us, or so we thought. Being a recovery mechanic I was driving at the rear of a 6-vehicle packet consisting of 4-ton troop carriers and 110 Land Rovers heading for Basrah. A scruffy looking skinny boy, not much older than eight or maybe nine-years-old, stood beside the road filling large plastic containers with stagnant water from a huge puddle measuring about ten-metres across, created by the coalition after dropping a bomb that not only obliterated its target, it also hit a water pipe beneath the road.

Under a scorching sun the stench coming from the crater was no different to an open sewer. A cloud of mosquitoes danced above the NATO made pond as other boys and girls filled similar containers for their families to wash, drink and cook with. To make matters worse an Ox stood in the middle taking a piss. We came to a halt about one-hundred meters further up the road because the lead vehicle needed to check where we were on the map, which we did from time to time. In other words the young Second-Lieutenant navigating had deviated from the route and made us lost – again. The scruffy boy clocked our packet, dropped his containers and started to frantically wave his arms to grab our attention.

Grinning from ear-to-ear, he ran towards us shouting: "Mister, Mister, water, water!" All Iraqi children shouted that when chasing us, and for good reason. Under Saddam's regime clean water was a rare commodity for the majority of the population. All they could use for cooking, washing, cleaning and even drinking was the dirty, contaminated water from canals, rivers and stagnant ponds. The only clean tap water available was piped into hospitals, government buildings, offices and hotels.

In fact, any establishment that was owned by Saddam's notorious Ba'ath party and his Al-Bu Nasir tribe. Only those fortunate to be in Saddam's tribe or a member of the Ba'ath party were allowed to purchase residential plumbing. If you weren't a member, which was most of the population, including the Shiites and Marsh Arab tribes, you stood no chance.

We all had difficulty coping with such desperation for something as common as clean water, so we felt compelled to help the poor lad in anyway we could. When the boy reached our leading Land Rover he continued to greet us shouting: "Mister, Mister, water, water!" He then grabbed a handful of Dinars from his scruffy dark grey trousers and waved the wad of worthless cash at us. Unexpectedly he spat on Saddam's head printed on the front of the bank notes shouting: "Saddam gone, we love Bush, we love Blair!" I could have thought of a better word to describe my beloved Prime Minister, but under the circumstances I thought it best not to confuse the poor lad.

He worked his way down the packet, swapping various Dinar notes for US dollars, still shouting: "Saddam gone, we love Bush, we love Blair," and even, "Blair feeds us, Blair feeds us." When he reached Stuart and I sitting in our Foden recovery vehicle he repeated shouting his sales pitch, urging us to buy his worthless Dinar notes.

We each gave him a five-dollar bill for two 250-Dinar notes, estimating he must have made about fifty dollars from all the lads in the packet. It was worth every penny, though, if only to see him smile from ear to ear. And because we carried an abundance of bottled water, albeit desalinated, he also walked away with as many two-litre bottles his skinny arms could carry. More often than not it was the parents that coaxed their children to approach us. After all, soft hearted squaddies were more likely to buy a worthless currency from children rather than adults.

We knew as soon as the conflict started the Iraqi Dinar became worthless over night and inflation would skyrocket, causing a loaf of bread to cost thousands of Dinars. Subsequently tens-of-thousands of Iraqi civilians starved, unable to buy food and provisions with their useless currency. The average wage for an Iraqi citizen that wasn't a member of Saddam's Ba'athist party was the equivalent of little over ten- dollars per month. So Iraqis were quick to realise they could make a fortune selling their worthless Dinars as souvenirs to us unsuspecting squaddies. The young entrepreneur we met made a fortune out of us, enabling him to provide food for his family for many months.

Darren was totally gobsmacked by my story and was about to ask a question, but some arsehole overhearing it butted in. "I'll buy it off you!"

"What?" I replied.

A stumpy, fat middle-aged man standing behind Darren attempted to thrust a £5 note in my hand, repeating, "I'll buy that Iraqi banknote off ya."

"It's not for sale," I replied.

Darren turned to face Stumpy. "Did you hear him tell the story behind this banknote?"

"Yeah, I heard him, so what? He was only talking about an Iraqi kid." He then looked at me. "Go on, sell it to me. I'm offering you good money for it. Worth a lot more than five-dollars."

"Piss off!" I snapped, "It means more to me than anything you could offer."

"Why? It's only a fucking Iraqi banknote you bought off some kid. You must have others."

"I have a few more, but I'm not selling them."

"C'mon, sell me one, you selfish git."

I couldn't believe what I was hearing. If he'd heard the story I told Darren, he was unbelievably stupid not to recognise the concept of sentimental value. At that moment he'd made up my mind. This stumpy, overweight, dickhead reflected the attitude of the small-minded people of my country. The majority of which appeared to live in my small, pathetic town.

"Do yourself a favour and fuck off," Darren replied.

"I only want to buy it off him!" Stumpy fumed, with a little anger in his tone.

"I've had enough, I knew this would happen if I came out tonight."

I grabbed the Dinar note from Darren and made my way out of the bar, quickly followed by Darren.

"You're all murdering bastards, anyway. Did you hear me, squaddie?" Stumpy shouted, "you're all child-killing, raping, murdering bastards!"

"Hey, ignore him. C'mon, have another drink. We could go somewhere else if you like?" Darren said, following me out.

"No, take me home. This was a big mistake, I shouldn't have come out."

Darren and I sat in silence as he drove me home, but my mind was by no means quiet. I couldn't get Stumpy out of my head.

When Darren stopped outside my house I said my goodbyes, walked through the front door and went straight to bed, but I couldn't sleep. I lay awake most of the night squabbling with my conscience over Stumpy, Helen being pregnant, my 'dear John' letter from my boss, and the return of many questions relentlessly running through my head.

I could feel anger surge through my veins yet again. The temptation to go back into the club and beat the shit out of Stumpy was incredible, but I knew I shouldn't, otherwise I would have proved to the other patrons that Stumpy was correct and I was nothing more than a murdering bastard. Let's face it, Piers Morgan, the once chief editor of the Daily Mirror, would have had a field day printing headlines such as: Iraq war veteran continues to murder innocent victims back home. Giving Piers the perfect excuse to redeem himself from those false pictures he printed of British soldiers supposedly beating and torturing Iraqi PW's in the back of an army truck.

As I lay in bed with many questions racing through my mind, the rapidly growing demon deep within decided to make an appearance, laughing as it taunted my thoughts, telling me how easy it's going to be to steer my pathetic carcass towards self-destruction. And the crazy thing is, putting aside the fact it sounded just like David Tennant, I felt like letting it. My world was collapsing around me, and I begun to care not a jot.

CHAPTER 4

GIZZA JOB

Before I knew it the early morning sun pierced through gaps in the curtains whilst birds perched on my silver birch sang their first chorus of the day. I lay still for a while, staring into space. For a few tranquil moments the war seemed a million miles away. I then noticed my plastercast, instantly signalling the many memories of the conflict to come flooding back in an instant: Scud missiles hitting our location, snipers taking pot shots at us, Stuart forgetting where he buried our cans of coke to keep them cool...

I reached for my wristwatch lying on top of the bedside cabinet; it was almost 6am. I decided to get up, have a wash and get dressed, thinking how I was going to spend my day. Be positive, I thought, put the weekend behind you, it's now a new day to the start of a new week. My first plan of action was report to my OC (Officer Commanding) at the TA centre.

Depressing the button on the intercom fitted to one of the gateposts, I buzzed the front office.

"Hello."

"It's corporal Mervin, Angela," I answered, recognising her cheery dulcet tones.

Angela had been 'in service' with the TA for what seemed centuries. A curvy woman in her late forties, who'd once been married to the army but had since left, only deciding to stay on as a civilian to help with the mountain of paperwork the army loves to dish out.

"Kev, come in," she replied all excited.

The magnetic lock on the gate released its grip allowing me to push them open and drive through into the courtyard. Memories of half-a-dozen or so squaddies in CS95 (Combat Soldier 1995) uniform walking down the front entrance steps, one of whom was me, came flooding back. It was from when we all met one evening to have our pre-deployment meeting and receive further instructions about our forthcoming mobilisation. After the meeting some of us, including myself, left by the front entrance.

I drove down the side of the building where the car park and parade-square at the rear came into view, along with brick sheds lining the square that housed our vehicles and various bits of kit. I parked the car and walked towards the rear entrance. Entering the building brought back further happy memories as my footsteps on the concrete floor echoed down the long, dimly lit corridor. I could almost hear the lads walking with me, laughing and joking as we headed to the bar after our midweek training evening.

I reached the end of the corridor and walked through the two creaking swing doors into the main hall. The highly polished floorboards, worn down by years of highly polished boots, seemed to welcome me home as I walked across them towards the administration office, knocking twice on the office door before walking in.

"Hi, Angela, how's things?" I cheerily said as she sat at her computer typing whatever it was she was typing.

"Never mind that, how are you?" she asked, then looked at my plastercast.

I explained everything over a cup of tea. Angela knew of my arrival because the TA Centre received a signal from Glasgow HQ about my casevac but she didn't know any of the finer details. So I was under strict 'Angela' instructions not to leave the office until I told her everything.

After telling my war story and that Helen was pregnant, which was a big mistake because she wanted to know how Helen was doing, when the baby was due and other pregnant related questions men can't possibly understand, I asked if she would allow me to see the OC.

I knocked on the door of the adjacent office. "Enter!" a deep booming voice bellowed.

I walked in wearing a smile, equalled by my OC. A tall yet slightly overweight man in his mid fifties, with what was dark hair but now almost grey.

"Great to see you, corporal Mervin."

"Likewise, sir," I replied standing to attention. I didn't salute because he was dressed in civilian clothes – a light grey suit – so he wouldn't have expected me to. Inadequately dressed, the army term it.

"Sit down, Kev," he said, already falling into his informal mode, "fancy a coffee?"

Even though I'd already had a cup of tea with Angela, it was only polite to accept. As I made myself comfortable the OC dashed out of the office. A few minutes later he returned with two coffees and a folder containing details of my casevac report.

"Now then," he said clapping his hands together and rubbing them, "let's see what we have here." There was a few minutes silence whilst he studied the notes. "It appears you are out of the war for good. 2RTR battlegroup doesn't want you back because of your injury."

"So what do I do now?"

"Go home, relax, and enjoy your family," he jovially answered.

"Can I return to my TA duties?" I hopefully asked.

"No chance, not until I've had the all-clear from Glasgow, and judging by this report that won't be for a further five weeks."

"So in the meantime I can't do anything?"

"No," he answered assertively, "and you can't return to work either because you are officially still on operations until your demobilisation date in July." He paused for a second to take a sip of his coffee. "Helen came to see me about a letter you received from your employer," he added.

"I think I know the one."

"You've read it, then?"

I didn't need to answer him. The sudden concerned look on my face said I did.

The OC couldn't help but notice, and grew another concerned look on his own face. "I can't promise anything, but I'll see what the army can do to help."

I thanked him, but the way my luck was going I decided not to cling onto any glimmer of hope.

"Have a look at these," he said, changing the subject once again, with hope of cheering me up.

He passed me a bundle of blueys (letters) the lads had sent him from Iraq. We called them blueys simply because the A4 size piece of paper that folded into itself making an envelope was light blue – actually some were white – but the nickname 'bluey' squaddies gave them seemed to have stuck. All the lads called-out from our company were split up and attached to different units of various battlegroups, but their blueys said the same thing: Everything is fine, all okay, and maybe the odd squaddie humour story (law and common decency dictates I cannot recite them) thrown in to make light of the conflict.

We tended to steer away from writing about the conflict, if only to stop our families from worrying. I suppose it was only natural to do the same when we wrote to the OC. We needn't have bothered. He was no stranger to war, serving in Kosovo, Bosnia and other conflicts, and most certainly qualified to understand the horrors of war and the effect it has on a soldier's mind.

I drank my coffee and left the TA centre a little happier than I was when I arrived. Reading blueys from the lads certainly cheered me up, even though they weren't addressed to me. My next stop was to visit my employer – or rather my ex-employer. I thought about writing him a letter, but he could easily tear it up and deny all knowledge of receiving it. So I thought about telephoning him, but he could just cut me off. My best option was to confront him face-to-face, leaving him no option but to explain why I'd been sacked. I could then let off a bit of steam and explain the error of his ways, and boy, was I looking forward to that.

I went through a hurried off-the-cuff script in my head of how I thought the conversation would go. I knew we'd have the odd cross word to start with, but after we'd both calmed down and had a coffee, then hopefully all will be forgotten, concluding with a reconcile of my employment when I'm demobilised. After all, surely he'll understand my predicament and surely he'll be patriotic enough to realise sacking me wasn't the best move he'd made.

Yep, I convinced myself that is how the conversation would go. I was happy. When I reached the industrial estate, however, for some unknown reason my heart was in my mouth and I broke out in a cold sweat. I suddenly felt that it wasn't the best idea I've had, and it will only end in tears.

My preconceived notion of how our conversation would go was quickly hijacked by yet more paranoid thoughts. David Tennant was telling me to turn back, even questioning why my boss should welcome me back. Other voices begun to scream at me, shouting: your country hates you, don't bother to try and get your old job back, your country hates you because you killed all those innocent women and children. Your country hates you!

I started to believe them, to the point of almost convincing myself that I was to blame for all the civilian deaths in the war.

Before I knew it I was driving in the car park, and because it was available, instinctively parked in my old parking space, only this time I wasn't turning up for a day's work. I pulled on the handbrake and turned off the engine, instantly turning off the voices taunting me. Staring at the glass-fronted building I took a deep breath, grabbed the door handle and was about to step out of the car, but something held me back.

Whether it was my demon playing or just plain fear, I was frozen to the spot. Scared of walking into the building to face people that knew where I'd been, only to be hissed and cursed as I walked by them – my proverbial hostile public. I needed a few minutes to gather my thoughts.

Okay here goes, I muttered to myself. I climbed out of the car and made my way to the front entrance. Each step became heavier and heavier as I thought of those 'people' in the building sneering at me. I really didn't want to do this, but I suddenly felt as if someone was giving me a helping hand; as if I were gently but firmly pushed towards the building. An inner strength, maybe.

"Mornin,' Ruth," I said cheerily walking into the reception, "is Bob available? I would like to see him."

"Can I help you?" Ruth replied from behind her modern, highly polished glass- top desk. A middle-aged lady caked in heavy makeup, collar-length blonde hair that came out of a bottle, and wearing a smart red suit accompanied a rehearsed welcoming plastic smile.

"You don't remember me, do you?" I replied, which was hardly surprising. I'd only been working for the company a short time –

about ten weeks – and met Ruth on only two occasions. One of which was at my job interview.

"No, sorry, I don't."

"It doesn't matter. Can I see Bob? I'm Kevin Mervin."

Ruth's welcoming smile suddenly changed to a look of horror, as if she'd heard my name before. "Oh right, I'll see if he is free," she awkwardly replied, dialling Bob's extension number.

Ruth must have heard something about my sacking, and if she did, that meant the whole company did, because Ruth had a reputation for spreading gossip.

"Sorry, he can't see you, Mr. Mervin, he's too busy."

Yeah right, of course he was. I could imagine the look on his face when Ruth told him I was standing in reception. I came all this way especially to see him and wasn't about to be fobbed off with some lame excuse that he was too busy. And more to the point I would have worked myself up into a nervous, quivering wreck for nothing.

"No matter, I'll see him some other time, perhaps."

And that some other time was right now.

I smiled at Ruth and walked outside, but instead of heading towards my car I carried on to the rear of the building, hoping the rear roller shutter door wasn't locked. It was, and it was pointless banging on it because the noise in the workshop would have drowned out any attempt of trying to attract attention.

I waited for a few minutes with hope that one of the lads would sneak out for a crafty fag, allowing me to enter the building, but that might not have been for hours. Instead, I decided to forget about this potentially combustible idea. After all, I'd have only made matters worse by charging into the building, cornering my ex-boss and shouting obscenities at him for sacking me. So maybe writing or phoning him was a better idea.

I walked back to the car as my head continued to spin with thoughts of my cowardly ex-boss refusing to see me. A further thought jumped into my head, if only to calm me down a tad, reminding that my immediate situation wasn't that bad after all. I was, technically, still employed by the regular army, so at least I had a few months of income before my demobilisation in July.

After demobilisation, however, if I failed to convince my boss he'd made a huge mistake sacking me or able to find further employment, I faced the prospect of the dole queue. With that in mind I decided to drive to the Jobcentre and see what they had to offer, and find out which benefits I were entitled to should the need arise.

So far my day wasn't going too well. I needed a few positives to counteract the negatives, and the thought of visiting one of the most depressing establishments in the country didn't enthral me with confidence. I hated Jobcentres. The only vacancies available were those that had been advertised elsewhere, but failed to entice any potential candidates. So the Jobcentre was a last resort for employers to grab the attention of any potential job seeker desperate to find work – in walks me.

Entering the building I was, putting it bluntly, gobsmacked. The old tatty blue notice boards with rows of old tatty vacancy cards attached were replaced with modern touchscreen computer displays mounted in beige plastic pillars. Half a dozen or so were scattered around the open plan floor space, which had been completely redecorated and modernised since I last visited in 1991. Gone were the old 'customer' serving kiosks, behind, what seemed, bulletproof glass. Gone were the worn-out grey lino floor tiles and gone were the dull grey coloured walls covered in peeling paint and obscene graffiti. Even telephone numbers scribbled in biro on the windowsills belonging to young ladies offering various pleasures – for a price – were nowhere to be seen.

I took the opportunity to familiarise myself with the new modern surroundings whilst I waited for one of the touch-screen displays to become free. At first I was pleasantly surprised. I could no longer smell stale cigarette smoke and urine, see any cigarette burns in the new navy blue carpet, and there were no patronising signs saying 'sign on here', which roughly translated meant 'for handouts queue here'.

The clientele, however, hadn't changed. The obligatory teenage single mother with three scruffy toddlers, sat in front of a desk shouting the place down. At the top of her voice she demanded more handouts because 'she knew her rights' as she kept saying. And because it was around the time of year pupils were taking their exams, swarms of thickies, which every school has its fair share, grabbed the opportunity to leave school early without bothering to take any exams. Only to head straight for the 'handouts' counter to see what they could scrounge from the state before paying anything into it; spending it wisely on drugs, alcohol, cigarettes and computer games. Welcome to Blair's Britain.

Ignoring the commotion, I picked up a week old copy of the local newspaper and sat down on one of the carefully arranged blue cushioned chairs. Facing me was a row of civil servants sitting behind desks serving 'customers' and taking shed loads of abuse. One of which made it blatantly obvious, and seemed quite proud of the fact, that he'd just come out of prison and wanted every benefit he could possibly scrounge, apart from help to find a job. All the excuses came out as to why he couldn't work. I could think of only one – he was unemployable because he was outrageously thick.

"Can I help you, sir?" a soft voice asked.

I took no notice and carried on reading my paper. After all, why would someone be calling me 'sir' in a place like this? I was under the impression job seekers were still called 'next!'

"Sir, can I help you?" she asked again.

I looked up and yes, it was me she was talking to. "Oh right, you took me by surprise. I'm waiting to use one of those machines over there." I pointed to the touch-screen displays.

"Are you here to claim any benefits?" she quietly asked, as if I'd be embarrassed should anyone overhear. She'd be right.

"Well, I might be."

She frowned at my reply. "Maybe I can help. Come with me."

I followed the thirty-something year-old civil servant dressed in a smart dark blue suit and her black hair pinned up like a head-mistress style bun, to one of the desks across the open-plan floor space. Above her desk was a sign saying 'New Claims.'

"Take a seat, sir, and I'll see what I can do for you." She sat behind her computer and placed some sort of ID card in the side of the keyboard. "Do you know your National Insurance number?"

I did, and gave it to her.

"Can you please confirm your full name, date of birth and address?"

I did.

She paused for a while to study the screen. "Okay, Mr. Mervin, I see you are employed. Is this correct?"

"Yes, well, sort of."

Miss Smart-Suit frowned again. "But you wish to make a claim for unemployment benefit."

I didn't exactly word it like that, but I could see where she was coming from.

"Maybe, I don't know yet. I'd better explain, hadn't I."

She nodded, agreeing with me.

This was going to be fun. Where do I start? So I thought it best to explain my present problem then work backwards.

"I'm in the TA and was called out to serve in Iraq. Before my call-out I started a new job, but had only worked there for ten weeks before my call-out. When I returned home I discovered my new employer had sacked me. The army is going to see if they can save my civilian job, but I'm here to find another one just in case they can't. I'm also here to see if I can claim any benefits should the need arise." There, said it, in a nutshell.

Miss Smart-Suit sat in silence for a moment, not really sure of any reply to my predicament.

"How did you hurt your arm?" she eventually asked noticing my plastercast.

"Oh this, I fell off my recovery truck."

"Was this in Iraq?"

"Yes," I nervously replied, wondering where she was going with this.

I became suspicious of her questioning. At first I thought she was making polite conversation, but there was more to it than that.

"Were you employed by the TA or the regular army during your call-out?"

Wow, I wasn't ready for that one. It felt as if she was fishing for information, looking for weak points to trip me up.

"Employed by the regular army," I answered.

I was about to explain why this was but thought better of it so not to confuse her.

"Are you still being paid by the regular army?"

I knew she'd ask that question.

"Yes."

Miss Smart-Suit paused for a moment as she thought about my answers. This interview or interrogation as it became, was like a game of chess; both of us pre-empting each other's next move.

"And you say you no longer have a job because your civilian employer sacked you for being called-up."

"Yes."

"And you have a letter to prove this."

"Yes, in a manner of speaking."

"What do you mean by that?"

"My boss didn't exactly word it like that, although it meant the same. He basically meant that because I hadn't returned to work since my last day of leave the company could no longer tolerate the amount of time I had off work."

Miss Smart-Suite looked totally confused. "But you were called-up, so surely the army told your employer of your deployment?"

"Yes, they did, in the form of a letter, leaflets and instructions on what to do about my position within the company."

"But they sacked you, regardless."

"Yes."

She paused again to contemplate my answers. "When will you stop being paid by the regular army?"

"When I'm demobilised, which will be in July."

"You will then be back in the TA and become a civilian again?"

"Yes."

Another pause as she contemplated my answer.

"Will you excuse me, I'm going to have a word with a colleague, I'll be right back."

"Yes, of course, luv."

She doesn't know what to do, I thought, feeling smug. But did I really want all this attention? Five minutes later Miss Smart-Suit returned to her desk.

"I've discussed your matter with a senior colleague and we both agree that you cannot claim unemployment benefit when you are demobilised from the regular army because you will have made yourself intentionally unemployed."

That I did not expect.

"Say again."

"It means that you will have intentionally left your last employer, the regular army, and therefore make yourself unemployed. You will then have to wait a qualifying period before you can claim any unemployment benefits, which may take up to thirteen weeks."

"What?" I was stunned. "How can that be? I'm a TA soldier who was called-out and attached to a regular unit. When my tour is over I'm demobilised, become a TA soldier again and return to being a civilian. I don't have any choice. That's how it's done."

Of course, Miss Smart-Suit ignored what I said and just recited a few lines from what seemed a government script. "You will be leaving your last employer by your own admission and therefore will not be eligible to claim unemployment benefit."

"What about my civilian job, is there anything you can do about that?" I asked.

"Your previous civilian job has no bearing on you claiming unemployment benefit because the army will be your last full time employer."

"So there is nothing I can do regarding my civilian employer prior to my call-out."

"That will have no bearing on any future claim you make regarding unemployment benefit," she added, trying to disguise her smug grin, giving me the impression she too opposed the liberation of Iraq.

It was tempting to make a sarcastic remark about the teenage single mother and the jailbird still shouting and screaming for handouts, which they were no doubt awarded without any awkward questioning.

The system, and Miss Smart-Suit, failed to recognise or chose to ignore my situation, and further more, couldn't care less. I was totally shafted and there was nothing I could do about it. So much for Tony Blair protecting reserve soldier's employment rights. I felt like a social outcast – the proverbial dole scrounger, yet not allowed to claim benefits.

To be an outcast living in Tony Blair's socialist Britain had an entirely different meaning. All you had to do to qualify under his regime was fight for Queen and Country. Even during Gordon Brown's socialist republic dictatorship veterans were no better respected. My mind was finally made up; I hated this country and everyone in it.

"Is there anything else I can help you with, Mr. Mervin?" Miss Smart-Suit asked.

What a stupid question, which deserved nothing more than a sarcastic answer.

"Yes, get me on the next flight to Iraq, cos' I felt more welcome there."

Miss Smart-Suit obviously didn't like my reply and promptly vacated her seat to help someone more important, such as an ex-con or scrounging school leavers.

There was little point hanging around so I decided not to use the touch-screen displays and made a sharp exit from the building. Whilst driving home I reflected upon my situation, but couldn't get my head around it. What was I supposed to do should the army fail to reinstate my civilian job, and how will Helen and I cope if my money ran out before I could find further employment?

I had a mortgage and bills to pay, a family to feed, and Helen was pregnant. Rob a bank? Tempting thought. After all, they've robbed me over the years. But no, not really an option. It was time to take a reality check and think about which remaining options I had. Difficult to do when all I could think about was Helen, my boss, Miss Smart-Suit's attitude, and the way my government had swept me under the carpet to the point of denying I'd ever existed.

CHAPTER 5

UNSUCCESSFUL ON THIS OCCASION

I went home to think things through. First and foremost I had to keep positive. Try to look on the bright side and forget about the incredible attitude of Miss Smart-Suit and even Stumpy from the working men's club. Above all, definitely keep Helen in the dark about my – or rather our – predicament. It was pointless upsetting her. Besides, what would it have achieved? I also decided to write to my old boss and ask if it was possible to make an appointment to see him, making a polite and proper approach, I suppose. And should push come to shove I could always use my HGV (Heavy Goods Vehicle) Class 1 licence to find work.

Since the mid-1990's Britain has suffered a huge shortage of HGV drivers – hence the sudden surge of former eastern-bloc immigrant truck drivers filling the gap – and the reason for this is quite simple. Since Tony Blair's reign, to become a HGV Class 1 driver you now have to take three driving tests, with each test costing anything around £1,000 including training. Thanks to the army I was actually paid to do my training and test, which I needed to drive a 27-ton recovery truck and tow casualty vehicles and trailers on public roads.

Once you have your Class 1 licence further costs continue should you wish to retain it. Every HGV driver now has to have a digital driver card or 'Digi-card' as it's known, costing around £50. It records daily and weekly driving duties, which is then downloaded onto a computer at the end of each shift, replacing the old analogue tachograph cards. After every 5-years, however, it has to be replaced, costing a further £30, not including the extra £10 for an updated photograph, which is also required on your driving licence. Then there's the HGV medical, which has to be taken when you reach 40 years of age, and every 5 years thereafter until the age of 60 years. After which, a medical is required every year, costing approximately £60-£100 each time.

Incredibly the government have thought of something else to rob the wallet of HGV drivers by introducing an obligatory DCPC (Driver Certificate of Professional Competence) costing around £300 – £400, that has to be renewed every 5-years, so the government are confident HGV drivers can drive their trucks safely and professionally. And there's me thinking a driving test was more than adequate. But once again, the EU decided that not enough money was being made out of the transport industry.

As you can see, driving a truck for a living is a costly career move, not to mention the irregular working hours and shift patterns to contend with. My only remaining options were to apply for vacancies advertised in my local rag or face another interrogation by Miss Smart-Suit at the Jobcentre. I opted to apply for vacancies in my local rag.

I bought a copy and feeling optimistic I applied for jobs similar to my previous experiences – working in HGV workshops, parts departments, forklift driving and even telephone sales. In fact anything, so long as it wasn't HGV driving. My CV also needed updating, but how was I supposed to do that without mentioning my call-out to Iraq and recent sacking from my last employer? Naively I told the truth.

Over the following week I applied for fifteen vacancies, yet only two bothered to reply, both saying the same thing: Sorry, you have been unsuccessful on this occasion. I knew I was qualified for most of the vacancies and over qualified for others, so why wasn't I getting any interviews? I didn't know until later. My mind was well and truly focused on finding further employment, and because I was so focused I'd almost forgot about Iraq. Although I was occasionally reminded by news bulletins, such as the news clip of President Bush strapped in a jet fighter landing on an aircraft carrier 1st May 2003, emphasising his belief that the war was over and all is tranquil in Iraq.

Saddam Hussein, or rather his Generals, did in fact surrender to the US-led coalition on 16th April. The remaining Fedayeen militia and the odd Iraqi soldier die-hards loyal to Saddam, however, continued to fight the coalition because it was their turn to live in fear of the oppressed Iraqi population that had a huge axe to grind. And boy, were they grinding.

Finally, twenty-two job applications later, I received a letter instructing me to attend an interview at 10am Monday 26th May. The vacancy was for a stores manager position at a printing and packaging engineering firm that supplied and installed packaging machinery. Not exactly my ideal job but at least it would pay bills and it didn't involve driving an HGV.

Suited and booted I arrived for the interview and sat on one of the grey plastic chairs. A low level table with glossy 'packaging machinery' magazines placed neatly on the glass top took centre stage in the modern air-conditioned reception, and a 'help yourself' coffee machine stood next to the factory floor entrance. The temptation to grab a coffee was almost unbearable but my attention was quickly diverted towards a smartly dressed attractive young lady. Maybe in her mid thirties, and not unlike Miss Smart-Suit from the Jobcentre, she walked into the reception from the factory floor and stood in front of the coffee machine.

"Mr. Mervin?" she said with a soft, almost inaudible voice.

"Yes luv, that'll be nice, white with 2 sugars," I jovially replied, hoping she'd actually do the honours and get me a coffee.

She frowned and ignored my request. "Come this way, please."

Following her through the factory floor entrance we walked alongside a row of glass partitioned offices. The factory floor was loud and busy with air tools whirring and whizzing, drilling and riveting bits of packaging machinery. I looked at the workforce to see how happy they were, remembering some vague interview tips given to me by my old careers' officer from secondary school. Why I suddenly remembered him I don't know, but his tips had always sprung to mind at previous job interviews.

He told us to first notice the cars in the car park. If they looked old and tatty that's a sure sign the wages were low. If they looked new and some were even sporty the wages will be good. Second, checkout the workforce to see what kind of mood they're in. If they looked as miserable as sin that's also a sure sign the conditions are terrible and the management is screwing them into the ground. Since leaving school I discovered that his words of wisdom have turned out to be a load of bollocks.

I followed Miss Smart-Suit-Two into a sound-proofed boardroom towards the rear of the factory, with huge double glazed windows facing the shop floor – no doubt to keep an eye on the work force.

"Please take a seat, Mr. Mervin, I'll be right back."

"Off to fetch the boss, eh?" I replied in an attempt to raise a smile on her face.

She didn't respond. In fact I'm sure I noticed a rather disgusted look on her face.

I pulled out one of a dozen black leather padded chairs from under a large polished oak boardroom table and sat leaning over it whilst Miss Smart-Suit-Two, in a classic pre-interview fashion, left me alone for a few minutes to gather my thoughts. I grabbed the moment to execute another early 1980's careers' officer top tip by making a mental note of my surroundings, in particular the display cabinet at the top end of the room. I memorised some of the brand name cartons and packaging in the cabinet made by their machines in a feeble attempt to impress the interviewers should they ask if I knew a little about the company.

"Mr. Mervin, sorry to have kept you waiting," a sharp and booming voice cried out entering the boardroom.

I was taken by surprise and jumped up from my seat, almost feeling myself standing to attention.

"Sit down, Mr. Mervin, and make yourself comfortable," the same voice bellowed, which I could now see came from a small fat man in a dark grey suit, aged around fifty or so. "Been in the wars, have we?" he added, taking note of my bandaged hand as he made his way around the table.

I didn't comment.

He drew a chair opposite and plonked his fat arse on it, placing my CV and application form in front of him. Although vertically challenged, maybe 5ft 4-inches tall, his confident manner came across as being the big boss man. Sitting next to him was Miss Smart-Suit-Two, whom I thought was his assistant manager. Boy, was I wrong.

"Let me introduce myself, I'm Brian, the factory manager. Sitting with me is Vincenza, the owner of the company, who I believe you have already met."

Oh shit, I'd cocked-up the interview before it'd even started. I smiled at her, which was reciprocated with what can only be described as a 'you sexist pig' stare.

"Would you like a coffee?" Brian asked. He then looked at Vincenza to do the honours.

"Milk and sugar, luv?" Vincenza sarcastically asked, emphasising the word *love* whilst continuing her stare of contempt. She certainly had it in for me from the start, and seemed unhappy with Brian's 'I'm the boss' attitude.

"Yeah please, two sugars," I nervously answered.

Vincenza left the boardroom to fetch the coffees. Brian, who certainly gave the impression of being a tad sexist, didn't even notice her leave as he continued to read my application form. I couldn't help but break into a smile. I liked the way he expected the owner of the company to fetch the coffees just because she was a woman.

I attempted to hide my smile by looking down at my tie, but when I looked up a few seconds later, instead of seeing Brian I was sitting opposite a sergeant dressed in CS95 uniform. I was back at Chetwynd barracks where I spent the first few days of pre-deployment training. The Sergeant was sifting through a mountain of paperwork. Then, without looking up, asked which regiment I was to be attached with.

"SDG's, " I answered.

The SDG (Scots Dragoon Guards) was the original regiment I supposed to have been attached with (known as a detachment) prior to going into Iraq. But like most of my unit, we ended up swapping and changing at the last minute, eventually finding a detachment with 2RTR (2nd Royal Tank Regiment).

"What?" Brian muttered under his breath, looking a tad confused.

A dark blue sleeve belonging to Vincenza suddenly appeared from behind and placed a vending machine cup of coffee in front of me.

"Your coffee, Mr. Mervin."

I picked it up from the table, but it wasn't from the one in the boardroom; it was a folding table you have on an aeroplane to eat your mid-flight meal from. I was now seated next to the Lieutenant I shared a flight with coming home from Iraq. My hand begun to shake uncontrollably, spilling almost half of its contents down my shirt and onto my lap.

"Are you okay, you've gone very pale?" the Lieutenant asked.

My head snapped towards his words with confusion written all over my face.

"Yes, I'm fine, sir," I instinctively replied, still bemused as to why I was sitting next to him.

Without warning I returned back to reality sitting opposite Brian, appearing somewhat amazed as to why I called him 'sir'.

My unexpected trip back to Chetwynd barracks, only to be then sitting beside the Lieutenant on my flight home to Blighty, coupled with the fact I was supposed to be conducting myself in a professional manner at a job interview, made me feel faint. Blood drained from my head causing me to break out in a cold sweat. This was not the right time to have a flashback, if there is ever a right time, let alone have two rolled into one. That had never happened before, and it scared me.

"Why did you suddenly shout out SDG's, what's that? And why did you call me sir?" Brian asked.

Oh boy, embarrassed or what.

"Well, the SDG's are the Scots Dragoon Guards, I'm sorry for shouting it out, I must have been thinking of something else."

Vincenza sat next to Brian, but her 'sexist pig' stare was replaced with a sudden 'get this mad man out of my factory' stare.

I took a few sips of my coffee. The sweet taste brought the colour back to my cheeks, but the few minutes of silence that followed didn't help the awkward situation. Neither of them spoke a single word; they just stared at me, wondering if I was about to pass out or lash out.

"Do you want to continue?" Vincenza eventually asked, albeit a tad nervously.

"Yeah please, I'm okay now. Must be the thought of being interviewed, the pressure, you know."

I was making a feeble excuse, but it didn't alter the fact they thought I was some crazed lunatic.

"Right then," Brian said, eager to get the interview started, let alone over with, "tell me a little about yourself."

Still feeling a little delicate I went through the usual bullshit – school, college, previous employment experience – then reached the point of explaining the story about my last employer, and paused.

"Carry on," Brian prompted, but in a somewhat precarious manner, probably wondering what I was going to say or do next.

"Well, as you can see on my application form I've explained what happened with my last employer."

He scanned through my application. "Oh yes, must have missed that bit."

Silence filled the air once again, adding to the already uncomfortable atmosphere.

"Ah, I see you were called-up for Iraq. Can you explain in more detail?" Brian asked glancing at my plastercast, seemingly wondering if my injury had anything to do with it.

I started to explain, then out of nowhere – *bang*!

Without warning I instinctively jumped out of my chair to find cover. For a split second I thought we were under a mortar attack, then realised the loud bang came from the factory floor, as a piece of heavy machinery dropped a few inches from a chain lift onto the concrete floor. I gingerly climbed back into my chair, facing two shocked and now very nervous interviewers across a boardroom table.

"I'm sorry, maybe I should forget about this interview and leave." I said, concluding I had well and truly cocked it right up.

Further looks of nervousness came from the opposite side of the table, especially from Vincenza.

"We've nearly finished, anyway, Mr. Mervin, I only have to tell you the salary and a few other things about the vacancy and that's it. Unless Vincenza has any questions?"

Brian looked at Vincenza for a reply, whom looked back at him with eyes the size of saucepan lids, slowly shaking her head. It was clear to see both wanted this interview to finish so they could boot me off site. Not two minutes later the interview came to an abrupt end.

As I drove home I decided not to tell Helen about the interview. I thought it best to keep her spirits up and pretend it went okay.

My situation, however, remained the same – becoming increasingly desperate.

"Hi, did it go well?" Helen shouted as I walked through the front door.

"Yeah okay, nothing out of the ordinary. I have to wait for a letter to see if I got it or not," I replied, picking up post from the hallway table. I sifted through the letters as I walked into the front room where Helen was ironing. "Looks a good job, though," I added, keeping up the charade.

"You've had a phone call from that MP bloke," Helen replied changing the subject.

I forgot about him. I wrote to my local MP (Member of Parliament) to see if he could help reinstate my civilian job. I explained the situation, and that I tried to see my ex-boss but he refused to see me, adding that I'd wrote to him but never received a reply. Of course, I never expected a reply from my MP either.

"What did he say?" I asked.

"It was his secretary, but she asked if you could pop into his surgery on Friday at three o'clock, for a chat."

Finally, it seemed my luck was changing for the better and my spirits begun to lift a little.

I sorted the mail in order of importance and sat down on the settee to read them. Amongst the pile were two more rejection letters, one of which caught my attention as to why I'd been refused, and I couldn't believe it. Because I was in the TA the company feared that if employed I might be called out again, leaving the business in a compromising position.

"Good news?" Helen asked.

"Not exactly, no."

"Replies from your job applications?"

"Yeah, but they say the usual: you have been unsuccessful on this occasion... blah, blah, blah."

I thought it best not to tell her I'd been rejected because I was in the TA.

"Never mind. At least you stand a good chance with the one you went for today."

I smiled at her, not really knowing what to say, and couldn't help but think I was never going to find a job. I had to admit I was scared. Not only of my flashbacks seemingly intensifying, but also the future and what it may bring for my family. It appeared my only chance of finding employment was help from my MP.

I opened the last envelope marked with a NHS stamp. The formal letter inside invited me to arrange an appointment with my local hospital about my injured hand, thankfully arranged by the army. Ever since my arrival home I'd been bombarded with telephone calls from an over concerned army constantly nagging about my health, resting my broken thumb, and that I was in good health.

They were beginning to be a pain. I even received telephone calls from various colonels quizzing me on mental issues and asking if I needed to see an army psychiatrist or a counsellor. Tempting as it were to ask for psychiatric help, I thought better of it, deciding to cope with my flashbacks on my own. Call it bravado or just plain stupidity, but I simply felt asking for help would be admitting I'd failed the army and was going slightly nuts.

I telephoned the number on the letter and made an appointment: Monday 2nd June at 11am. Hopefully by then I'll feel a little better in myself, have a positive response from a potential employer and all will be well in the world. Then maybe, just maybe, my family and I will be able to put my war behind us and get back to some sort of normality.

CHAPTER 6

IT'S ONLY POLITICS

Sir Mike Jackson, retired Chief of General Staff, whom I met during my pre-deployment training at Chilwell, once mentioned that his soldiers were overburdened by a Labour government that does not seem to appreciate them, whilst leaving soldiers with too many commitments. He also mentioned that the Labour government neglected to ensure that soldiers were properly accommodated and properly paid, and did not provide the troops with satisfactory equipment.

Sir Mike Jackson, who served in the army for 43 years and is highly respected by soldiers, warned that poor treatment was making it difficult to recruit men and women into all three Armed Forces. He also accused the Ministry of Defence of adopting a politically correct stance, exacerbated by Tony Blair and his arrogant socialist government.

It is blatantly obvious that there was a huge anti-military clique amongst Tony Blair's treasury and cabinet members, most of whom regarded spending money on the Armed Forces as a diversion of funds from the social budget. Especailly when most, if not all of Tony Blair's disciples, followed the concept that socialism was the way forward and that the military symbolised evil capitalism; convieniently forgeting about their mentor, Stalin, and his approach towards spending billions on the Soviet army.

Gordon Brown, the Chancellor during Tony Blair's reign and unelected Prime Minister soon after, must bare full responsibility for the Treasury's renouncing attitude against the British Armed Forces, since he was personally responsible for reducing the number of infantry battalions at a time when the infantry was desperately needed in Iraq and Afghanistan. Comrade Brown, however, as always, had his childish tantrums when accused of not understanding defence. History, however, proved that he didn't have a clue.

Ignoring warnings from other parts of the political spectrum, he arrogantly continued to reduce defence spending towards a dangerous all-time low, inevitably compromising the army's fighting strength and its capability of even defending the UK, let alone carrying out operations abroad. It left many unanswered questions as to why Brown would do this, suggesting he lacked serious understanding of how the British Armed Forces operated and what their requirements actually were. But comrade Brown wouldn't back down. After all, he was the leader – albeit unelected – and therefore right. Everyone else was simply wrong.

Brown treated all wings of the Armed Forces terribly, to the point of contempt; preferring to waste billions of tax payers hard earned cash on projects that created social popularity for the Labour party: the Millenium Dome, writing off African debts, sucking up to minority groups, religious leaders... the list went on and on and on.

When the pot was empty, however, with two conflicts to fight, Brown had to face reality and scratch around for cash, desperately seeking funds to finance overseas operations, if only to temporarily appease outraged public voters. But from where? He couldn't be seen cutting back on public services, not after a decade wasting tax payers' money on pathetic pilot ideas.

In desperation and his own selfish way of thinking he forced the MOD to go cap-in-hand to – can you believe it – the National Lottery trust fund with a begging bowl and kindly ask for some kind of grant to help towards funding the two conflicts. It's beyond any level of intelligence that an unelected Prime Minister (in effect a dictator) could actually stoop so low and turn down funds for the Armed Forces. The same Forces preventing terrorist cells from Al Qaeda attacking mainland Britain having to approach the private sector and beg for money.

General Jackson knew that operations in Iraq and Afghanistan were going catatrophically bad due to Labour government cutbacks, and that soldiers and airmen were being needlessly killed because Tony Blair and comrade Brown couldn't, or perhaps refused to borrow any more money for equipment to enhance military effectiveness, or even devise a strategy to extricate soldiers from the situation in which a socialist government policy had embroiled them in the first place.

To rub salt into the wound Brown left the army to fight two wars with low-cost equipment, including CBA's (Combat Body Armour). This basic yet vital piece of kit was, unbelievably, beyond what the government could afford at the time. Incredibily, there wasn't even any money available for a much needed recruitment campaign.

Media reports showed that Tony Blair was popular with the Armed Forces because he made a personal effort to visit them in theatre, appearing genuinely grateful for what they were doing on behalf of his socialist government and the British people back home. Comrade Brown, however, came across as being made to visit soldiers, if only to boost his popularity and get much needed votes for the forthcoming general election. In reality, he came across as not caring a jot about the vital work troops were doing in Iraq and Afghanistan, or elsewhere around the globe.

It's hardly surprising he was never popular with the Armed Forces, as he was clearly out of his depth when dealing with voters wearing uniforms. And it was obvious to everyone else, other than Brown and his massive following of socialist disciples and 'yes men', that the defence of the United Kingdom was severely neglected under his unelected leadership.

Many of Brown's ministers at the time of his leadership also failed to recognise the need of the MOD, its importance in defending the UK and even the meaning of morale amongst the troops. They frequently confused toughness for high morale, and it is simply not the same. Morale stems from good leadership, discipline and comradeship. It is not about feeling good because you have an illusionistic leader at the helm of 10 Downing Street.

When other cabinet ministers returned from jollies visiting soldiers on operations, they simply reported to their leader that all is well and morale is high, therefore we must be doing something right. In reality they were missing the fact that troops were being polite and would never admit to suffering from any government cutbacks. They never do, and never will. It's tantamount to admitting defeat and asking for help, which British soldiers simply have no concept of.

Because of the Labour government's lack of understanding they continued to make further cuts to the Armed Forces, to the point of risking lives of TA soldiers by axeing their training for six months. This meant that TA soldiers due for deployment to Afghanistan in April 2010 were told that the MOD could not afford to pay for any more vital combat training before they left, just because Brown wanted to save a miserly £20million. A drop in the ocean considering the TA is vital for the defence of the UK and its government.

Senior officers warned that such a decision would cost lives because Britain's 'weekend warriors' will fall behind in their preparations for combat. Serving TA soldiers predicted that units would disband, thousands of reservists would quit and recruitment would dry up, rendering the TA useless in combat. Brown, however, was more interested in gaining popularity from civvy street voters by spending £12billion on a pointless VAT cut to render his political reputation, yet unwilling to spend a mere £20million to train the TA whilst still at war.

Friday, May 30th 2.30pm. Suited and booted I felt as if I was going for another job interview. I gathered my rejection letters and a copy of the 'Dear John' letter from my previous employer should my MP wish to read them, and drove to his office hoping I was armed with everything needed to put my case across. He was my last hope to reinstate my job and I didn't want to leave anything to chance.

I parked outside his surgery, which was nothing more than an end-of-terrace Victorian house with a bay fronted sash-window and a bright red front door – naturally. I depressed the button on the intercom and waited for a reply.

"Can I help you?" a friendly female voice asked.

"Yes, hello, I'm Kevin Mervin, I have an appointment to see Mr. Crawford." I checked my watch and was actually ten minutes early.

"Please come in, Mr. Mervin," she replied, buzzing the door lock to release the mechanism.

I walked into the hallway, which was not unlike any other Victorian terraced house, greeted by a fifty-something year-old smartly dressed lady waiting at the entrance of the office, which was originally the front room.

"Mr. Crawford won't be long. You're a little early," she said in a polite but sturdy manner. "Please wait in here," she added, ushering me into the reception, which was originally the back room of the house.

Above the fireplace on the chimney-breast proudly hung a large portrait print of Tony Blair, dressed in a dark blue suit and wearing a red tie, dominating the magnolia painted wood-chipped wallpapered room. Oh, the temptation to draw a comedy beard and moustache on it was almost impossible to ignore, but I managed to resist, if only because I never had a pen.

I sat on one of the few dusty wooden chairs erratically placed around the walls of the room and picked up a magazine from the glass-top coffee table. The room resembled an old doctor's waiting room I visited from to time as a child, less the painting of Tony Blair, of course. Even the magazine I picked up wouldn't have looked out of place – a copy of 'People's Friend'. Flicking through it, not at all interested in its contents, Mrs Fifty-Something, whom I presumed was his secretary, entered the room, smiled and limply outstretched an arm to indicate I should walk through to the front room.

"Go right in, Mr. Mervin," she said, "Mr. Crawford will see you now."

I returned a smile, threw the magazine back on the table and walked into his office. Behind an old Victorian dark wooden desk placed in front of the fireplace stood Mr. Crawford. He looked like a typical MP with rosy cheeks, collar-length grey hair and dressed like my old geography teacher, including a tweed jacket with brown leather patches on the elbows, dark brown trousers, white shirt and of course wearing a red tie.

"Mr. Mervin, please sit down," he cheerily said.

I walked over to the chair adjacent to his desk as he showed a hand to offer a welcoming handshake. I shook his clammy hand the best I could with my left and sat down, as did Mr. Crawford.

"Now then, what can I do for you?" he asked, momentarily staring at my plaster cast.

"I take it you know why I'm here," I presumed.

Mr. Crawford's cheery welcoming smile suddenly changed to a blank expression, giving away he didn't have a bloody clue as to why I wanted to see him.

He gave a vacant glance towards Mrs Fifty-Something, silently screaming for some kind of explanation. Sitting behind her desk next to the front window, she frantically shuffled around a pile of paperwork then handed him a letter – my letter.

He quickly scanned over it. "Oh I see, and you are here because?"

My brilliant idea of seeing an MP to help reinstate my job seemed to fall at the first fence. I assumed he must have read my letter and wanted to help. After all, why go to the trouble of writing a letter and invite me to see him? Instead, he came across as being totally ignorant to my situation.

"As you can see in my letter, I want to know if you can help get my old job back. I've tried every possible avenue but drawn a blank. As I see it, you are my only hope."

Mr. Crawford sat back in his seat holding the letter and let out a long sigh. "To be honest, I can't see what I can do. As you say, you've tried every avenue. Besides, I was never in support of the invasion of Iraq in the first place."

"Liberation you mean," I quickly corrected.

"Eh?"

"You said invasion. It wasn't, it was a liberation."

"What makes you say that?" he questioned.

I had a feeling this would happen – become immediately sucked into some political argument over the war. He was 'Old Labour' after all, and most definitely against, as he saw it, the invasion of Iraq. He even attended the anti-war march in London on the eve of the conflict, so I knew I wasn't going to win any Brownie points by contradicting his moral beliefs. I had to return to the reason why I wanted to see him.

"Look, Mr. Crawford, I'm in a corner here and beginning to realise there is no way out. I've tried to find further employment but it seems no one will employ me, so can you help, or do you know anyone who will lean, politically, on my boss and persuade him he was wrong to sack me for being called out."

He let out a laugh. "I don't think so, Mr. Mervin, if your boss sacked you, that's nothing to do with me."

"Yes it is," I snapped, "you're my MP and your boss has repeatedly said that the likes of me have nothing to worry about because our jobs are protected by law. Or is that yet more political bullshit?"

The expression on Mr. Crawford's face looked like a cat's arse sucking a lemon, and his cheeks glowed with anger because how dare I, a mere part-time squaddie, blaspheme our illustrious leader, Tony – the Second Coming – Blair.

Before he could get a word in edge-ways I threw my rejection letters on his desk. "Here, take a look at these."

He glanced through the letters, mumbling as he read them.

"What do you think of the one that won't employ me because they fear I might be called up again, or how about the one from my boss?"

He didn't reply. Instead he stared out of the bay window for a few seconds, obviously thinking of some politician's answer – yet more bullshit.

"Mr. Mervin, I fully understand your predicament," see, bullshit, "but I really don't know what I can do to help. You lost your job through, what seems, some loophole, which I have no real answer for. Sorry, but may I offer my best wishes to you and your family –"

"Stop!" I shouted, raising a hand as if to signal him to halt, "your refusal to help has no bearing on your moral beliefs, then?"

"Of course not," he snapped, "I'm not simply refusing to help, I just can't see what I can do to help. Can you?"

I never expected to think of any ideas myself. That was his job. I had to think of something quick, no matter how outrageous.

"Okay, write a letter to my boss stating that as my MP you disagree with the disciplinary action taken against me and should therefore seriously consider withdrawing such decision to terminate my employment, or words to that effect. That'll do for a start. Then write another letter to show any potential employer, stating that my application must be treated without bias or conviction because I went to Iraq."

Fat chance he'd agree to it, but thought it was worth a try.

"I can't do that."

Told you.

"Why not?"

Again he paused, staring out of the window to think of an answer, and before he came out with yet more political crap I jumped in first. "Okay, can you find out if it's possible for me to claim unemployment benefit?"

Ignoring me, he looked at my letter again, reading the few lines explaining my visit to Miss Smart-Suit at the Jobcentre.

"Mr. Crawford, I hate to admit it but I'm becoming increasingly desperate here. I've been sacked from my job because I was called-up, unable to find work because I was called-up, and can't claim unemployment benefit because I was called-up. You must be able to do something for me."

Never thought I'd see myself begging for help from an MP, but I was.

As Mr. Crawford read through my letter all I could think was that my country had turned its back on me, and for what? Was it because I went to war, contributed to the liberation of a nation from a tyrant, but failed to find WMDs? And yes, I took what the nation said and thought of the conflict personally.

"If the Jobcentre said that you can't claim any unemployment benefit, and they must have given you some good reason as to why, then there is little I can do to persuade them otherwise," he firmly said, placing my letter on his desk.

I threw up my arms in submission, totally losing the argument to someone who either failed or refused to grasp my predicament.

"Tell you what, how about going public," I suddenly suggested, grasping at any crazy idea that came into my head, "we could go to local and regional newspapers, radio, even television. Let's embarrass my boss, and yours. I'm game if you are."

He frowned at the thought of such a ludicrous suggestion. After all, how could a Labour MP that marched against the liberation of Iraq shoulder to shoulder with the likes of George Galloway and Clare Short, support a soldier who'd fought for it? I would have received a more positive response if I suggested monkey tennis.

He leant forward on his desk and clasped his hands together. "I don't think that would be beneficial to either of us, Mr. Mervin," he whispered in a low voice, as if he was warning me not to even dare think of doing that, let alone go ahead with it.

"I give up," I said throwing up my arms in submission again. "Okay, what do you suggest I do?"

"Mr. Mervin, I fully understand your situation but there really is nothing I can do." He checked the time on his watch, maybe hinting to terminate this train crash of an appointment. "I do have other people to see, so I think you should go home to your family and sort out your problems from there."

"Tell you what, Mr. Crawford, how about if I wrote to your boss, good ole' Tony, to see what he thinks," I said sarcastically.

"Mr. Mervin, by all means write to the Prime Minister, but he will only tell you the same as me," he chuckled, "now please, I do have other appointments," he added, waving an arm gesturing me to leave the room.

"You mean Tony Blair has no problem sending the TA to war, but couldn't give a shit about us when we return home, only to be dumped in the gutter and forced to ask for help? Help that we shouldn't need to ask or even beg for in the first place!"

"Mr. Mervin, there's no need for that."

Oh yes there was.

"What am I supposed to do? By July I'll be demobilised and will lose my only income, thanks to your precious, whiter than white, purer than the driven snow, boss."

He sat back in his chair and appeared to be in deep thought. For a moment I thought he finally succumbed to my situation and was about to pull some proverbial rabbit out of the political hat; but no, he wasn't.

"Is your wife working?"

"Yes, why?"

"At least you have some money coming in, so things aren't that bad."

I couldn't believe it. It seemed he was attempting to find some moral get-out clause and make out I had nothing to worry about. I had to face it, he wasn't at all interested in me. I was no longer his or Tony Blair's problem. At least I knew where I stood – I was on my own.

He handed back my letters, which I took as my cue to leave. I snatched them from his hand and simply left without saying a word. What could I say? Thank him for his wise advice?

On the way home Helen came to the forefront of my mind. What was I going to tell her? Should I explain that our situation was becoming increasingly dire as each day passed? No, of course not. She was pregnant and upsetting her further wouldn't be a good idea, considering she lost our last baby at such an early stage of pregnancy.

My last and only hope, which I was determined to avoid, was to find some agency driving work before my demob date on the 4th July. If not I would have no income and therefore no means of paying the mortgage, bills, food... the list went on. With that in mind I felt as if I was being sucked into a deep, dark black hole, with no means or any idea of how to get out of it.

CHAPTER 7

NHS: TELL ME WHERE IT HURTS

Monday, 2nd June 10am. I gathered my army medical documents and drove to the local hospital. After finding a parking space and paying some extortionate fee for the privilege, I made my way to the main reception. Showing the receptionist my letter she acknowledged my appointment by giving directions as to where to go – follow a maze of corridors through the building eventually coming to a department for clumsy folk.

"I'm here to see doctor – " whomever it was written on the letter with some unpronounceable name, and showed it to the nurse behind a desk.

The nurse took my letter and medical documents and politely asked me to take a seat with the other accident prone patients, aged eight to eighty, all with some kind of broken bone, bump or bruise. Crutches, slings, neck braces and plastercasts were abundant. I sat on one of the plastic chairs and picked up a magazine from the table in front of me – a caravan magazine – that I never thought I'd ever read. I hated the bloody things. In fact, if Jeremy Clarkson from *Top Gear* walked in to the waiting room at that precise moment and caught me reading such literature he would have insisted I were shot at dawn.

One by one patients hopped, hobbled and virtually crawled to a cubicle at the far end of the waiting room when called by a nurse. Moments later they miraculously reappeared, almost skipping across the floor grinning from ear to ear, pleased to be free of plastercasts and bandages. I only hoped my appointment would go so well.

After an hour of waiting and countless pages on the six-berth Pathfinder-7 with a built in hot and cold running water system, boredom was setting in fast. Every time the cubicle door opened the remaining patients sat upright seemingly *willing* the duty nurse to shout out their name. Unfortunately, it was yet another nurse walking through with an arm full of paperwork.

"Mr. Mervin?"

I ignored my call. The write-up on the all singing, all dancing four-berth Countryman with fitted solar panels and a wind generator was just too riveting to put down.

"Mr. Mervin!" the duty nurse said again, peering from around the cubicle door and sounding a tad more assertive.

I could almost feel her authoritative glare as she scanned the remaining patients for a 'Mr. Mervin'. A glare that would have otherwise been saved for a student nurse administering an enema instead of an aspirin to a poor and rather unsuspecting patient.

I thought it best to quickly discard the magazine and make myself known. I casually raised my good arm and made my way towards her; she was still wearing a glare that could bore a hole in a railway sleeper. I raised a smile in an attempt to ease her mood, but it didn't even make a dent. She was obviously having a bad day.

"Wait here, the doctor will be with you in a moment," she snapped, showing me the examination bed as she walked out of the adjacent door.

I sat on the bed and took in my surroundings, making me feel faint. I knew I would sooner or later; I hate hospitals. In fact, I thought I was doing well to make it as far as the waiting room without passing out. I don't know why hospitals make me feel that way; they just do. Maybe it's the smell of detergent, the thought of patients being operated on only a few metres away or just the surgical instruments lying around. Whichever, my irrational phobia quickly caught up with my surroundings and made it quite clear I was going to react accordingly.

Doctor Unpronounceable decided to make an appearance. "I see you've injured your thumb in Iraq," he said without looking up from my casualty notes.

"Yes," I answered, trying my best to fight against my phobia.

He looked at me to acknowledge my reply; quickly noticing I wasn't feeling too good. "You okay, Mr. Mervin?"

"Yes, I'm fine, just not keen on hospitals, they make me feel, you know, queasy."

"You'd better lie down," said a surprisingly concerned nurse standing behind him. The same nurse with a face like thunder that called out my name.

I lay back on the bed and immediately started to feel the benefit. The sudden rush of blood to my head quickly resumed a healthier colour to my cheeks.

"Are you a regular soldier, Mr. Mervin?" Doctor Unpronounceable asked.

"No, TA, but I'm actually classed as regular at the moment because I'm effectively still on operations and signed to my regular unit in Iraq, until I'm demobilised in July."

Nurse Attitude, as I now named her, and the doctor, looked a tad confused to my reply, so I had a stab at explaining what happens when a TA soldier is called-out on operations and how the TA works.

I was fighting a losing battle here; neither of them had any idea that TA soldiers were called-out on operations. They both thought we were nothing more than a home defence force – a last resort should the Soviets invade, which is supposed to be a redundant concept since the fall of the Berlin wall back in 1989. Their ignorance surprised me considering many NHS doctors and nurses serve in the TA, many of whom continue to serve overseas in various operations. Obviously not these two.

"Was it worth it?" asked Nurse Attitude.

"What?"

"The invasion of Iraq."

Oh boy, yet another media suckered individual hell-bent on calling it an invasion.

"We didn't invade, luv, we liberated it. And yes, it was worth it. It had to be."

"Not from where I was standing," she sharply replied.

"And where was that, from the comfort of your own living room?" I snapped.

"We shouldn't have gone there in the first place," she said, conveniently ignoring my sarcastic reply.

"Maybe not you, that's for sure, but the Iraqis were pleased we did. I know that because they told me. What did they tell you from your living room sofa?" I added.

Again, she ignored me.

"Mr. Mervin, place your arm flat on the bed and wiggle your thumb," the doctor instructed, trying his utmost to ignore our conversation whilst he manipulated my hand.

Nurse Attitude stayed silent as she read through my notes, if only to appear professional in front of the doctor, but a smirk suddenly grew across her face as she said the most outrageous comment I'd heard since my arrival home. "Mr. Mervin, I think it would be best not to mention anything about your involvement in Iraq to any other members of staff or patients. We don't want them upset, do we?"

I didn't know how to react to that; or the doctor. I was certainly insulted by her remark and I think the doctor felt a little embarrassed.

"Do you suffer from any shooting pains when you try and move your thumb?" the doctor asked, seemingly changing the subject to simmer down the atmosphere.

At first I ignored the doctor's question. The temptation to have a go at Nurse Attitude was beginning to test my temper to its limit, but thought it better to stay calm. I didn't want to give her any ammunition. Besides, she and millions of other civilians had already made up their minds about the liberation, albeit misguided, so no matter what I said I wasn't going to change her ignorant mind.

"No, nothing, feels a little stiff, but there's no pain," I eventually answered.

"In that case, Mr. Mervin, I think your cast can come off. Your thumb seems to have healed correctly, although you may find some movement restricted."

Doctor Unpronounceable looked at the nurse and nodded, signalling her to fetch the tools needed to take off the cast. In other words, fuck off and keep your opinions to yourself.

"Sorry about Staff-Nurse Pickering and her political views. When she feels strongly about something, especially Iraq, she tends to let everyone know about it."

"She's entitled to her opinion, I suppose, but she should engage her brain before putting her mouth in gear."

The doctor frowned at me, as if to ask for an alternative explanation he could understand.

"What I mean is, she seems to reflect the opinion of journalists and newspapers that know sod all about the conflict."

"And I suppose you lot have all the answers."

I didn't like the tone of his voice, or his comment, if it was one. But I wasn't about to argue with someone holding my freshly healed thumb in his hand.

"Can you make a fist?" he added.

I gave it a go, but my thumb could only bend half way. "It's a bit difficult to."

"It will be. Your hand has been in one position for six weeks, so you'll need physiotherapy. I'll ask Staff-Nurse Pickering to arrange an appointment with our therapist. In the meantime we'll take an X-ray to make sure everything is okay."

"Can I sign off the Zed list, then?"

"Zed list?"

"The army placed me on a Zed list, which means I'm downgraded and restricted to softer duties. And because I was sent home that means I can't do a bloody thing."

The doctor rummaged through my folder. "I have a form here to complete, some kind of release form with other notes of your injury, which I suppose will tell them you are now fit for duty. I'll fill it in then you can give it to your Commanding Officer. Does that mean you will have to go back to Iraq?"

"Dunno."

"Well, if you do, be more careful next time."

I took the hint and returned a smile.

Nurse Attitude reappeared with a pair of what can only be described as garden shears, and headed straight for my arm.

"Don't worry, Mr. Mervin, I know what I'm doing."

The look of panic on my face certainly gave the nurse something to smile about.

"Lay your arm flat on the bed and relax."

Yeah right. Why did I have a feeling this was going to sting a bit. But I needn't have worried, she cut through the cast with ease and didn't even leave as much as a scratch.

"There you go, all done," she said in a way a mother would say to her son after ripping off an old band-aid.

I lifted my arm off the bed and rubbed my healed thumb, instantly smelling an odour of bandages and old plastercast.

The doctor completed my 'fit for duty' form and muttered something to the nurse before disappearing out of the cubicle.

"You're to have an X-ray, so gather your things and follow me," Nurse Attitude abruptly ordered.

I jumped off the bed and followed her down the many corridors to the X-ray department. I couldn't help but chuckle to myself as I watched the nurse's fat legs rub together in her black nylon stockings, sounding like a steam train struggling to climb an incline.

"Wait here," she commanded.

I sat on one of the plastic chairs outside the X-ray room whilst Nurse Attitude handed my notes to a guy in a light blue smock behind a desk and whispered something in his ear. He looked at me and frowned, obviously taking an instant dislike to whatever the nurse whispered. When she'd finished explaining to him what I can only presume was whom and what I was, she walked over to me.

"You won't be kept long. We have a busy X-ray department and don't want NHS resources clogged up by soldiers. We have real patients with real needs to treat, you know."

Difficult as it was I somehow ignored her comment.

"What about my physio appointment? The doctor said you'll make it for me."

"Me? No, that's up to you, I have civilian patients to look after."

I was about to react to that particular comment but was too late. She'd already about-turned and begun to chuff away down the corridor.

"Mr. Mervin, this way," the X-ray guy eventually said after keeping me waiting for almost half-an-hour.

He ushered me into the dimly lit room towards another plastic chair next to a padded table.

"Sit down and place your arm flat up-right on the bench."

I did what I was told as he slid a lead plate under my arm and positioned the X-ray machine inches away from my hand before disappearing behind a glass screen.

After a few clonks and clangs he re-emerged to reposition my hand to take another photograph.

"Staff-Nurse Pickering told me you were in Iraq," he quietly said.

Here we go again.

"Yes, that's right."

"So, why are you here, should you be in some military hospital?"

"There isn't any, they've all been closed down."

"Does that mean all TA soldiers have to go to NHS hospitals?"

"Well, yes, I suppose so, including regulars."

"If you ask my opinion, none of you lot should be treated by the NHS. It's bad enough with the amount of civilian patients we already have, let alone casualties from an illegal war."

He must have had the same views as Nurse Attitude, and he obviously didn't like the idea of me, a child murdering thug, clogging up NHS resources.

I was getting pissed off with all these jibes and sarcastic remarks. Tempting as it was to make a fist with my newly healed thumb and try it out on his jaw, I decided to keep quiet. Instead, I bit my tongue once more, whilst I endured further remarks about the 'invasion' as he also called it, and why he was so disgusted with the amount of civilians killed by indiscriminate shelling and bombing by coalition soldiers. Clearly he, like the rest of my country watching the conflict on television, had all the answers.

"What was it like?" he asked.

"What?"

"The war, what was it like?"

"You've just told me yourself, so why would you want to know what I think?"

A childish reply, I know, but he deserved no better.

"No, I mean, what was the scariest part of the war for you?"

"You really want to know?"

His expression changed to one of excitement, as if he was about to be privy to some exclusive war story. "Yes, of course I want to know."

I smiled, slowly leant forward, only to suddenly grab his throat, giving my thumb its first test of strength, and stared wide-eyed into his eyes. I'd finally lost it.

I could feel anger coursing through my veins, instantly awakening my demon within. It taunted me as I struggled between seriously damaging this pathetic excuse of a human being and my sanity. I knew what I was doing, and I knew it was wrong. Furthermore I wanted to stop, but I enjoyed watching him choke; desperately gasping for breath as his head changed to a deep shade of crimson.

Remembering his question I answered, "coming back to this pathetic country and putting up with having to listen to wankers like you."

His eyes appeared as if they were about to pop out of their sockets. I had more strength than I thought. It was then my demon backed down, giving me the strength to tap into sanity and release my grip.

I stood up, let go of his throat and kicked the plastic chair across the X-ray room in sheer frustration, quickly deciding that the chair should take the brunt of my anger rather than him.

The X-ray bloke jumped back in surprise and staggered a few steps towards the glass screen whilst massaging his throat. "You're fucking mad!" he screeched, "I'm calling security."

"And what do you suppose they'll do, throw me out? Tell you what, don't bother with the X-rays," I took out a £20 note from my wallet and threw it on the floor, "here, I'll pay for the photos you've took. After all, I don't want to be a fucking burden on the NHS."

I left the X-ray room, grabbed my notes from the reception desk and headed for the car park, deciding not to make an appointment with the physiotherapist. I didn't fancy returning to a place where I wasn't welcome, convincing myself I'd do just as good a job as any physiotherapist. Besides, I'd already tested the strength of my thumb and it seemed okay to me.

Driving home I reflected on what I did to the X-ray guy. My MP decided to spring into my thoughts and replay what he said, or rather didn't say – his refusal to help. Miss Smart-Suit and the ex-convict from the Jobcentre suddenly decided to make an appearance, quickly followed by Vincenza and Stumpy from the working men's club. Why they all haunted me in one go, I don't know, but I couldn't get rid.

I didn't notice the Zebra crossing fast approaching. The whole scenario seemed to be in slow motion as the young mother, already half way across the road, cradled her little girl in a feeble attempt to save her from the impending impact. The girl, about the same age as Rachel, stared at me with wide, petrified eyes. Her mother too, stuck fast like a rabbit caught in the headlights of a car, frozen in total fear.

I stamped hard on the brakes and the screeching tyres caught the attention of passers-by. Shit, I wasn't going to stop in time. The mother managed to grasp the reality of what was about to happen and made a split second decision to make a dash for safety, leaving her bags of shopping behind. I pressed harder and harder on the brake pedal, but it was no use, if she doesn't move quickly I'll hit them both.

Instinctively I attempted to steer away from hitting them and headed towards the curb side, hoping the mother didn't decided to turn tail and head back the way she came. A split second later I passed over the crossing and ploughed into the bags of shopping left behind in the road. The sound of the bags hitting the lower part of the bumper and being dragged under the car was loud and sudden. In an instant daylight disappeared and I could smell the desert air – I was thrown back to when I'd ploughed through a Fedayeen militia roadblock, hitting two pick-up trucks full of tomatoes.

I finally came to a halt and the engine stalled. I looked around in a somewhat confused state. Why wasn't I in my Foden, where was Stuart, and why did I stop? I should have kept driving to clear the impending shit about to unfold. No time to think about that, I needed my rifle before the choggies (Fedayeen militia) opened fire first. I searched the back seat for my rifle, but it wasn't there. Shit, where is it? I had no choice but to leg it.

I attempted to start the engine but it just continued to turn over and over without sparking up. Too late. Round after round of enemy fire hit the bodywork. Any second now I'd be cut to pieces by automatic weapons.

"Oi, open the fucking door, you twat!"

The smell of desert air suddenly disappeared and was replaced by daylight, along with hysterical banging of fists and kicks over the car. I was back in the UK but wished I wasn't. Half a dozen or so eyewitnesses frantically tried all four doors, but the central locking device must have kicked in on impact with the shopping bags.

"Open the fucking door!" the same voice bellowed.

I looked to my right and could see a red-faced middle-aged bloke staring right at me. His eyes bulged with anger and spit sprayed the window as he continued to shout and scream obscenities. He was obviously a tad upset. Looking around the car I could see other men shouting and screaming through the glass, banging their fists on the roof, desperately trying to get at me. Shit, they wanted blood.

Reality returned and I quickly realised what I'd done. I unlocked the door to step out of the car and explain what had happened. As soon as the door locks disengaged two burly-looking blokes, clearly builders or civil engineers of some description brandishing shovels, dragged me out of the car.

"Thought you'd try and drive off, did ya?" one of them shouted.

"You'll wish you had," added his mate.

Before I could explain, and where I'd begin I didn't know, someone kicked me in the back and I fell to the ground, quickly followed by further kicks and punches from the rest of the mob. I curled up into a tight ball and prayed they'd get bored very quickly, but remembered the shovels. I could do nothing about them but wait for the inevitable whack across my head.

"Leave him alone!" the young mother shouted from across the road, "he doesn't deserve this, he tried to stop."

The lynch mob stopped kicking and started to mutter amongst themselves as the young mother, still carrying her daughter, ran over to what seemed my rescue.

"He tried to start his car and fuck off," one of the builders replied.

"No one was hurt, and why do you think he was trying to start his car?" She pointed down the road, clearly concerned about the tailback caused by the incident. "Look at the queue, he was trying to move it to one side and let the traffic pass."

Actually, I wasn't. As far as I was concerned I was being sprayed with automatic fire and wanted to get the fuck out. But if she says I was trying to move my car from the middle of the road to let traffic pass, who am I to argue.

"He's a mad driver and needs teaching a lesson, darlin'."

"Someone call the police!" a proverbial little old lady screeched, whom I'm sure was part of the bloody lynch mob.

"And I'll tell them about you lot picking on an innocent man," the young mother added.

Hearing the police were about to be called made the majority of the crowd quickly disappear. They were clearly a tad nervous of the law getting involved, although the lynch mob didn't really care or give a shit about the queue of traffic patiently waiting to pass.

"Look at this," one of the other builders said, slightly out of breath as he returned from moving my car. He brought with him my casualty notes, shoving them under the nose of his mate. "He's a fucking soldier, look."

I managed to stand up, with a little help from a wheelie-bin, and dusted myself down.

"Who you with?" the builder asked studying my casualty notes, referring to which regiment.

I ignored him to thank the young mother for stopping the ritual kicking.

"I'm sorry about that, I lost concentration and didn't see you."

"I was half way across the fucking road! What d'ya mean you didn't fucking see me?" she snapped.

"Hey, he's been to Iraq and was injured," the builder interupted, scanning my casualty notes.

I snatched them from his hand. "These have nothing to do with you."

For a split second I thought he was about to wrap his shovel around my head, but he didn't. He just sneered then walked off with his mate, quickly followed by the remaining mob that were thirsting for my blood only a few minutes before.

I looked at the remains of the young mother's shopping spread across the road.

"Let me pay for your loss, it's the least I can do. How much?"

I grabbed my wallet and was about to give her a predicted £20 note, which was all I had left after stupidly shelling out for my X-ray photos.

"Fifty quid," she quickly replied.

"How much?"

"Well, it didn't come to that, but I'll need to get a new jacket for my daughter. It's ruined no thanks to you."

One of the sleeves on the scruffy looking jacket did have a small tear and it was suspect as to if I'd caused it, but I wasn't going to argue. Looking into the eyes of the young child, however, reminded me of the children in Iraq dressed in rags.

"I'll have to get some money out of a cash machine."

"There's one up the road," she said, pointing at the shop she'd been to earlier.

I withdrew £50 from the machine, quickly snatched from my hand by the young mother.

"Once again, I'm sorry for nearly knocking you over."

"Don't worry about it, I'm not."

"How about your daughter, is she okay?"

I looked at the young child clinging tightly to Mummy's legs. She seemed okay, with no cuts or bruises evident.

"Make sure you buy something nice for your daughter, won't you."

"Fuck that, she can go to her gran's, the miserable little madam. I've got an extra fifty quid here so I'm off out tonight," she surprisingly said without giving any moral judgement or concern over her daughter's wellbeing.

Without a bye-or-leave the young overweight mother, dressed in black leggings and a dirty pink tracksuit top, dragged her daughter down the pavement, clearly in a hurry to palm the youngster off with her mother so she could go out on the piss.

I also didn't hang around. Some of the lynch mob returned when they realised the police hadn't been called, and judging by the look on their faces they still wanted to have a go at me. I jumped back in my car, which thankfully started first time, and headed home.

Considering Helen's condition I never told her about my little fracas. I didn't want to burden her with yet more worry, and keeping Helen in the dark was becoming second nature. Instead, I said everything went okay and my thumb was now healed. What I didn't say, and once again keeping something else to myself, was the question raised by Doctor Unpronouncible at the hospital: Will I be returning to Iraq now I'm fit for duty?

If I was ordered to, how would I tell Helen, and how would she react? In many ways I wanted to go back. After all, my country showed nothing but contempt since I returned home and at least I'd be earning. With that in mind I placed my 'fit for duty' form into an envelope and posted it to the address provided. Within a week or two the army will make the decision whether or not I should return to continue my tour.

CHAPTER 8

LEFT OUTSIDE ALONE

When it suited the political climate, journalists and the print media couldn't wait to jump on TA soldiers returning home from tours of Iraq and Afghanistan, craving for that horrific war story to try and better their equally blood-thirsty counterparts.

Within hours of disembarking their aeroplanes, battle-weary squaddies eager to return home to their loved ones were preyed upon by waiting journalists and reporters, without even being given the chance to remove their boots from aching feet. The journalists acted like hungry vultures encircling an injured animal. Radio and television quickly climbed upon the bandwagon to grab personal accounts of the war, only to manipulate them to suit their political persuasion.

I was interviewed on numerous occasions by the print media, radio and television, promising my point of view would be voiced. Of course, it rarely was. Like many interviewed about the liberation – from the humble squaddie to retired generals – journalists, reporters and television presenters were more interested in putting across their own opinions to feed their disillusioned information hungry followers.

Television production companies were also quick on the uptake when it came to expressing their own opinion about the war, to the point of leaving sections of an interview on the cutting room floor simply because many soldiers' anecdotes didn't agree with their politics. I too had experience of this when a certain television production company made a documentary for Channel 4 about the TA in Iraq and Afghanistan, presented by Colonel Bob Stewart – Commander during the Bosnia conflict – now turned politician.

After a day's filming telling my story to Bob, along with how I thought the TA had been treated by the government, media and the general public, it was suddenly dropped from the programme. Maybe I was being too honest and the production company didn't want the public to know the hard truth, or maybe I didn't reflect the political climate at the time.

The msot self-opinionated person I was ever interviewed by had to be George Galloway MP, whom I was told once served in Her Majesty's Armed Forces. He interviewed me on his Sky television programme, The Real Deal. As we all know he can be a tad controversial on certain topics, especially concerning the Middle East.

Our politics and views on Iraq were poles apart, although he did have a few opinions of the conflict that made sense, one of which was the political mess the US government had made of the conflict, turning it into an utter quagmire.

When the producer of George's programme invited me to his studio in London for a live interview, I jumped at the chance. I'd listened to George's night time discussion show on TalkSport radio many times, where he presented himself as being fair and balanced towards any debate – providing you agreed with his politics.

To be a listener is one thing but if as a caller on his show you contradicted his stance on any subject he would simply cut you off, then proceed to play down your original questioning or opinion by injecting his own perceived reasoning. So to be interviewed by the most controversial Member of Parliament, broadcaster and political presenter in modern British broadcasting history, and in a circumstance where he couldn't cut me off when I disagreed with his bullshit, I had to grab the opportunity.

My preconceived thought on what I was letting myself in for seemed to be correct. When I arrived at his studio – nothing more than a converted cellar under an office block – the producer I spoke with on the telephone greeted me. I can only describe her as some middle-aged new-age traveller, with long green hair and dressed like a first year sociology student. All fired up to ban the bomb, save the whale, spread the latest eco-fashion gossip and the evils of oil and Jeremy Clarkson.

Ushered down stairs to the dark depths of George Galloway world I was introduced to another producer of the programme for a brief on what will happen during the 'live' interview, at which point George arrived. And there he stood – the sharpest dressed politician this country had ever seen, not a thread of tweed or corduroy in sight. He quickly introduced himself then disappeared, and that was the last I saw of him until the interview. As for the briefing, all I was told was that George will ask a few questions about Iraq. That was it.

During the interview I quickly realised, and correctly predicted, that George was only interested in putting across his opinion. And as a presenter of his own television programme he certainly came across as a tad egotistical. At one point he accused me of being some kind of agent sent by Tony Blair's government to infiltrate his program and spread their propaganda.

A preposterous accusation to say the least, but it proved to me that he didn't care what anyone else said, even those that had fought in Iraq at the time. His attitude was that his views of the conflict were correct and therefore everyone else is wrong. Not unlike comrade Brown's attitude towards running the country during his unelected administration.

Whilst he played with his Subha Islamic prayer beads under the desk and out of shot of the cameras he continued to pour his political persuasion over my answers. He would then try to twist and manipulate my replies and constantly interject biased views by saying to his viewers that hundreds-of-thousands of innocent Iraqi civilians had died horrific deaths because of the 'invasion'. And in typical George Galloway fashion he gave the impression that we – the coalition – were nothing more than murderous thugs. He even praised the groups of 'freedom fighters' as he called them, for fighting the invaders – predominantly the UK and the US.

I took such an allegation to heart and tried to explain to George and his viewers that 'freedom fighters' were supposed to fight for freedom, which would reflect that we, the coalition were just that. But the 'freedom fighters' George admired had no interest in saving a nation from tyranny. They wanted to continue it on their own terms to gain control and dictate rule over a petrified population, not unlike the Taliban in Afghanistan. And like the Taliban, George's 'freedom fighters' tortured and killed their own country folk because they dared to speak out.

During the liberation of Iraq these 'freedom fighters' were and still are supporters of the Ba'ath Party regime. Saddam Hussein paid these followers – known as the Fedayeen militia – to keep his evil control over the population. If anyone dared step out of line they were dragged to some barren wilderness, which Iraq has plenty of, then systematically tortured before being brutally murdered.

George fell silent and I quickly realised he was listening to what I was saying. I continued with a few further facts about his precious 'freedom fighters', such as about locals that were once terrified of these thugs who could right now tell the coalition where they were hiding. But if caught doing so by the Fedayeen, they were brutally murdered.

Often we would find evidence of this, including the charred remains of children forced to drink petrol then shot in the stomach with a tracer round, instantly causing the torso to explode. Or husbands forced to watch their wives repeatedly raped, only to have a pistol forced into their vaginas and shot after the militia had their fun. Leaving husbands to relive the sheer agony their wives had to endure before dying in front of petrified eyes, perpetually allowing the nightmare to haunt them for the rest of their lives.

Infants were also thrown alive from rooftops or into fires or canals to teach tale-tale-tit parents a lesson they will never forget, and to send a message to others to keep their mouths shut, otherwise the same would happen to their children. The Fedayeen militia, like many other factions in Iraq, were hellbent on keeping control of territory in any way they deemed fit, no matter what the cost.

These same groups of murdering bastards carried out numerous atrocities for decades, ordered by Saddam Hussein so he could keep control through fear. And let's not forget George Galloway once travelled to Iraq, stood in front of Saddam and saluted him. Saluted the same man responsible for hundreds-of-thousands of deaths during his dictatorship, including the gassing of hundreds of innocent civilians in 1988, and George had the nerve to call these thugs of Saddam 'freedom fighters.'

Maybe George should travel to Kuwait one day and see if he can get away with naming the Fedayeen militia as 'freedom fighters', or has he forgotten about the 'invasion' in August 1990 by Saddam Hussein and what the Iraqi generals and militia inflicted upon the Kuwaiti population. Or maybe walk with the Kurdish population in northern Iraq and tell them that he once shook hands with Saddam, and that the US and UK Governments had no right to invade Iraq. My guess is that he wouldn't walk out alive.

Needless to say it was pretty obvious George and I have very different views upon the liberation. His audience were also predictable with their reactions after I explained what George's 'freedom fighters' did to their own people. Text and emails came pouring into the show, and the telephone lines were jammed with callers thirsting for my blood. After all, I was insulting George's brainwashed followers and daring to question his knowledge of the invasion. One caller, who clearly watched the conflict on television, accused me of being brainwashed by the government and not having a clue as at to what I was talking about.

I came to the conclusion that there are none so deaf as those that wish not to hear. In other words the caller was of the same ilk as George and wouldn't be told any different purely because of his politics or religion, even if the facts contradicted his argument. There was, however, the odd newspaper story, radio and television programme that concentrated on individual cases with sympathy and understanding, although presenters were still determined to have the last word. Nevertheless, on rare occasions TA personnel had the chance to put across their grievances over the airwaves leaving listeners and viewers to make up their own mind.

In the early 1990s there was a feeling that the reservists were a good value for money; getting a ready-made military force on the cheap. Such a thought has come to an abrupt end, especially when reservists are being called upon to fight alongside their regular counterparts in numbers never seen since the Suez crises. In 2005 the Tory opposition reported in parliament that 600 reservists per month were leaving the armed forces, equating that around 20,000 had left since 2003.

It was also mentioned that recruitment had fallen sharply by 12% between 2003 and 2006 and didn't increase by much a few years after, even with a token £3 million given by the government for a recruitment drive. A somewhat feeble attempt to keep the public happy that it was actually doing something about the problem, which of course soon dried up with no other funding available.

I feel these figures may be misguided or even exaggerated. Perhaps, once again, sabotaging related statistics to emphasise a political argument. However TA and reserve soldiers hung up their boots for the last time for various reasons, and some not dissimilar to mine, leaving the TA under strength by about 7,000. In 2007 there were around 32,000 reservists where there should have been 39,000. It is sometimes argued that the youth of today are too weak and feeble to join the armed forces, or maybe no longer have the British bulldog spirit to stand up and fight for their country. In some ways such an argument has an element of truth about it. That maybe due to comrade Brown and his weak and feeble socialist government having a somewhat relaxed approach towards law and order, reflecting his seemingly despondent attitude over a decade of rule.

I think he made it abundantly clear it was far more important to waste billions of pounds on, let's say, propping up failed banks, rather than support an army that is there to protect us from, let's say, the Taliban or terrorist cells attacking the UK. Another little dig, I know, but I see it as being a correct reflection on Brown's past dictatorship and his pathetic disregard towards Her Majesty's Armed Forces.

Not to put the blame entirely on Brown's shoulders, because as we all knew he liked to pass the buck, a study in the retention figures during his unelected reign showed that many left the TA during recruit training. This maybe a reflection on the mental attitude of the student simply because they didn't have the balls to continue the training; quickly realising that being a soldier and fighting a real war is definitely not like playing a game on an X-Box. After all, you only have one life in a real war, not three, and you can't pause to have a can of Tizer when you feel like it before resuming the game.

I also recognise that many reservists completed the recruit training realising what it means to be in the British army and turned out to be brilliant soldiers and officers. This has become apparent in Iraq, Afghanistan and other conflicts around the world in past decades. As for reserve soldiers leaving the army simply because they served in Iraq or Afghanistan, their reasons for doing so are far more complicated and unfortunately unavoidably political.

To name but a few: TA soldier, Scot Garthley, was wounded during the first hours of the Iraq conflict. On 20th March 2003 a scud missile exploded close by, taking fifteen or so other soldiers to dig him out of the crater caused by the explosion. Immediately he became a casevac and taken to a field hospital and treated for his injuries. An orthopaedic surgeon informed Scot that he had a collapsed disc and would need further investigative surgery to ascertain the finer details of his spinal injury.

After initial treatment he was flown back to the UK via Cyprus where he was admitted to an NHS hospital in Birmingham. And that's where, as he put it, everything went terribly wrong. Admitted to A&E he was first told, as many other battlefield casualties were when admitted to NHS hospitals around the country, to remove his uniform as it offend other patients. Apart from the fact he didn't have any other clothes to wear, he regarded the comment as insulting and deeply offensive. Eventually a registrar found time to see Scot, only to hand him a walking stick and told to go home and take three weeks bed rest.

Scot tried to explain that he had a medical report from the army, written by two orthopaedic surgeons, stating that his injuries were serious and require a little more treatment than a walking stick and three weeks bed rest. The registrar's reply was that he'd been instructed to keep beds for gunshot casualties only and therefore couldn't offer Scot a bed. Consequently Scot had to leave the hospital with his walking stick and go home.

Sitting in a NHS wheelchair with no transport arranged to take him home he was, in effect, marooned. The only option he had was to telephone his girlfriend and ask her to drive all the way from Scotland to a city she didn't know and pick him up. At which point Scot realised that his family hadn't been informed of his injury or his arrival back to the UK. It was later discovered that under normal rules the defence medical services should have arranged for Scot to be admitted into a

NHS hospital with his type of injury. That didn't happen, and this is where communication between regular and reserve forces fall foul.

The regular unit Scot was attached with in Iraq did its job by airlifting him back home for treatment, and as far as they were concerned that was the end of the matter. After all, Scot was now in a NHS hospital and will surely receive appropriate treatment for his injuries. Meanwhile his TA unit wasn't immediately informed of his injury or told he was on his way home and therefore wasn't able to arrange transport.

Unfortunately, Scot's problems didn't end at arranging his own transport home.

Whether it was down to the army or NHS cutbacks, it would be a further eight months before Scot received any treatment. And because of the seriousness of his injury he needed treatment fast, so he had no alternative but to pursue private healthcare, which of course cost him his own money. Having private health care, however, he soon discovered his spine needed to be pinned, plated and fused, as well as a further dozen or so operations.

As I see it, neither the regular army or the TA broke any rules. His unit in Iraq arranged to have him air lifted to hospital in Birmingham, so surely it was up to the TA to take over from then on. The TA however, as far as they were concerned, had Scot mobilised with the regular army – as we all were – and therefore was the responsibility of the regular army until demobilised. Conclusion: Lack of communication.

Former TA soldier, Anthony Bradshaw, was haunted by memories of Iraq. In a repeated flashback that appeared from nowhere, he sees the skin of an Iraqi child peeling from her body. Anthony's condition worsened and he became a recluse. Scared of stepping into the outside world he feared mortar rounds exploding around him, and was scared children playing nearby would end up burnt, just like the little girl he saw.

Anthony was in the Pioneer Corps, tasked to build camps and transport supplies throughout the battlegroup. As he transported much needed supplies to the field hospital at Shaibah his vehicle packet came under fire from Iraqi forces. He could hear soldiers from his own convoy screaming at him to get out of his truck and take cover as 7.62mm shorts snapped overhead and mortars exploded around him.

He felt numb as his flashbacks of bombs falling on Basrah were scrambled with everything else he witnessed, seemingly appearing surreal. He started to get more and more angry with himself, but couldn't understand what was wrong. Eventually Anthony's condition was recognised as PTSD and subsequently discharged from the TA. But as soon as he walked onto Civvy Street the army simply ignored him.

Hoping the NHS might come to his rescue now that he was a civilian, he soon discovered that they were not much better. He was simply given a few pills and sent on his way; not even considered for counselling. Unfortunately, Anthony is now nothing more than a statistic of hundreds of TA soldiers that returned home from Iraq and Afghanistan suffering from combat stress but had to cope with their suffering in silence.

David Corrigan, an ex-regular soldier from County Durham, was a medic in the TA. He came under fire as he retrieved battlefield casualties during a fierce firefight. Travelling at night with 16-Air Assault battlegroup and under tactical conditions, David and his colleagues recovered 25 casualties in 45 minutes, with injuries that included gunshot and shrapnel wounds, burns and broken bones, before becoming a casualty himself.

In pitch black, with mortars exploding all around and bullets cracking above his head, David fell out of the back of his armoured ambulance and injured his knee. Undeterred he continued his duties until his injury became unbearable and had no alternative but to seek medical attention. After initial treatment at Shaibah Field Hospital 48 hours later he was airlifted back to the UK and taken, with all of his kit, to the garrison town of Catterick in North Yorkshire.

Unceremoniously dropped off at a supermarket miles from where he lived he had to telephone his wife to collect him, which was the first his wife knew of David's arrival home. He then faced similar problems to Scot, having to arrange his own medical care if he wanted his knee treated quickly. It required, like Scot's spine, numerous operations. Yet again a total breakdown in communication between the regular army and TA, and definitely a lack of care.

Graham Craddock, another TA soldier, was flown back to the UK suffering from heat exhaustion – a common occurrence in Iraq – where temperatures often peaked at 50 degrees Celsius. When Graham returned home his wife, Clare, noticed that he wasn't the Graham she knew before he was called-out. In effect he returned home a completely different person.

Graham's medical officer at the Shaibah Field Hospital described his condition as nothing more than heat exhaustion. After further investigation it appeared he might have also been suffering from psychological problems due to the effect the conflict had on him. After many months of travelling from Manchester to Preston barracks for further assessment the army decided they couldn't help due to lack of resources in psychological care. Once again, Graham was forced to sort out his own medical care, or rather his wife did, referring him to her own GP. And fortunately for Graham, Clare's GP was a mental health specialist.

After four assessments Clare's GP diagnosed Graham as suffering from PTSD and even wrote to tell his Commanding Officer of the diagnosis. His wife said, Graham is nothing more than a stranger in his own house. He never goes out, doesn't socialise and won't even answer the telephone. Even his own children don't recognise their daddy any more. Graham predictably lost his job and became, due to his mental state, unemployable. But his story doesn't end there.

When a regular soldier is injured and requires many months recuperation he can apply for sickness benefit from the army – as you would in Civvy Street – to the extent of SSP (Statutory Sick Pay). If the injuries are severe, such as an amputation, a soldier can then use his army pension or insurance to sustain some kind of living. For a TA soldier it isn't quite as simple. Reservists injured on operations do have an insurance scheme they can fall upon during long periods of sickness or continuous recuperation. However, qualifying for such a benefit is extremely difficult. The initial obstacle is to to prove you are eligible. This can be virtually impossible when such an application is passed back and forth from TA to regular army administration, each claiming the other holds responsibility. For example, veterans from Operation Granby – Gulf war of 1991 – waited over 15-years for their pensions.

In extreme cases TA soldiers returning from Iraq suffering psychological problems have not only distanced themselves from society altogether, some have committed suicide. In 2004, 13 months after returning from a tour in Iraq serving as a medic in the medical corps, Peter Mahoney put on his uniform and service medals and asphyxiated himself in his car, surrounded by photos of his four children.

His wife, Donna, found a leaflet lying beside him – the very same issued to us all when we were demobilised, explaining the psychological trauma in war. Peter had ripped up his copy, but Donna wanted the information to be sent not only to soldiers, but also families of all soldiers, so they too could recognise any change in their loved ones returning from active service.

He regularly wrote blueys to his wife, where she could feel the emotion in his writing, often alienated and lonely. They would start by explaining the day's events, then adding that his battlegroup were hit by Scud missiles on a daily basis. But as always, ending that he was safe and had protective clothing should chemical weapons be used against them.

As time went on his blueys became more and more distant and withdrawn.

He would emphasise that he will not, under any circumstances, die in Iraq. Adding that he and his wife had plans for when they grew old together, and she should never think he was going to die. After a while he said in another bluey he was feeling low, explaining that he was here (in Iraq) in body but mentally absent. He went on to say that he craves peace and tranquillity, to regain some sort of sanity, and how he longs to get back with his wife and family.

When he eventually came home Peter's war continued to haunt him with memories, such as when he was on a task to collect supplies. Some of the soldiers within the vehicle packet gave a little girl a bar of chocolate. When his vehicle packet returned along the same route some twenty minutes later, they found her hanging from a street lamp-post because she took some chocolate from the coalition.

At first Peter's family didn't notice much of a change in his personality, but after a while they noticed he was becoming angry and even racist, often walking off on his own. Bonfire night was one of these occasions, which would have been a particular difficult time. November 5th may bring great joy for children, with fireworks whizzing and exploding into bright, wonderful colours, but for Peter it was a different story, as it was for many returning home.

The sudden bang of a huge rocket from a near-by firework display and the small crackling of a repeater giving the effect of an automatic weapon can remind many of us of the gut-wrenching feeling we felt during a firefight. Such reminders have the potential of being so traumatic it can throw us back into the war and make us dive for cover, whilst those around laugh or look at us as if we'd gone mad. Peter's experiences changed his personality, which took a huge toll on Donna and his family. He became increasingly angry and aggressive, and when asked to see a doctor he just refused. The outcome was a tragedy for Donna and Peter's children.

It is believed that hundreds of TA soldiers returned home from Iraq and Afghanistan with psychiatric problems. It is also recognised that TA soldiers suffer more than regular soldiers because the transition from military to civilian life is so violent and abrupt, they simply lack the same support offered to regular soldiers.

Lack of communication? To a certain extent, but more a lack of care and understanding for TA soldiers and their needs when returning home from a conflict.

PTSD is an extremely complex illness. It is difficult to diagnose, in either a regular or TA soldier suffering from such a condition. It also has to be said that mental care in the regular army is poor to say the least, which reflects the enormous problem the MOD have with a lack of government funding and priorities to its budgets in, as they saw it, more urgent cases.

In fairness the RTMC at Chilwell had thousands of TA and regular reservists pouring through its gatehouse during the mobilisation of Operation Telic, so the odd mistake or misjudgement was bound to happen. And it has to be said that medical staff and officers at Chilwell worked around the clock to look after casualties returning home, which I was one.

Of course, contingency plans back in the UK were put into effect for casualties as soon as a signal was received from battlegroups and individual units in Iraq. My return home was reported to Chilwell within hours of the aeromedical evacuation taking off from Kuwait City airport. The following day not only the RTMC, but also DIVHQ (Division Head Quarters), TAHQ in Bordon, the Army Personnel Centre in Glasgow and my own TA unit were all informed of my return. It's a shame that other casualties were let down due to a lack of or indeed a breakdown of communication.

Although I managed to cling onto my sanity – albeit close to rack and ruin – other TA soldiers weren't so lucky. They found it impossible returning to Civvy Street, exacerbated by their mental wounds still sore and wide open. They were left to face their fears, only to quickly spiral down a slippery slope and fall victim to flashbacks and paranoia.

A 39-year-old Sergeant Major had been in the TA for twenty years, but unfortunately resigned after serving in Iraq because he suffered from PTSD. He flew from Basrah at 1pm and landed at Brize Norton at 08.30am BST. He was then put on a coach for Chilwell. During his demobilisation he discovered that the army pay office in Glasgow deducted maintenance for his ex-wife through the CSA but never paid her. To make matters worse, his employer was instructed to take 85% of his salary in deductions and subsequently left him with only £280 a month to pay bills, feed his girlfriend and young family. To make matters worse, by the time he returned home from Iraq he had been blacklisted for any credit or future loans.

Not surprisingly he had a mental breakdown, eventually seeking help from his doctor because he couldn't sleep. It took a further six weeks to get his medical records from the army, and in their opinion suffered from PTSD, but not caused by the war; it was from the fallout from his civilian life waiting for him upon his return home. Boy, do I know that one. He was duly signed up for a course of counselling and spent a week in a psychiatric unit because he felt his head was going to explode and even considered taking his own life.

A TA soldier from the North-East of England was forced to take action against Cummins Engine Co., after he was made redundant within days of returning home from Afghanistan. Thirty-seven-year-old Simon Sunderland was coming to the end of a 12-month tour when his bosses at Cummins told him – by email – that he was being made redundant. His union vowed to fight the company, warning that they could be in breach of the law.

Simon felt he'd been kicked in the teeth, naïvely thinking he was coming home to normality. His tour begun in May 2010 but when he returned to the UK at the start of March 2011 he was still under the employment of the army for a further two months, and was looking forward to a holiday with his family. His civilian position as a production line worker was to be held, by law, until he returned from duty. But he lost his job, along with a further 400 staff at the US-owned engineering company.

It's ironic to think that Simon was serving in Afghanistan alongside American soldiers and it was an American company that made him redundant when he returned home from fighting an American war. Maybe it's questionable that he could have been made legally redundant, but morally, should he have been? Simon was in Kabul during his time in Afghanistan and previously completed a six-month tour in Iraq. He hoped to find similar civilian work elsewhere but didn't hold too much optimism, especially living in the North-East of England where jobs are scarce to find.

A TA soldier (name not known) returning from his second tour of Iraq initially showed no signs of PTSD. On his first tour a civilian stabbed him in the groin during a riot in Basrah. On his second tour his base was repeatedly hit by mortar attacks, and within a short period back home it wasn't long before he showed obvious signs of combat stress: mood swings, nightmares, flashbacks, chronic insomnia and other linked symptoms.

He lost his temper over the tiniest of things and couldn't deal with serious problems, such as bills and mortgage payments. Asked about his civilian job as a van driver and he simply replied: "I can't give a fuck anymore. I just turn up, do what's expected and go home."

When he was provoked in a pub a fight started and he bit off a man's ear. He was drinking twice as much as he used to, his marriage was strained and he could no longer cope with civilian life in a country where few understood, appreciated or were interested in what soldiers had to endure. He couldn't settle down and asked if he would go back to Iraq, his answer would be an immediate "yes".

For a long time he refused to admit he had a problem. His wife and friends finally persuaded him to visit a doctor. When the doctor gave him a form to fill in he threw it away; concerned it would have a knock-on effect with the TA. And if he had to see a psychiatrist and they recommend he took time off, he questioned if it would have effect on his civilian job, and would it be added to his civilian medical record? As far as he was concerned, if you ignore it, it will go away.

None of the three friends he served with at the time had any idea he was eligible for an assessment at Chilwell or that there was one available. The MOD, however, said that it made strenuous efforts to publicise the programme. Meanwhile, his friends and many others in the TA felt that the moment they were demobilised the MOD lost all interest.

32-years-old private Forshaw, like many other reservists, was sent to Iraq amongst strangers. His mother said that after he returned home to suburban Surrey, he had no friends who had shared the same experiences. Nobody, including the TA or the MOD contacted him to see if he was coping with the sudden transition back to civilian life. He was not the type of person to share his problems with others, and knew that to have done so might trounce his chances of returning to Iraq for a further tour.

One afternoon Dave Forshaw drove his Land Rover to a woodland park in Esher, Surrey, removed his shoes and closed the windows. He then started a chainsaw and lay there whist the fumes from the two-stroke engine suffocated him. He was seen in his car the following morning by people walking their dogs but they assumed he was sleeping. When he was still there the following day help was summoned, but of course, it arrived far too late.

The police found his MOD90 (army identity card) inside the car and a letter from an Australian colonel commending his conduct after his vehicle was hit by a roadside bomb in Basrah. The colonel mentioned in his letter: "I was astounded at David's composure as he went about the business of comforting his comrades". Private Dave Forshaw was unscathed, but all three of his passengers were injured.

On the day the body of her son was found, Janet Dawes, the mother of Dave Forshaw, discovered a note that he had left in a wardrobe in his bedsit in Mitcham. He was dyslexic, so she believes he must have spent many hours writing it. He asked for the flag of St George to be draped over his coffin, for the song 'Everybody Hurts' by R.E.M. to be played at his funeral, and for his ashes to be scattered at the Emirates stadium of his beloved Arsenal football team.

Dave, normally a gregarious, fun-loving man, went on to say in his note: I'm leaving a lot of good friends and family behind and taking the easy way out, but for once in my life instead of making other people happy I am making myself happy. The best time of my life was being in the army and fighting for my country, England.

Mrs Dawes said that her son, a decorator, had always wanted to join the regular army, but was told he was unable to because of his dyslexia. He decided to have a go at joining the TA and when he took the same entrance exam as he would to join the regulars, he amazingly passed. In October 2005 he was called-out for Iraq and served two 6-month tours with only four weeks off in between.

When he returned home in November 2006 he was at his happiest, at least on the surface. Then the decline began. He could not settle back into civilian life, he drifted from one job to another, ran up debts and stopped attending training sessions with the TA. He became moody and on some days he would hide himself away. He began eating alone and visited his mother less. All he wanted was to return to Iraq or Afghanistan, but his efforts to go back as a soldier or private security contractor were repeatedly thwarted. He wanted to live a life of real purpose but it wasn't there; so he ended it.

The military did not send an official representative to the funeral of Private Dave Forshaw, and he will not appear on the official list of Iraq war casualties. He may or may not have been suffering from PTSD but he was, in his own quiet way, a victim of the conflict, and in that he is not alone. As he wrote in his suicide note: The help was there but I did not take it.

23-years-old James Piotrowski, a Lance Corporal in the Irish Guards, was yet another victim of combat stress. Formerly seen as one of the most promising recruits of his intake and praised for fighting in Iraq with 'pride, loyalty and compassion', James faced a Courts Martial for possession of a personal rifle 5.56mm, commonly known as the SA80(A), which he smuggled out of his barracks. He was jailed for 7-years for a firearms offence and assaulting a military police officer, despite a medical report submitted by his lawyers stating that he was suffering from PTSD.

When he returned from Iraq he suffered from nightmares and panic attacks, and was described by his mother as being a 'lost, lonely soldier.' In a letter to his local newspaper after the court-martial, James's father wrote: I am not saying he didn't deserve a custodial sentence for these serious offences, but the military have been totally and utterly clinically negligent in their treatment of my son and many other veterans, which is absolutely outrageous. He went on to say: young men returning home from conflicts are receiving no help to return to normal soldiering... creating a timebomb of human agony for them to endure.

Justin Smith, who served in the Coldstream Guards and suffering from PTSD upon his return home, said that he was given good psychiatric care in the army, but was told he would have to pay for private therapy when he was demobilised. They said it will cost £250 and he would have to pay £50 towards the total cost. Justin confronted former Prime Minister, Tony Blair, in a live debate on television.

The Prime Minister subsequently wrote to Justin saying: "although it may be of little comfort, the government has made improving NHS mental healthcare a priority".

Under the government's guidelines, cognitive behavioural therapy (CBT) which helps patients control their thought processes, is one of the recommended treatments that should be available on the NHS. The problem is that many veterans put on waiting lists were waiting up to 18 months.

What is worrying is that the number of soldiers showing symptoms of PTSD is increasing rapidly. Thirty-years after the Falklands conflict there were less than 400 seen to have suffered from PTSD. The rate of soldiers suffering now has increased ten-fold, which may be due to quicker and better diagnosis of the symptoms. It also has to be taken into consideration that it may take fifteen years for a regular soldier to seek help for combat stress. For TA personnel it could take even longer.

As for professional help available, there isn't really an infrastructure in place to help. TA soldiers also have more difficulty with readjustment problems than regular army soldiers who tend to remain in a military environment – often among the same group of people they served with on operations.

Unlike the United States, where a generation of Vietnam veterans introduced the notion of PTSD, there is still government suspicion of the concept in the UK. Little information about the mental health of UK troops is readily available, and information is even more scarce for TA soldiers, yet the symptoms of PTSD in TA soldiers continues to rise. Around 75,000 UK troops served in Iraq during its liberation in March 2003, many of whom have done multiple tours, with a large percentage being from TA units. It's a shame that when TA soldiers return home from operations they are left outside alone.

CHAPTER 9

RETURN TO CIVVY STREET

Friday, 4th July 5.00pm. Demobilisation day. The army didn't require my return to Iraq. Instead I was ordered to report to a local doctor authorised by the MOD to examine TA soldiers for enlistment, recruit courses, etc., where I was finally passed fit for duty. A week later my medical documents were sent to my TA unit from Div HQ and put in writing that I was no longer required on Operation Telic because 2RTR battlegroup were disbanded on the 7th May and returned to Germany. So as far as the army was concerned the war was well and truly over for me.

Now I knew, officially, I would not be returning to Iraq, pressure to find work became priority as Helen became more and more distraught over our financial situation. But I found it difficult to concentrate on my family whilst so many thoughts continued to whiz around my head, and the distance between reality and my delicate state of mind rapidly expanded each day.

"Are you going to sort out that army stuff in the garage?" Helen shouted from the kitchen in a somewhat disgusted manner, just because I left it in a pile and hadn't cleaned it up since coming home.

I ignored her and continued to watch television.

"Kev!"

"Yes, alright!" I snapped.

The inevitable forthcoming unpaid bills dropping through the letterbox had become very real and Helen was quickly losing faith in my optimism to find work. I too was losing faith as cracks were now evident in our marriage. We would argue over the most stupid of things, mainly bills, and of course my army stuff, as she called it, left in a pile. To save Rachel hearing further raised voices from Mummy and Daddy, I went into the garage to sort out the kit I needed to take back to the RTMC. Apart from the mountain of paperwork issued by the army for my demobilisation, I came across some keepsakes and memorabilia in my brown grip (kit bag).

Yes, I know I mentioned none of us brought back any war trophies, but hey, I meant weapons, ammunition, goats, camels, Iraqi women, things like that. All I brought back was a handful of sand from the desert that I kept in a steel flask and some Subha prayer beads given to me by a grateful father for taking care of his young son, which I treasure. I also had some vehicle number plates, courtesy of a few civilian commercial vehicles Stuart and I recovered for humanitarian work, and an Iraqi flag. Stuart found a couple of them just lying around inside a Ba'ath Party government building in the centre of Basrah. Well, that was his excuse for finding them, and he was sticking to it.

Underneath these keepsakes were my CBA, a couple of empty rifle magazines, my bayonet and two well-used NBC suits, which was one piece of clothing I was glad to see the back of. Neatly folded at the bottom were my two sets of desert combats. I took them out, along with the NBC suits, and gave them a good shake. Sand and dust filled the garage making me cough.

I dropped the clothing on the floor and placed a hand over my mouth in an attempt to stop the dust getting up my nose. The dim light bulb reflected a dull glow as dust floated in the air, reminding me of the many sandstorms we had to endure in the desert. It then dawned on me that by the Monday I would no longer be a regular soldier; I will be returned to Civvy Street and become a TA part-timer once again.

Helen stood in the doorway leading into the garage from the kitchen. "Here, I thought you might want this," she said wearing a smile as she handed me a mug of tea.

I returned a smile, as if to say I'm sorry for snapping at you.

"So, this is it then, your last day as a regular soldier."

"Yep, by Monday I'll be a civilian again."

I thought that was the end of our conversation and continued to pack my kit, but no, Helen had to have another dig, which was, as usual, over money.

"You do realise next month's pay from the army is your last one."

I gave a sigh. She knew I was aware of that, and I was sick of her reminding me.

"Yes, of course I know."

"Well, you'd better find a job quick. We have loads of bills to pay next month, and the mortgage, and the way things are going, we won't have enough."

It was obvious she had those employment rejection letters on her mind.

"What d'ya think I've been doing since I got back?" I shouted, but thought it best to try and calm down otherwise we'd be arguing over old ground again. "Look, when I get back after the weekend, I'll be able to concentrate a little better on finding work."

"But you need a job now, for God sake!"

"Stop your nagging, I'll sort it, okay."

"Yeah, yeah, so you keep saying," she said rolling her eyes, thinking I hadn't noticed, "you lost your last job, so who's fault is that? It isn't mine, Rachel's or anyone else's but yours!"

Helen suddenly snapped, smashing her mug of tea on the garage floor and splashing everything, including my kit, in hot tea.

She began to cry and under any other circumstance I would have consoled her, but I no longer cared. Her comments hit a raw nerve and without me realising it paranoia decided to have another stab at my subconscience; reiterating Helen's words that it was my fault I lost my job and couldn't claim any benefits.

Putting aside my thoughts and trying my best to look as if I cared about her feelings I had to say something to calm Helen down, but what? I was rapidly running out of ideas, and a sense of humour. Too late, she'd stormed off slamming every door in her path.

"Sod it," I muttered to myself, "I'm not chasing after her."

As far as I was concerned it wasn't the time or place to start throwing accusations at each other, so thought it best to have a chat when I returned after the weekend. Besides, a weekend apart would do us both a world of good, or at least I thought it would.

My orders for demobilisation were simple: Report in civilian clothing to the gatehouse at the RTMC, Chertwynd Barracks, Chilwell, Friday 4th July by 23:59hrs, returning all issued kit and bring all relevant paperwork.

Some of my kit was already retained by 2RTR, such as my rifle due to my spell at the military hospital in Shaibah. As for my desert combats, which were issued by 2RTR battlegroup in Kuwait a few days before the conflict, they were mine to keep. The desert boots were also mine, purchased from an army surplus store prior to my pre-deployment training, thanks to a warning from our OC at the TA centre advising us to buy our own boots because large sizes were in short supply.

I repacked the brown grip with everything I needed to return to the QMS (Quarter Master Sergeant) and threw the grip in the boot of the car, along with my TA issued doss bag and wash kit. A bed would be allocated during my weekend stay, but I had a feeling it wouldn't include blankets, which is why I thought it best to take my sleeping bag, just in case.

I checked that my MOD90 army ID card was in my wallet, otherwise I wouldn't be allowed to enter the barracks, and jumped in the car. Rachel peered through the bay window, frantically waving at me with tears in her eyes. I tried my best to explain to a four year old that Daddy wasn't going away to war, but she was having none of it. Rachel overheard Mummy and Daddy arguing and even watched me struggle with my kit as I loaded the car, so God knows what was going through her fragile little mind. I glanced at my silver birch before I drove off and remembered I did the same when I left for my pre-deployment training. For a split second I felt as if I was going to war again.

As I reversed down the driveway I blew Rachel a kiss and smiled in an attempt to reassure her confused mind that Daddy will be back soon. Rachel's usual response was to smile back, no matter how sad she felt, but on this occasion all I got in return was a sad little girl face with large blue water logged eyes staring straight at me, convinced Daddy wasn't coming home. At least when she does see me again I'd be home for good, I thought. In the meantime my frightened little princess had to endure a further few days without me. To Rachel that meant, yet again, an eternity.

My drive up the M1 should have been, I suppose, enjoyable. After all I was to be demobilised and returned to Civvy Street, which meant no more long spells away from my family and no more risking life and limb in some pathetic war. The rest of my platoon were also due home, it was fantastic to know that all survived – remarkably in one piece. And they had regular work waiting for their return, which meant, putting aside personal difficulties, they stood a better chance to pick up their family life from where they left off. My future, however, was uncertain and played heavy on my mind. Before I knew it I reached Chertwynd Barracks.

"Do you have your ID?" asked a MOD Plod (security officer) at the gate.

I showed him my MOD90 and he waved me through the barrier. In an instant further memories came flooding back to my pre-deployment days, as I thought they would. I parked in the almost empty car park and lit a cigarette before making my presence known, just as I did when my mother dropped me off. The biting cold air of February was replaced with a warm light wind and the trees were in full green livery, but the typical army barracks ambience hadn't changed one bit.

A steady stream of replacement TA and regular reserve soldiers called-out for Op-Telic 2 flowed through the gatehouse entrance. I watched a few of them as they de-bussed and grabbed their kit from cars and minibuses just outside the reception hanger; all of them standing out like sore thumbs. They were pasty white, looking nervous and apprehensive of their imminent future.

As they said their goodbyes, wives and girlfriends could no longer restrain their tears. A mother, which I presumed, gave her young squaddie son a huge hug and kissed him on the cheek, embarrassing the poor lad in front of his mates. I let out a giggle. My mother did the same when she dropped me off, and it's a tad more embarrassing when you're 36-years-old.

I looked at my watch: 6:15pm. Leaving my kit in the boot of the car I made my way towards the reception block adjacent to the hangar and reported I was here for demobilisation, although I was tempted to say I was here for pre-deployment training. I gave a young corporal standing behind a desk my paperwork, where she made a few squiggles and stamped it, then placed it all on top of a pile in a tray.

"Is that it?" I joked, alluding to the notion that I was now de-mobbed and could go home.

"No, you've only been booked in," she replied, smiling at my pathetic joke.

She gave me yet more paperwork with instructions on what will happen over the weekend, and a rough photocopied map of the barracks indicating which buildings to report to during the demobilisation process.

"Accommodation is here," she said, pointing to the building on the map, "breakfast will be at 0800 hours. I presume you can remember where the cookhouse is."

I returned a smile as if to say, too bloody right I know.

"You have time to grab an evening meal if you wish, and the rest of the evening is yours, but you are confined to barracks during your demobilisation process. The bar is open, but don't get pissed," she added.

I thanked her for the information and made my way back to the car, but instead of fetching my doss bag and finding a bed in the accommodation block, I sat in the driver's seat and seemed to go into some kind of trance. Why, I don't know, and I certainly didn't have a flashback. I just sat there, motionless, staring into space. For how long, I don't know that either, but the fading light indicated it must have been a good few hours. I needed to get a grip of myself.

I could hear the bar buzzing with music and laughter. That's where I needed to be. Let my hair down and talk with others that have experienced the same as me. Sure enough the bar was full of squaddies, some for pre-deployment training whilst others for demobilisation, and they were easy to tell apart. Those going to Iraq stood in large groups, excited and full of adrenaline, all psyched up to go to war, if not a tad nervous. Those for demobilisation wore deep tans and sat quietly in even deeper thought. Huddled in smaller groups around tables, occasionally leaning forward listening to each other's war stories and experiences over the din of the battle virgins.

I grabbed a pint and opted to sit with a group of demobs, introducing myself to four guys sitting around a table. They arrived that afternoon after catching a red-eye from BIA (Basrah International Airport) to Brize Norton, before hopping on a coach to Chilwell. They'd been awake for almost 36 hours, only taking the odd nap here and there, and like me had nothing to do until the morning. None of them knew each other before jumping on the plane, but when they landed it was if they were long lost pals. That's the army for you – making friends in the army was easy, and they stay friends for life.

As soon as they de-bussed, settled into the accommodation block, a quick wash, a bite to eat, and whilst still dressed in dirty desert combats, they made their way to the bar for the first beer in six months. The beer continued to flow as we swapped stories and generally had a laugh. It was a great relief to have a drink with a bunch of guys that held no prejudice or conviction, spit in my face or called me a murderer over something civilians knew nothing about. I felt as if I'd come home.

The following morning, I somehow awoke in my doss bag fully clothed and in the accommodation block. How, remains a mystery. And how my wash bag managed to unpack itself on the bedside cabinet I don't know, but my thumping head may be a clue as to why I couldn't remember. I needed some breakfast, a squaddie breakfast with all the trimmings to soak up the beer and hopefully, with a little help from a couple of aspirin, cure my headache. The guys I drank with the night before were nowhere to be seen, so god knows what happened to them. I had a wash and shave and made my way to the cookhouse.

"Kev, over here!" I heard a familiar voice shout.

It was Ian, one of the lads from the night before, sitting on his own at one of the dining room tables, only this time dressed in civilian clothing.

I made my way across the cookhouse holding my breakfast tray piled with artery clogging stosh and sat with him. As we tucked into our fry-ups we chatted about last night's drinking session. Apparently Ian carried me over his shoulder back to the accommodation block whilst someone else fetched my doss bag and wash kit from the car.

"D'ya know what we're supposed to do today?" he asked as he chewed on a sausage.

Ian was about my age, although looking a tad older with his grey crew-cut hair. He too was with 7th armoured, attached to the LI (Light Infantry), also carrying the rank of Lance Corporal. He'd been in the regular army for 12 years, decided to leave, but hated every minute of Civvy Street. He wanted to go back in the regular army but his wife didn't agree because he had found a well paid job – some kind of warehouse manager – so he opted for the TA instead. Two-years later he was in Iraq.

I took out a folded timetable from my back pocket and scanned the day's activities. "We're to report to reception at half-nine with appropriate paperwork for a briefing, then we're split into groups. I suppose to speed up the process."

"Yeah, and it still takes two fucking days," Ian sarcastically replied.

I checked my watch. "C'mon, we'd better get going, it's quarter past."

We rushed the last of our fry-ups and legged it to our first port of call where we met thirty or so other guys, all eager to get their demobilisation over with. They too arrived the day before, and we were just the first party. Through the early hours of the morning a steady flow of coaches arrived from Brize Norton filled with battle-weary squaddies for demobilisation.

The door finally opened and we were shown into a room filled with rows of plastic chairs. Once settled we were addressed by a captain who explained what the weekend will entail and what is expected to happen during the demobilisation process, taking his instruction from hand-outs given to us when we arrived.

Day one: Registration. Report for 0930hrs. After which we're to split into groups and moved between various cells on the timetable. My group's first day consisted of a welcome brief to ensure all paperwork and kit had been brought back, and all soldiers for demobilisation understood what the process consisted of.

Welfare brief: Applications for additional payment such as travel, overseas allowances and Longer Separated Service Allowances (LSSA).

Insurance claims on kit and/or injuries, annual leave and outstanding pay. There were also details given on the Army Welfare Services (AWS) should any soldier require immediate help with family problems and personal support, which included help from the Army Families Advice Bureau (AFAB).

Recruitment brief: For any soldier wishing to extend their operational tour or transfer to a regular army unit.

Employment brief: For soldiers with concerns of civilian employment. In addition, Sabre (the legal wing of the army) was at hand to help anyone with such issues. Boy, I certainly needed help from those guys.

By now, after numerous coffee and fag breaks, our heads were spinning with all the information bombarded at us. We were pleased lunchtime arrived, allowing our brains to cool down and let some of the morning's information to sink in. I for one grabbed the hour break to talk to the Sabre guys and see if they could help. I gave them all the information I could muster and they said they would get back to me by the end of the day. I took it as read that finally something was going right for me. With the British Army helping who needs MP's or the Jobcentre, which were as useful as wearing soggy socks.

It felt as if a 10-ton load had suddenly been lifted from my shoulders. I couldn't wait to return home and tell Helen that all will be okay. Finally, I'll be getting my old job back. I did think of telephoning Helen but thought no, it'll spoil the surprise. Besides, I didn't have all the finer details and I was prematurely counting my chickens before they'd hatched. Even so, I felt confident the army would be able to help.

After lunch part-2 of our fun day commenced: Weapons and de-kit. Return SA80(A2) rifles and/or LSW's (Light Support Weapon), bayonet, scabbard, magazines, cleaning kit and webbing – if issued by the RTMC. My rifle, however, was retained by 2RTR, which I gave all the relevant details to the QMS. I handed back my CBA and issued green kit clothing, but the army let me keep the brown grip. Nice of them.

Afterwards, if anyone had any welfare, recruitment or employment issues unresolved from the morning's lectures, they were to report to the appropriate cells for either results, answers to earlier questions or further briefing. Of course I was one of those that needed an employment issue resolving. The remaining had the rest of the day to themselves, and considering it was only 6 o'clock that meant plenty of drinking time. But, and isn't it always so with the British Army, we were ordered not to drink excessively because of our medical in the morning.

Ian and the rest of the gang disappeared to the cookhouse for their evening meal whilst I virtually skipped to the welfare office to see the Sabre guys, convinced they'd managed to pull that proverbial rabbit out of the hat, which my MP and other government officials failed to do. How wrong could I have been. Sabre couldn't help either. And thank heaven I didn't telephone Helen earlier with, what I thought would be, fantastic news. They came up with the same excuse I'd heard many times before: because I was employed for less than 13 weeks my employer had no legal obligation to keep open my position when I returned home.

I didn't bother with my evening meal; I'd lost my appetite, which was no surprise. Instead, I went for a walk around the barracks in an attempt to think things through. I came to a decision, although somewhat coaxed by my situation and left without any alternative, I had to find a HGV driving job with an agency. And as they were so desperate for drivers they didn't give a shit if I'd been called-out to Iraq or even fought for the Fedayeen militia, so long as I had a current Class-1 driving licence.

The problem was I would have to leave the TA because my weekends, or at least the Saturday, will no doubt be taken up when working nights for a driving agency. Not unless I was lucky enough to find a driving assignment that hadn't been taken by the blue eyed arse lickers and find weekday work only. Driving agencies, I have since learnt, are notorious bullshitters. Promising the perfect shift only to have you on their books and tell potential clients that they have a full complement of drivers ready and available.

As for some of their clients, you wouldn't pay them to work for. The worst are the so-called 'blue chip' companies. They appear whiter than white on the surface, but to be assigned to them as an agency driver is no better than working in a Pakistani sweat shop. You're certainly not treated any better. And the most sadistic, painfully thick and notoriously ill-educated of all their own full-time employees have to be the transport manager and clerks, chosen for their arrogance. Oh yes, agency driving was one career move I wasn't looking forward to. But needs must when the devil farts in your face.

"Hey, coming for a drink, Kev?" Ian asked, standing in the doorway of the bar.

I'd walked an entire lap of the camp and didn't realise I was now standing right in front of it.

"Yeah, why not," I replied, follwing him into the building.

"Are you okay?"

"Yeah, just want this demob crap to finish so I can get home and start my life again."

"I know what you mean. I now have a divorce to sort out, so a new life would be nice right now."

I was counting the change in the palm of my hand to buy a pint without breaking into a bank note, but lost count when I heard Ian say he was getting a divorce.

"You mean you are getting a divorce because you were called-out?" I guessed.

"Yep, everything was fine, or so I thought. Then back in April I received a bluey from the missus, a 'Dear John'. Some of her friends decided she needed a night out to cheer her up. She met a bloke at a nightclub, one thing led to another, then, put it this way, he certainly cheered her up. They started to see each other on a regular basis, and the rest, as they say, is history."

"How the fuck did you cope with news like that, stuck 3,000 miles away in the middle of a war?"

"It wasn't easy, not at first. But as the days went on it became easier to forget about it, especially when we were busy, which believe me, helped. But now I'm back in England – ," he paused for a few seconds, staring into space. I knew that feeling only too well, " – I dunno, Kev."

My problems, if only for a brief moment, slid into insignificance after hearing Ian's sob story. At least I had a wife and family to go home to, albeit an argumentative one. Other than a close family bereavement I can't think of anything worse for a squaddie fighting a war thousands of miles away from home, only to unexpectedly receive a 'Dear John'.

Ian wasn't the only one to receive similar bad news. I'd met a few lads in the battlegroup, and knew of others elsewhere within 7-Armoured that had opened a bluey, which would otherwise bring much needed smiles and laughter, if only to have that important link home, instead bring tears, anger and frustration. A bad cocktail of emotions for a squaddie to absorb when armed to the teeth and about to go into battle.

Many stories spread around the battlegroup of individuals receiving 'Dear Johns' only to immediately ask permission for a flight home. Of course, their requests where denied. Some resorted to desperation, even self harming to blag a casevac flight back to Blighty. Some kept their thoughts to themselves, which made matters worse. On one occasion a soldier decided he'd had enough and calmly walked into a CP (Command Post) tent full of officers, including the one that refused him a ticket home. He pulled the pin on a grenade and boom! Seriously injuring the occupants, including himself.

Thankfully Ian didn't react the same way. Like he said, he kept himself busy by keeping his soldiering head well and truly switched on.

"Fancy another pint?" Ian asked.

"Yeah, why not, sod the medical in the morning."

Ian paid for the drinks and passed me a pint. "Here's to failed marriages, cheers, Kev."

There wasn't anything I could add to that, and I didn't really want to, so I sipped my pint and quickly changed the subject to more trivial things, such as cars, music and funny war stories; avoiding anything to do with marriage, women and home life.

Time ticked by and without realising it we'd drank a gallon each, and had a good hour left before the bar closed.

Day 2: Report for 0900hrs. Medical & Clinical run-ups, Med/Stress questionnaire & debrief, MO (Medical Officer) appointment, should you need one after a medical. After lunch: Update on allowances & leave entitlement, further medical treatment and advice (if required), help on employment and further training recruitment, onward travel (go home).

The following morning I was surprised not to have a blinding hangover. Well, maybe a little one. Ian, on the other hand, was suffering badly. After all, I'd been home for two months and reaccustomed myself to the taste of alcohol. Ian hadn't touched a drop for six months.

We managed to drag ourselves to breakfast, along with some of the other lads we'd been drinking with, but Ian remained silent whilst the rest of us swapped friendly banter. He sat staring out of a cookhouse window, almost withdrawn from reality. No need to guess why.

"You okay, Ian?"

Ian turned his head, only to stare into his mug of tea. Seemingly his thoughts were a million miles away. "Yeah, I'm fine, Kev, just thinking." He then asked a question, to no one in particular, but it took me by surprise. "Has anyone experienced any weird thoughts about the war, like flashbacks, that sort of thing?"

"Give us a chance, mate, we've only just got back," one of the other lads replied with a mouth full of fried egg, treating Ian's question as a light hearted joke.

I certainly didn't take it as a joke and wanted to know more. "Have you experienced something, then?" I asked.

"Yeah, but you don't wanna know about it. I shouldn't have asked, sorry," he replied, feeling a little embarrassed.

"No, I do want to know, tell me what happened." I urged, looking at him straight in the eyes.

"You serious, Kev?" he asked, relieved that he could finally confide in someone to talk to and not take the piss.

I was a tad concerned with the other two overhearing our conversation but I needn't have been. They totally ignored us and more interested in stuffing their faces.

"We'll talk later," I said softly.

Ian could see I was serious and wanted to talk to him in private. He returned a slow nod, acknowledging without anyone else noticing. The others finished scoffing and took their empty plates to the awaiting trolley next to the kitchen door, leaving Ian and me to finish ours.

"Don't be late you two," one of them said as they walked away, "you don't want to miss your medical, do you," he sarcastically added, waving his sample bottle at us, which we all had to fill with our first piss of the day.

"He's right, we'd better get this medical over with," I said, "but we'll talk later, okay?"

Ian nodded. "Have you experienced the same?" he asked.

"Yes, on numerous occasions, but we'll talk later. I'm just pleased I'm not the only one."

"Me too, Kev, I thought I was going nuts."

We made our way to the medical building with our freshly filled sample bottles, which must have resembled rocket fuel judging by the amount of alcohol we consumed the night before. On the way we all gradually clumped together in a large group, laughing and giggling about the demob process, the war, and swapped childish anecdotes about pissing in a small sample bottle. It was then I realised I lost sight of Ian.

The medical reception was full of lads waiting to be seen by various MO's, each carrying their medi-cards and sample bottles. Once invited into the adjoining cubicles we were asked to hand over our samples and medi-cards then strip to the waist. The usual tests were carried out – poke and prods, the proverbial 'breathe in and out' then 'cough' whilst our balls were cupped. A few questions were asked concerning our health in general, such as if we'd suffered any medical ailments whilst on operations or any psychological problems since.

Our next port of call was the main hall, where we were due a pep talk by one of the officers concerning returning home from operations, probable psychological grievances about facing the public and returning to Civvy Street before being released into the community. A little late for that as far as I was concerned. I'd been effectively back in Civvy Street for almost three months.

We were ushered to sit in the rows of plastic chairs where a captain took centre stage to take the brief. He ordered a corporal to hand out a leaflet – a med/stress questionnaire – which included advice on common reactions to stressful and traumatic events: Fear, anxiety, stress, anger... the list went on. At first, the captain was full of the joys of spring. It was if he was pleased to see so many faces coming home from the war unscathed. He too had recently returned from a stint in Iraq and knew exactly what we experienced, so at least he stood with us on common ground.

He joked about the countless goats and how they became increasingly attractive as the weeks unfolded. Oh, how true. I cannot recall one decent looking Iraqi woman, or any who seemed to be under the age of eighty-five. He went on to talk about the heat and made a joke about the IA drills we had to do in the midday sun. Soon enough the topic of conversation became a tad more serious, explaining the mixed emotions we'll experience when we leave the barracks. The unwanted attraction of stupid questions from the public and maybe the print media, and how we can cope with our thoughts before they become scrambled with paranoia.

Everything he said, however, I'd already experienced, apart from how to cope with my thoughts, which is why I brought up the question: For those that have already been casualty evacuated home and experienced these mixed emotions over the past few months, what are they supposed to do?

His face dropped and he didn't really have a straight answer, other than to ask anyone else in the group if they'd arrived home before their demob date due to a casevac. Around 6 or 7 out of 100 or so raised their hand, so statistically this little problem needed addressing. He suddenly looked concerned and asked our unique group to stay behind for a chin wag if felt we needed to.

Putting aside this slightly embarrassing chink in otherwise perfect demob process armour, he continued his rehearsed patter covering some do's and don'ts: Don't bottle things up, try to discuss concerns as they come up; don't use alcohol to cover up any problems; don't isolate yourself; do take time out with friends & family; do try to fit in with normal routines that your family have established whilst you were away... and many more do's and don'ts that effected us all one way or another.

He also mentioned where to find professional help and to see our GP or MO if we feel a must to do so; talk about any psychological problems; take time with rebuilding relationships – wives, husbands, girlfriends, boyfriends; how to confront the reality of civilian and home life; coming to terms with your experiences and memories… again, the list went on. And again, some of these remedies had arrived too late.

We were now getting a tad bored. Yes, many of us would have touched on these experiences, but we were British soldiers after all, and British soldiers simply do not admit they can't cope; they see it as a weakness, a failure. After all, we'd been trained to fight wars and whatever they dare throw at us, and we now had first-hand experience.

Dealing with trauma of war, however, is very different and outrageously complex. All the military training ever created can never teach how to deal with it; that is purely down to the individual and his or her personal strengths. Hopefully, being a soldier, sailor or airman, military training brings out the survivor within, which, I think, is the key to coping with the aftermath and fallout of fighting a war.

The captain closed his brief and even thanked us all for coming. If we didn't have any other grievances to resolve we could now go home. All our military kit and clothing had been returned, medical completed, pep talks done, leaflets, handouts and contact numbers given, so there were no need to hang around. But I didn't want to leave. I wanted to stay and go through the process all over again, if only to stay with the lads or even go back to Iraq, so long as I was with people I can trust. It was plain to see others felt the same, so we opted to have one last drink in the bar.

I looked around for Ian, but couldn't see him.

"You looking for Ian?" someone asked. It was one of the lads who sat with us at breakfast.

"Yeah, I lost sight of him after we left the cookhouse."

"I saw him in that briefing, so he couldn't have gone far. I'm Paul, by the way."

"Kev," I replied, shaking his hand.

Paul, yet another bloke in his mid-thirties and going slightly bald, was attached to an Engineers unit, and was a vehicle mechanic in Civvy Street. He spent most of his time working with VM's (vehicle mechanics) from the REME and recalls seeing Stuart and I bringing back vehicle casualties to a BLP (Back Loading Point) near Shaibah. He may have done, but I did explain there were quite a few Foden recovery vehicles knocking about.

We made our way back to the bar, and like me, Paul only risked a cola as we both had a long drive home; Paul longer than most, he was driving all the way to the south coast. The tables and bar were abundant with soft drinks, so it appeared everyone else resigned to the fact that they too were also going home.

"I couldn't help overhear your conversation at breakfast, you know, when Ian mentioned if we'd had any flashbacks," Paul surprisingly said, albeit slightly nervously, as if he'd wished he never mentioned it.

"Oh that, I didn't realise you heard. Well, maybe he was thinking aloud, not really knowing what he was saying," I casually replied, "why d'ya ask?" I didn't want to take the conversation any further just in case there was a wind-up coming my way, but I became curious to know if he'd had them too.

Paul took another sip from his coke, appearing to be a little uncomfortable with my questioning. "Oh nothing, just made me wonder, that's all." I could tell he wanted to say more, but wasn't sure how I'd react. "It's just that – "

"Just what?" I interrupted, hoping he was about to confess he'd also suffered with flashbacks.

"Nah, it doesn't matter."

"You've had them, haven't you," I prompted.

"Have you?" he immediately asked, hoping I wasn't about to take the piss out of his confession.

I put him out of his misery by admitting first. "I've had a few, started when I landed at Birmingham, and had them ever since."

Paul looked relieved. "I had a couple over the weekend, the first was when we landed at Brize Norton. For a fleeting moment I thought I was back in Kuwait. You know, when we first arrived," he said, referring to when we landed at Kuwait City airport around three o'clock in the morning on the 10th March, "as far as I was concerned I could see the Yanks guarding us as we disembarked the plane, and could even feel the warm desert air. In reality the guards were air crew pottering about with our luggage and it was bloody freezing."

"Why didn't you say something at breakfast?" I calmly asked, but really wanted to jump and skip around the bar pleased to be talking with someone who'd experienced the same, "all you said was, give us a chance mate, we've only just arrived."

"Yeah I know, but I didn't want to come across as some kind of delirious prick."

I knew what he meant. It's not the sort of thing you casually mention to total strangers over the breakfast table, especially to a bunch of squaddies returning from the same conflict. Paul and I, however, talked some more about our flashback experiences, which seemed to take a huge weight off both our shoulders.

"Maybe now, after talking about them, they'll stop?" Paul asked, hopefully.

I nodded, if only to limply agree with him, but we both knew they wouldn't.

We finished our drinks, said our goodbyes, and that was the last I saw of Paul. As for Ian, he must have sneaked off after the last briefing. Shame really. I only hoped he was okay and managed to cope with his flashbacks, and of course, sort out his family problems.

I collected my doss bag and wash kit from the accommodation block and took a slow walk to the car park, taking in my surroundings for the very last time. I felt as if I'd left behind a large part of my life at the RTMC. It was truly the end of an era. As I drove home the temptation to go back and start all over again was overwhelming. The thought of my family, however, was a much stronger emotion, and remembering Rachel standing at the window watching my car drive away hit me hard.

That thought alone was enough to make me put my foot down and get home as quickly as possible. I felt as if my life had turned a corner, and not for the best. At least I knew where I stood with my civilian job. I lost it due to some bureaucratic hiccup within the existing employment laws. And abiding by the rules, to go with the flow and obediently follow the system, didn't reciprocate any favours. Instead, my MP, civilian boss, job centre and even the general public didn't give a shit about my predicament. I simply learnt to return the favour by not giving a shit about them. I was on my own with only myself to rely upon.

I parked on my driveway and opened the front door expecting a four year-old whirlwind to grab my waist; but no, the house was empty. I checked the time – a few minutes passed five – so where could Helen and Rachel be? I thought of a few places, the obvious being shopping. I threw the gaggle of paperwork I inherited from my demobilisation on the hallway table and made my way into the kitchen. The kettle was cold indicating the house had been empty for quite a while. Decision made; make a cup of tea, turn on the television and slob on the settee.

"You're back then?"

I must have dozed off, it was now past seven o'clock.

"Where you been?" I asked getting up from the settee, "and where's Rachel?"

"Mother's!" snapped Helen.

Helen, as I guessed, had been shopping, and was literally throwing tins and packets of whatever into various cupboards around the kitchen. She was upset about something, and no doubt I was to blame.

"Okay, what's up?"

"Have a good time with your mates, maybe a few drinks and a laugh?" she asked, slamming the cupboard doors.

"What do you mean, have a good time? I was demobilised."

"Yeah, and in the meantime, as you threw money over the bar, no doubt, I've been going through our finances."

"Welcome home, Kev, did your demob go well?" I muttered under my breath.

Helen ignored my comment. I was beginning to think she too couldn't give a shit about my predicament. But then again, maybe she knew more than I thought. After all, she mentioned our finances and by the sound of it they weren't good. Helen, however, was never the best at looking after money. If it were there she would spend it. If not she'd moan and nag until I found a way of finding it, be it earned, begged or borrowed.

"We've had to pay the mortgage, credit cards and other bills for this month, and come next month, what happens then?" she asked.

"Look, although I've been demobbed, I've earned enough leave-pay to keep us going until the end of August, so we're still on top of things, for a little while, anyway."

"And then what?"

"Well, by then I should have found – "

"A job?" Helen interrupted, continuing to snap at my every reply.

"Yes, a job."

Helen didn't say anything. She just pulled a face as if to say, I've heard it all before.

I'd been back only a few hours and already she had to mention money, adding a dig here and there for not finding work. I could feel any little optimism I had about the future slip away into the ether. Trying my best to stay a little optimistic I attempted to reassure her that I was prepared to leave the TA and do a bit of agency driving until I found something more permanent. My plan worked and even softened her a little, but I knew deep down she wouldn't rest until I walked through the front door clutching a regular fat payslip.

CHAPTER 10

BREAKING POINT

Monday, February 2nd 2004. It had been a year to the day since my platoon were ordered into the office at our TA centre told of our impending call-out. And what a difference a year makes. Seven months after my demobilisation I still hadn't received any offer of employment, so I had no choice but apply for agency driving work.

As predicted the agencies I approached were only interested in my driving licence and couldn't give a damn about my past, or the fact I was in the TA. Great, I thought, I'll finally be working and able to support my family. What I didn't know was towards the end of the year driving assignments tend to dry up.

In between applying for full time work and pondering about leaving the TA, I applied far too late for any agency work. All available contracts to cover the Christmas and New Year rush had been filled by as early as September, and there were simply no positions left until work picked up again around Easter. Until then I continued to apply for full time vacancies. Anything from warehouse operative to refuse collecting, but I didn't receive one reply offering an interview or even a rejection.

As time went on I became complacent with the fact I would never find work. Leaving it too late caused a major concern with my, or rather our finances too. My army salary quickly dried up and we only had Helen's wage to keep us going, that wasn't enough to tread water let alone keep afloat and pay the mortgage.

Christmas and New Year had come and gone. Santa Claus managed to visit Rachel and gave her what she really, really wanted, and that was a Bratz doll, Groovy Chick bike, a doll's house and loads of other 'gotta have' fashionable toys. But the cost of Christmas left further bruises on our already battered finances, and like many other families up and down the country we spent money we didn't have. Buying the turkey, drinks and those much-needed presents for the family, only to put the expenditure on plastic, which just delayed the true cost of the festive season.

Putting our financial situation to one side, if only for a week or two, we were determined to make a great Christmas for Rachel and for our latest addition to the family, James, born November 2nd 2003. We were over the moon when he decided to make his appearance, especially Rachel. She now had a baby brother to care for and most definitely tease as he grew up. But I couldn't get out of my head the extra financial responsibility young James, unknowingly, brought with him.

Helen, however, conveniently forgot about our financial situation by spending a small fortune on prams, pushchairs, baby clothes and the latest must have newborn gadgets; once again paying for it all by using our flexible friend the credit card, which had already taken a bashing over Christmas. And coupled with the fact I was still unemployed and didn't qualify for any unemployment benefits, the pile of unpaid bills grew higher and higher. We'd already maxed our remaining credit cards to keep up with 'red' bills and even to buy food.

Inevitably we found ourselves missing the odd monthly minimum payments on two of our four cards, and because of this we were denied permission to increase our credit limit. To make matters worse we were unable to pay the mortgage for December and January, which totalled around £1600. In the short term it meant we had a decent Christmas and were able to forget about our problems. Back on planet earth, however, we'd started our unavoidable descent down that slippery slope of unmanageable debt, and didn't even have enough money for the next mortgage payment due by the end of February.

In the meantime David Tennant ran riot in my head, continuing to taunt my sanity and take delight in telling me I was useless. My suspicion of strangers also became increasingly intense, reaching the point of having an irrational hatred towards them. The thought of venturing outdoors, even walking to the corner shop, made me feel physically sick, so I became almost a prisoner in my own home. I'd conceded to the fact I was a failure and nothing more than a burden to my wife and family. After all, what use is someone that has been discarded by their government, unwanted by employers and renounced from society?

The date didn't help my balance of mind either; it was my first anniversary of being told I was about to be called out. And there I was, exactly one year on, standing in the middle of my garden trying to keep busy, supposedly picking up twigs and leaves that had fallen onto the lawn from trees next door. It wasn't long before uninvited memories – yet again – hijacked my mind: pre-deployment training, arriving in Kuwait, breaching the Iraqi border... Then the whole war whizzed past my mind's eye in a matter of seconds with amazing clarity. I could even hear the deafening sound of soldiers screaming in agony from their horrific battlefield wounds, which I constantly heard during my stint in the field hospital at Shaibah airfield. I then did something I thought I'd never do – I had a little weep.

Was I feeling sorry for myself? Some may think so. But no, it was far more complicated than that. It felt as if a lifetime of anger, fury, torment, frustration and personal defeat had been condensed into a few seconds, only to be dropped from a great height onto my shoulders, relentlessly pressing down, squeezing the last drop of hope and optimism out of my pathetic life. David Tennant embraced my emotional turmoil by patiently waiting for me to crumble beneath it, only to piss on my putrid carcass.

I'd always thought of myself as being strong willed. Whenever I felt down and cornered in the past, some unknown inner strength would quickly rise to the surface and temporarily seize control until I was strong enough to carry on and grab the helm with both hands. But that inner strength I subconsciously relied upon so many times before hadn't surfaced for many months. It was if it had been slaughtered. Cut down without mercy by my demon.

The effect of the increasing pressure to find work, debts piling up, being rejected from society and now the arrival of James, slowly but surely pushed me towards the brink of total mental collapse. I had to face reality, whatever reality was, by admitting I'd lost control and could no longer get a grip on what was happening around me.

With hindsight I may have been suffering from some kind of mental breakdown. Many, including a few within the medical profession, suggested PTSD. My mental state could certainly be perceived as showing signs of solitary introspection, paranoia and probably a bit of schizophrenia thrown in, and such symptoms are linked with PTSD. But only a psychiatrist would have had any inclination as to what was really happening inside my head, which wouldn't be a pretty sight.

I don't know for how long I was crying or for how long I was kneeling on the lawn, and hadn't realised it started to rain, but I was soaked to the skin. I raised my head and looked up at the house. I could almost see it sink into its own foundations before my very eyes in an inexcusable quagmire I had selfishly put my family into, and the very real threat of our home being repossessed.

"You coming in, you'll get soaked," Helen shouted from the kitchen window.

I jumped up and rubbed my eyes, hoping she didn't notice I'd been crying. The last thing I wanted was for her to see me quivering like a nervous wreck.

"Take your trainers off, I've just washed the kitchen floor," she ordered as I opened the back door, "I'm off to mother's with Rachel and Jamie, and won't be back till late afternoon. She's taking us shopping to buy some food for us, being as you don't have a job and can't provide for your own family."

Helen couldn't resist having the slightest of digs. Even her mother had a go at me for being useless and failing to provide for my family. She was one of those mother-in-laws that knew everything about anything, including the army and its tactics on the battlefield. She once told me that TA soldiers wouldn't be called out to fight in Iraq because they weren't proper soldiers.

If that wasn't bad enough when I returned from Iraq, and before I could get a word in edgeways, she said that some reliable source told her (so it must be true) that all TA soldiers weren't involved in the fighting and were kept behind in Kuwait during the conflict.

When I showed her my photographs with myself surrounded by Iraqi landmarks and road signs, however, she fell silent.

I didn't respond to Helen's dig. Instead I picked up the gaggle of shoes that littered the utility room and placed them back on the rack in appropriate rank and file. Helen loaded the car with Jamie's baby seat and other bits of kit whilst Rachel frantically searched for her Bratz doll, which was obviously desperately needed for the shopping trip.

"I love you, Daddy", Rachel shouted as she continued her search.

I looked up from my shoe inspection, encapsulated by her big, blue innocent eyes. It was if she was telling me that I wasn't myself, but everything will be okay.

"C'mon Rachel, Nanny will be waiting!" Helen snapped, shouting from outside the open front door.

I gave Rachel a hug – more so for me – and ushered her to the front door.

"Go on, darling, Mummy is waiting. I'll find your doll for when you get back."

Or at least I hoped I could now I committed myself.

Happy knowing that Daddy will find 'Penelope' the Bratz doll, Rachel ran to Mummy.

"Oh, by the way, there's some post on the table," Helen shouted, then slammed the door shut.

"Here we go," I muttered to myself as I walked through the kitchen towards the hallway table, expecting letters from credit card companies, the mortgage company, bills and vacancy rejection letters.

Yep, I was right, on all four accounts. I also expected all the bills to say the same as they had since my return home: This is your last chance to pay any outstanding payments or legal proceedings may proceed against you… blah, blah, blah. But no, they were far worse than that. I was right about the two letters from prospective employers, though. Both saying the usual: Sorry, you have been unsuccessful on this occasion.

One of the credit card companies, however, had passed my details to a debt collection agency, who stressed that immediate payment was due or they will be sending one of their agents to my house. This just made me laugh. In a way I was looking forward to them knocking on my door and demanding payment.

The letter from the mortgage company also threatened legal proceedings if I didn't catch up with my arrears, but offered one last chance to repay providing I get in touch with them straight away. I was pretty sure the next letter they'd send would be a repossession order if I ignored this one, so I forgot about the other threatening letters and jumped at the chance to phone my mortgage company and try to save my house from repossession.

As I reached for the phone it sprang into life. I hesitated at first, wondering who was on the other end. Maybe it's another creditor demanding payment. I shook the thought out of my head and answered the phone. It was one of the many, many driving agencies I'd signed up to over the past few months, and they were actually offering work. I couldn't believe it. Finally, out of all the crap that had been thrown at me, something was actually going right.

I wrote down the details of the company that needed a driver that evening and agreed I will be there at 8pm prompt. Unfortunately it wasn't on a rolling week to week basis or a continuous contract, and it was only for that night, but at least it was something. I had to get some sleep if I was to work through the night, but was too excited. Stupid I know, but I truly felt that all my problems were now behind me, all because I was offered a single nights work. The most I expected to make was around £70 after tax, and that was nowhere near enough to get me out of my financial mess, but at least it was a start.

Before I attempted to grab some sleep I had to phone the mortgage people to see if I could keep them at bay. Thankfully they agreed to give me until the end of March to catch up with the previous two outstanding payments, with the promise I would keep up with further repayments. Not the best of arrangements, but it was better than nothing.

I checked my watch – it was almost three o'clock, which meant I had four hours kip before I needed to get up, take a shower and get to work. I wrote a note for Helen explaining about the mortgage company and that I was in bed because I was working that night. Hopefully my note would cheer her up and put me in her good books. Trying to sleep and being excited, however, is nigh-on impossible, but

I knew I had to grab at least a few hours, otherwise driving through the night would soon take its toll.

It felt as if I had closed my eyes for only a few minutes when I heard the distinctive sound of a car door shut, then the dulcet tones of a four-year-old girl. The front door burst open, followed by a bit of shuffling and the sound of shopping bags being brought into the kitchen, then the shouting and screaming started.

"Rachel, leave that alone and help Mummy put away the shopping!"

"But it's my doll!"

Obviously Rachel must have found her Bratz doll the instant she walked into the house, which I forgot to look for. It was no use, there was no way I could fall back to sleep, so I got up.

"Were you in bed?" Helen asked as she noticed me walking down the stairs.

"I was trying to grab some sleep, I'm working tonight. Didn't you read the note I left you?" I asked, only to notice she'd placed a shopping bag over it, so obviously not.

"Working tonight? Oh, you can't, I promised mum you'd help set up her computer."

"What?"

"She's brought a secondhand computer, but doesn't know how to set it up, so I said you'll do it for her as soon as I got back from shopping."

"I can't, I'm working tonight." I checked my watch; it was now five-thirty.

"That's typical! You don't work for months then say you have to work just because my mum needs some help with her computer. It's the least you can do being she's bought all this shopping for us."

"What? Can you hear yourself? I planned a night's work to get out of setting up your mother's sodding computer. Where did that come from?"

I couldn't believe Helen. In fact, I simply couldn't understand her reasoning. I scanned the work surfaces of shopping bags strewed all over them, and yes, Helen's mother must have spent a small fortune. But the thought of spending a long drawn-out few hours with her, only to be criticised and constantly told what a complete waste of space I am, was one evening I wanted to avoid, working or not.

"I'll do it tomorrow," I said, if only to keep Helen quiet.

"No, you will do it now, otherwise it will make us look ungrateful," Helen grilled, expecting I'd drop everything for her precious mother and jeopardise a night's work. "Well?"

"Well what?"

"Are you going to help my mum with her computer?"

"Helen, I have to work tonight, and that's the end of it. I need to grab some sleep before I start at eight, okay."

I turned to face the stairs but Helen wasn't having any of it. She told her mum I'd help set up her computer, and as far as she was concerned that meant I had no say in the matter.

"You selfish bastard!" Helen screamed, "you selfish, selfish bastard!" A silence ensued, quickly followed by sobbing from a four-year-old. "Now look what you've done, you've made Rachel cry! Get out of my house, you useless, selfish bastard! Get out!"

I stood on the stairs trying my damned hardest to keep calm, but frustration and anger started to boil deep within. Maybe it was caused by Helen's pathetic outburst, or maybe I was getting close to loosing my temper. Whichever, I quickly pulled myself together and remained level-headed, thinking it was best to get out of the way and go to work, albeit a tad early.

Helen looked at me in disbelief – I'd dared to defy her. Her face was distorted with anger and tears flooded her eyes, but I didn't care. For twelve months I had agonisingly put up with Helen's sudden outbursts and relentless digs, and my feelings for her were now damaged beyond repair. I could no longer give a shit about this woman standing before me. I grabbed my toe-capped boots, jacket and workbag, and walked out of the front door, closely followed by Helen slamming it shut behind me.

"Daddy, please don't go," a little muffled voice shouted.

I turned to look at Rachel pressing the palms of her hands against the bay window as she watched Daddy load his car with work stuff. Then it dawned on me, the last time Rachel witnessed me loading my car with bags was when I left for demobilisation, and as far as she was concerned I was off to war again. I waved at her, mouthing I was going to work and will be back in the morning, hoping she understood.

Driving the twenty-minute journey to the industrial estate Helen's words echoed through my mind, coming to the conclusion that she was right, I was useless. Or rather my demon said she was right, and it wasn't going to leave me alone. My brief joy with gaining an extra two months to catch up with the mortgage arrears and having a night's work quickly slipped away as paranoia grabbed the chance to infest my mind once again. Only this time I let it do what it wanted to do. I no longer had any fight left in me to beat it off.

David Tennant quickly took advantage of my weakened state and kept repeating a question: What was I doing driving to a job that will last for only one paltry shift? In the scheme of things my demon was correct for once. Mentally calculating my debts they roughly totalled around £8,000, which prompted my demon to raise a further question: What would earning £70 tonight actually pay for? My mind continued to be taunted with the same question over and over again, and I tried to ignore it, but begun to believe in what it was saying.

Arriving at the RDC (Regional Distribution Centre), albeit a few hours early, I parked in the staff car park and as soon as I switched off the engine the relentless questions in my head also stopped. Walking across the yard, reversing bleepers rang out, as trucks reversed onto neatly parked trailers standing in unison on their loading bays. Forklift trucks whizzed past on the uneven concrete surface with pallets of produce bouncing around in trays and boxes, and shunter tugs chugged around parking empty trailers onto bays.

I entered the shabby transport office, which was nothing more than a small area cordoned from the rest of the warehouse by plasterboard partitioning, and was greeted by a typical transport clerk. When I say greeted, I really mean frowned upon because to them I was nothing more than agency scum.

The duty clerk, all of which believe they are managing director material, took my details and noticed I was a little early. She looked puzzled as to why, then turned to one of her colleagues and blatantly commented that I was a typical agency driver with no concept of time. Transport clerks aren't employed for their intelligence.

"So which rabble are you from?" she jeered, trying to sound in charge.

Tempting as it was to bite at her comment I thought I'd better not considering it was my first visit, so I answered her question and she ticked off my name on a list, not unlike a registration mark given at school. She then carried on reading her magazine, which I presumed had large print and pop-up pages.

I looked around the office and noticed a coffee machine next to the entrance, so I grabbed a few coins out of my pocket and scanned the menu on the front of the machine, noticing it only accepted company-issued pre-paid cards.

"Excuse me, luv, how do I get a coffee from this machine?" I asked the clerk, although I had a feeling I already knew the answer.

The duty clerk reluctantly raised her head from her magazine and sneered, as if to say how dare you disturb me. "Cards only," she snapped.

"So where can I get one from?"

She looked up again, getting increasingly pissed off with me interrupting her busy schedule. "You can't, it's for our drivers only, not you agency lot."

Puzzled as to why agency drivers couldn't grab a coffee from the machine and why they were treated with such contempt, I noticed one of their own drivers enter the office to use it.

"Ere' mate, could I buy a coffee from you, I'm gasping, and I don't have a card."

He looked at me as if I was something he'd just trodden in. Totally ignoring my request he grabbed his coffee from the machine and walked over to the counter with a handful of paperwork, presumably he'd returned from a delivery and was finishing his shift.

Another driver walked in, and he too placed a card in the machine, noticing I was leaning against it and asked, "Do you want one, mate?"

"I was under the impression agency drivers weren't allowed," I sarcastically replied.

He laughed. "Yeah, but I ignore this lot. They're only jealous because we earn more money than they do. It's always been like that."

"Oh right, so you're an agency driver too?"

He let out another laugh. "Yep."

"So how did you get a card?"

"I've been here for over a year now. After a few months we're put on an agency core driver list. I then came in one evening and for some reason there was a card waiting for me. All permanent drivers are issued one every week from the office upstairs, with twenty free drinks scanned on them. And for some reason they assumed core drivers are part of their clan. There's a few of us that now have them, but we keep our mouths shut." He then tapped his nose and winked, as if I've been privy to some huge transport department secret.

A little bemused to his reply I asked for a white coffee with sugar and reflected upon his comment about being here for over a year.

"I take it you're new here, then?" he added.

"Yeah, my first and only shift."

"Yeah right, you wish."

"What makes you say that?"

"Let me explain something to you. I'm Simon, by the way."

"Kev," I replied.

My new fat, fifty-something year-old mate ushered me to sit down so he could explain 'the ropes' and not only about how to get hold of a coffee machine card. Twenty-five percent of drivers are assigned from agencies, which is quite a lot considering they only had around forty or so full time drivers of their own, covering mainly the early morning and mid-afternoon shifts.

Agency drivers filled the bulk of night and early evening shifts because many of the permanent drivers didn't want to work through the night. He further explained that all new agency drivers were offered a single 'one off' shift so transport managers could see how they performed with their first run. If all went well they usually offered a rolling week-to-week contract. As for Simon, his rolling contract had lasted so far for over a year.

In an instant, unbeknown to Simon, the confidence I'd lost had instantly returned with the thought of having a full time job – well almost – by the end of my shift. Maybe, just maybe, today was the day all my troubles will be over. Well, it's said they come in threes, and I thought that was for bad news. In my case it was for good. First, the mortgage company gave me a little extra time to catch up with my arrears, second, was the offer of work, and third, the possibility of it becoming permanent-ish.

Whilst Simon explained a little more about the duties of a typical night shift, which was mainly trunk work, further drivers arrived filling the small transport office. They were typical drivers wearing high-visibility jackets, jeans, toe-capped boots and carrying small rucksacks or the like with maps, sandwich boxes and flasks sticking out of the top.

"Simon!" the clerk yelled.

"Ah, my load is ready." He got up to grab his paperwork and returned to his seat to see where he was going. "Ah, Carnforth."

"Where's that?" I asked.

"Off junction thirty-five on the M6. It's a truck stop, so you can grab a bacon butty on ya break in the café. We then meet up with the Jocks and swap our loadedtrailers for their empty ones to return."

"And that's it?"

"Yep. Piece of piss, innit." He read through his paperwork and took a mental note of the bay number then looked outside to see if he could see his trailer. "And there it is waiting for me. See ya later, Kev."

Simon grabbed his bag and made his way past the other drivers standing around waiting for their paperwork. As he walked out of the office three more drivers walked in, now it was standing room only. I estimated there were around a dozen drivers waiting for units and trailers, but within ten minutes the room emptied. I began to get a little worried. Perhaps my run had been cancelled. Then remembered I wasn't needed until eight o'clock. I checked my watch, it said quarter-to-seven, so I had over an hour to wait.

"Mervin!" the clerk shouted. "Here, you can take this load being you're already here."

I grabbed the paperwork and noticed I too was off to Carnforth. My truck was a nice surprise too – a Volvo FM with a sleeper cab, so at least I could grab a kip during my break.

I jumped in the driver's seat and noticed it had the old-fashioned tachograph reader rather than the new digital type. I wrote my details on the tacho disc and placed it in the reader. The disc was nothing more than a thin piece of card no bigger than a compact disc that recorded your speed, driving, waiting and working time. I switched on the ignition, checked I had a full tank of fuel and carried out the other usual vehicle checks before I coupled onto my awaiting trailer.

"You off to Carnforth as well?" a familiar voice shouted from a cab window over the noise of our truck engines. It was Simon, parked next to me.

"Thought you'd already left," I replied as I stood on the footplate hooking up my air and electrical susie lines.

"Nah, not yet. I like to waste half-an-hour to grab a bit more time on my shift. 'Ere, we can go up together if you like. I'll lead the way. I can introduce you to some of the Jocks when we get there."

"Sounds like a good idea," I cheerily replied.

All hooked up and ready to go, Simon and I made our way to security at the gatehouse before setting off on our four-hour journey. Simon was a tonic I badly needed. It was if he had been sent from above to restore my faith in humanity, make me feel that I'd been a total arse to think otherwise. An overwhelming sense of euphoria surged through my veins as I felt my past anxieties dwindle away.

Driving up the M6 motorway I started to think of ways I could repay my debts now I was working, and how I could treat Helen and the kids. Maybe go on a holiday in the summer. We hadn't done that for years. For the first time in a long time I wore a smile that wasn't fake and genuinely reflected that I was happy. I now had something to look forward to.

I pulled into the truck stop and dropped my trailer next to Simon's. The huge lorry park buzzed like a beehive; trucks dropping off and picking up trailers for many different companies and destinations. It even had an area for staying overnight, but God knows how drivers managed to get any sleep with the racket we were making.

"C'mon, Kev, let's grab a bacon butty and I'll introduce you to some of the lads in the café. They even have strippers here on some nights," he added as we walked to the main entrance.

"Bollocks!"

"No, seriously, although some maybe suspect."

We had our bacon butties and a chin wag with some of the other drivers, then made our way back to hook up to the empty trailers waiting for us.

"You can make your way back, Kev. I'm gonna waste another half-an-hour before I set off."

"Dragging out what you can, eh?"

"You got it, Kev, you got it," Simon replied with a wink.

I thought of doing the same, but I wanted to get back home as soon as possible to tell Helen the good news. I pulled out of the truck stop and made my way back down the motorway. It was almost half-past midnight and figured I'd be home by around five-thirty, so I'd still catch her in bed before she woke for work.

An hour passed and tiredness kicked in hard. I knew I should have grabbed some sleep during my break, but that wasn't to be, so I had to think of ways to keep awake and stay alert. I opened the window to let in the ice-cold wind, which worked for a while, but I became too cold so wound it back up again. Ten minutes later my eyelids begun to feel heavy. This wasn't good, so I had to reach for my emergency bag of sweets, which I wasn't planning to start eating until I was further into the journey.

I turned up the volume on the radio to listen to 'TalkSport'. Presenter, Mike Mendoza, was talking about Iraq and invited listeners to telephone the show and partake in the debate. This helped me to focus and keep awake because some of the comments were outrageous: we shouldn't have invaded Iraq; we killed thousands of innocent victims with indiscriminate bombing; President Bush wanted Iraqi oil... Similar comments were made throughout the show, and not one, other than Mike, defended the soldiers and the liberation.

I found myself actually shouting at the radio, desperate to telephone the show and join in the conversation. But I was driving, and there was no way I wanted to be caught by police using a mobile phone and jeopardise my new job. Instead I had to endure the 'tree huggers' calling in and insisting the British army were nothing more than murderers and every soldier involved should be hung for their war crimes.

I know I could have simply switched stations and listened to some music or even turned off the radio, but I was transfixed to these pathetic comments. The relentless droning of the 'tree huggers' combined with the droning of the engine, however, eventually made me feel sleepy once again.

I fought to stay awake but my eyelids grew heavier and heavier and I started to sway from lane to lane. A truck pulled up beside and honked his horn, but I didn't take any notice as I signalled to turn off the M6 at the approaching exit. The truck alongside frantically continued honking his horn to grab my attention, which he finally did. I looked at him and frowned, wondering what he wanted as I manoeuvred to turn off the motorway onto the slip road.

Suddenly, something grabbed my attention as I snapped out of my dream-state mind and noticed the junction never existed. I'd actually pulled over onto the hard shoulder heading towards a barrier. To make matters worse I was half way across the Thelwall viaduct spanning the Manchester ship canal.

I instinctively pulled the steering wheel to my right, making the trailer dance around a tad, but I managed to straighten up before driving off the hard shoulder and back onto the carriageway. The truck beside me, a Parcel Force lorry, raised his thumb to indicate if I was okay. I returned a thumb's up, indicating I was, but I wasn't. My hands were clammy and my forehead sweated profusely. I lit a cigarette, opened my window and turned up the radio, with hope my near-death experience gave me such a fright I'd now be able to stay awake for the rest of the journey.

Mike Mendoza continued to stick up for the British Forces and the liberation whilst callers gave their typical armchair warrior expertise as to how they would have fought the war. I tutted at their pathetic comments, then noticed something looking out of place on the motorway some 400-metres ahead.

"Turn the fucking lights off!" a voice bellowed, sounding like Stuart, the crewmember from my Foden recovery vehicle, shouting from the radio, "we're supposed to be driving tactical!" In other words, no lights on at all.

I instinctively turned off the lights and slowed down to a crawl.

"What do you think it is?" I asked.

"Bound to be another fucking ambush," Stuart sternly replied, appearing in the passenger seat.

Truck after truck sped past, sounding their horns and flashing hazard lights.

"Bloody idiots, don't they realise they're heading straight for it, and with their lights on they're making themselves an easy target," I commented.

Stuart ignored me as he poked his head out of the capola in the roof of the cab. "Hand over my rifle, Kev, I don't like the look of this."

I looked around the almost pitch-black cab but couldn't see his rifle anywhere.

"Kev, I need my fucking rifle!" Stuart shouted.

"I can't find it!"

"Too late, you're gonna have to speed up and charge straight through the blockade. Go for it!" he shouted, climbing back into his seat.

I put my foot down to gain as much speed as possible, hoping the chogies were pre-occupied with other vehicles approaching them and wouldn't see us until we'd ploughed through the blockade. Hopefully killing a few with the impact and causing enough chaos to get away before the remaining chogies could fire off a single round.

Cars driving dangerously close to my door tooted horns and shouted out of windows. One car drove straight in front, put on his hazard lights and slammed on the brakes, slowing me down to almost a crawl. He then speeded up and stupidly headed towards the blockade with his lights still on.

"Fucking idiot! He's gonna draw attention to himself, and us," I shouted, turning to Stuart for some sort of reply. But he'd gone, vanished into thin air, as did the blockade, the desert and the warm night air, only to be replaced with an icy wind. I'd had another flashback, which, as usual, came from nowhere.

Trucks and cars continued to sound their horns as they drove past, bringing me back to reality, yet still feeling confused as to why I was creating so much attention. As confusion gave way to reason I noticed my lights were switched off. I quickly switched them back on and gave myself a mental kick up the arse. I had to get a grip of these flashbacks, but how do I do that when they jump out from nowhere and don't realise I'm having them?

By the time I pulled into the yard it was half-past-four. I dropped the trailer on an empty bay, refuelled the truck and made my way to the transport office. I kidded myself my flashback was due to tiredness and promised I wouldn't have any more. After all, I could now put my life back on course with my new job. I placed the plastic folder on the counter and gave the duty clerk my tacho card so it could be photocopied. There must have been a shift change during the night as the grumpy clerk I met at the beginning of my shift was nowhere to be seen.

"Ah, Mr. Mervin," the young clerk said, "I believe you had quite an eventful night."

He was a scrawny looking character, maybe in his mid-twenties, and appeared to be the sort that relished having the power over his drivers, in particular agency drivers.

"What do you mean?" I asked.

He couldn't have known about my flashback, so he must be trying to say in his way that I'm perfect for the job and was about to offer a rolling week-to-week contract.

"You almost caused a pile-up on the M6 driving without your lights on."

How the fuck?

"Oh that," I replied, trying to play down the mishap, yet concerned as to how he knew, "I knocked the light switch by mistake, but it was only for a few seconds."

"Not what I heard."

"I don't follow," I replied, trying to play down the unfortunate incident, yet still wondering how on earth he knew.

"We received a call from a passer-by, saying you were driving for quite a distance without your lights on. He then said a car deliberately slammed on his brakes directly in front of you to slow you down and grab your attention, no doubt to wake you up. Because that's what happened, didn't it, you fell asleep."

It was pointless correcting him by saying I had a flashback. He wouldn't have understood, anyway. After all, he was only a civilian, a young one at that. So I had to agree and admit to falling asleep.

"I know it happens, but you have to make sure you get plenty of rest before you start your shift" he added, trying his best to sound pedantic, "and remember, our logo, name and telephone number are sprawled across those trucks and trailers in huge lettering."

Shit. I forgot about that. Still, at least I got away with just a bollocking.

"So thanks for last night and bringing back our truck in one piece, but we will no longer require your services."

"What?"

All hopes of paying my debts, catching up with mortgage payments, treating the kids and Helen, even going on a summer holiday were thrown away in an instant, all because of that fucking flashback. But I wasn't going to give up that easily.

"Look, mate, I may have slipped up but there's no need for that. I assure you I'll make sure I get plenty of sleep before tonight's shift."

"You've had your chance and blew it, not my fault."

"I can't persuade you to keep me on, then?"

"Like I said, you've had your chance," he replied with a cynical smirk, that I was tempted to wipe off, "and you are banned from site, never to return. You agency drivers are ten-a-penny, so you'll be easy to replace." he added, increasing the intensity of his smirk.

That was that, hired and fired within one shift. I couldn't help but think if I was one of their own drivers, would the outcome have been the same? No, is the answer, other than a stern telling off. But being an agency driver the company knew we were ten-a-penny, lowest of the low, scum drivers that are an unwanted necessity. Yet easy to hire and fire because agency workers have no employment rights, just more EU laws to obey than full-time workers. And my mishap was nothing more than a feeble excuse for the young lad to exploit his misplaced power and look fearful in front of other agency drivers mooching around the office.

My drive home wasn't the way I expected it to be. I should have been whistling with joy, grinning from ear to ear, knowing I'd managed to turn our life around and find a job. Helen would no longer be on my back continuously moaning, and bills could now be paid. But oh no, we can't have that. Instead, David Tennant threw in a flashback to spoil any chance I had of keeping a job. And this time my demon picked the occasion Stuart and I came across a blockade as we went to help some of the 2RTR guys with a casualty vehicle they needed recovering.

On our way to the recovery task a bunch of Fedayeen Militia parked two pick-up trucks across a railway crossing to give the impression they'd either broken down or had an accident. Their intention was to stop a coalition vehicle to either hijack or blow it to pieces, including the occupants. Stuart noticed them at the last minute and left us no choice but ram through the blockade. They opened fire on us as we charged through, totally destroying the pick-up trucks as we thundered past.

I parked on my driveway, switched off the ignition and sank into the seat knowing what to expect when I walked into the house – an explosion of insults, digs and nagging. I looked up and noticed all the curtains were closed, shutting out the outside world, as if to suggest some kind of metaphor – keep out, you're no longer welcome.

David Tennant started to laugh louder and louder, teasing and taunting my subconscience. Reminding how pathetic I was and that I'd never find a job because I was a useless waste of space. Nothing more than an oxygen thief, and who was I to argue. As far as I was concerned my demon was winning; I'd reached breaking point.

CHAPTER 11

THERE IS SOMEONE IN MY HEAD BUT IT'S NOT ME

I threw my car keys on the hallway table, took off my boots and went straight to bed feeling tired, demoralised and cheated. Only I could be almost offered full-time employment – albeit agency work – then hired and fired on the first shift. I thought it best not to mention anything to Helen, but at least I had some good news I could salvage from yesterday's fiasco – extra time to repay the mortgage arrears.

It must have been around lunchtime because I could overhear Helen telling Rachel she must finish her spaghetti hoops or she won't grow up to be a beautiful princess. I decided to get up, have a shower and make my way downstairs to tell Helen my good news.

"Oh, you're up then," she muttered from the kitchen, wiping up spaghetti hoops from the dining table. Obviously Rachel took a dislike to them.

"Want a coffee?"

"How did last night go?" Helen asked, ignoring my offer.

"Yeah, it went okay, but I don't think I'll be going back. I think it was a one-off."

"Huh, that figures. So will the agency be offering you any more work?"

"Dunno."

"More like you don't care!" Helen snapped, throwing the cloth on the table and storming out of the kitchen into the living room, leaving me to clear up after the spaghetti hoop Princess.

Now is the time to tell her some good news, I thought. "Hey, I forgot to mention, I spoke to the mortgage company yesterday," no reply, so I continued, "they said they will give us an extra couple of months to catch up on the arrears. That's good of them, isn't it?"

"And what use is an extra two months when you don't even have a job to pay them back!"

So much for my good news and hope of putting Helen in a good mood.

I could hear her sobbing, but the lack of feeling I had for her rapidly surfaced and I chose to ignore her emotions. Instead, I cleaned up Rachel's mess, wiped her down with a damp cloth and lifted her out of the chair so she could play with her Bratz dolls.

Helen came back in to the kitchen clutching a couple of letters. "How are you going to pay these?" she yelled, still with tears running down her cheeks, thrusting the letters into my hand, "these came this morning, and look, they're threatening letters this time. You know what happens next, don't you? We're going to be cut off!"

I read the letters from the gas and electricity suppliers, both seemingly gloating that we have only one more chance to pay up – or else. It's as if they don't want us to so they can take great enjoyment cutting us off and laugh at our misfortune whilst wallowing in their billions of profit they make every year.

"And don't you dare say you will sort it, because I've had it up to here!" she added, gesturing a hand against her forehead as some kind of indicator to show how pissed off she is.

I stood motionless holding the letters, but wasn't at all bothered with their contents. I didn't even attempt to console or reassure Helen, I just stood in silence.

"You don't care, do you, you just don't fucking care!"

She was right, I didn't. I'd tried my best but failed. There was nothing more I could do to bring our lives back to normal, so the only thing left was give up trying.

"I'm going to mother's for the rest of the day so you'd better think of something quick to find some money or I'm leaving you."

I let out a chuckle.

"You think it's funny, do you? I mean it, sort something out soon or I'm leaving you to rot in your own self-pity!"

I tried my hardest to ignore her comments and stop giggling, but for some reason they came as a blessed release. The thought of her leaving sounded like a fantastic idea. Oh, the peace and quiet.

Helen grabbed some baby things, strapped James into his pram and with Rachel in tow slammed the front door behind her – again. I was now on my own with my thoughts, but there wasn't any. Instead of thinking of something constructive to do I switched on the television and slumped on the settee. As usual I left the television tuned onto a news channel, and there it was, nothing but Iraq, Iraq, Iraq. And as per usual a so-called expert blurted out his reasoning as to why the peacekeeping process wasn't working.

The telephone sprang into life, diverting my attention from the gripping expert on the television. I checked the time and noticed I'd been watching the same bulletin repeat itself over and over again.

"Kev, it's Darren, you coming out for a drink tonight?"

"I dunno, Darren, considering what happened last time, remember?"

"No, not the club, I mean into town."

Even the thought of going into town for a drink filled me with dread, but what harm could it do, I thought.

"Yeah okay, but I'm skint, I can't afford it."

"Don't worry about that, I'll lend you a few quid," Darren replied, "I'll be round at eight, so be ready."

I replaced the handset and for a split second felt almost guilty of blowing Darren's borrowed money on a night's drinking. But thought nah, what the heck.

Instead I went back to bed to grab a few hours kip before hitting the town.

I must have been more tired than first thought. I woke up with the house in total darkness. I switched on the bedroom light and noticed it was almost seven o'clock, so I had a quick shower, splashed on a bit of aftershave and made my way downstairs, noticing Helen hadn't yet returned home.

I didn't care. Her not being home saved me from her nagging questions: how can you afford to go out on the piss, yet we can't afford to pay any bills? Or, it's okay for you to spend money we haven't got on beer, yet you won't feed your family…

Darren rang the doorbell at eight o'clock precisely. "You set?" he asked as I answered the door.

"Too right I am, c'mon, let's go," I firmly said with Helen's nagging voice ringing in my mind, let alone ears.

"Bloody 'ell you're keen, aren't ya?"

"After what happened last night, so would you be."

I explained to Darren about the little mishap during my night shift, and that I'd blown any chances working full time for the company and the agency whilst he drove. I also brought him up to speed with a few other escapades, things that happened, or rather didn't happen, whilst searching for full time work.

We found a pub to our liking and I couldn't wait to get a pint down my neck.

"I'm in the chair," I said making my way to the bar with Darren's money, "what'ya having?"

"Usual," Darren replied, as he scanned the room for a clear table so we could sit around it and continue our conversation.

I grabbed our drinks and made my way to Darren, where he had found a deserted table in the corner of the bar.

"Cheers," I said as I gulped down my pint before sitting down, "I'll grab us a couple more."

Before Darren could say anything I was at the bar ordering two more pints just as Darren started his first.

"Oi, take it easy," Darren said as I returned with the drinks, "the rate you're going, it's as if there'll be no tomorrow."

"Suits me," I replied in between gulps.

"For fuck sake, Kev, I know it's frustrating not finding work but things can't be that bad, can they?"

I thought for a moment. It's all very well moaning and groaning to him about what a shit week I'd had or how pissed off I was being out of work, but did I really want Darren to know the ins and outs of my marriage with his sister? Did I really want him to know about my flashbacks, paranoia, or how I felt about them – the public? The immediate answer was, no, of course not. After all, they were my problems, not his.

I decided to change the subject by talking about the two bits of skirt standing at the bar, both dressed in very short black dresses where certain areas would have been better hidden with a belt. Darren and I giggled like naughty schoolboys when the girls clocked us looking at them. We never stood a chance chatting them up anyway.

Instead we carried on drinking and admired their taste in clothes.

As the beer flowed it didn't take long before Darren predictably diverted the topic of conversation towards Iraq. It wasn't his fault. We both couldn't help notice a wall mounted television in the corner of the pub switched to the Sky News channel, blaring out news bulletins of the day's events. He was bound to ask.

"You wish you were back there, don't you," Darren surprisingly said.

"Bloody 'ell Darren, where did that come from?"

"I'm right, though, aren't I?" I couldn't deny it, he was. "What hold does that shit-hole have over you?"

"I dunno, it just does," I shrugged, not really wanting to answer his question.

I started to fidget and play with a beer mat, thinking this great idea of Darren's to come out for a pint was, yet again, a bad one. I half expected 'Stumpy' to walk in and that would have really been the icing on the cake.

"Helen popped round to see me earlier," Darren said between sips of his lager, eager to change the topic of conversation again, and giving suspicion as to why he really wanted me to come out for a drink with him, "she reckons you're going mad."

"Go on," I beckoned, remembering Helen accusing me of getting a night's work simply to get out of setting up a computer for her mum – and I'm supposed to be the one going mad?

"Well, she seems to think you can't be bothered to find work and just, you know, given up hope."

I could slowly feel myself shake once again with anger. Not at Darren, but towards Helen for not only misunderstanding my feelings and emotions, but also gossiping. I hated being talked about, especially when the person spreading the idle gossip – wife or otherwise – knew nothing of the shit I had to put up with, and not just Iraq. Also the seemingly endless shit since returning home.

"Now, before you have a go at me, hear me out," Darren added with some urgency, as if he knew I was about to jump down his neck for interfering, "I suggested it might be a good idea if you re-mortgaged the house, and before you say you don't have a job, it might be possible to get a mortgage if you self-cert."

I laughed at his preposterous notion of even considering re-mortgaging the house. I was finding it hard enough to repay the existing mortgage, let alone apply for a new one.

"Was it Helen who came up with this ridiculous idea?"

"Actually it's mine, because I've done it myself when I needed cash a few years ago, remember?"

I did. Darren was once made redundant from a building firm and found it extremely hard to find further work within his trade. Instead he too did a spot of agency driving, which took the sting out of his financial predicament for the short-term, but he slowly continued to sink into a quagmire of unpaid bills – including mortgage repayments. With three growing children and a wife to support he had to do something quick so he looked into re-mortgaging the house even though he didn't have a job.

Out of the blue he'd paid off debts, re-decorated the house, bought a new kitchen and bathroom, had a family holiday and traded in his old and knackered car for something almost new. Within six months he'd found full time employment so his mortgage repayment history remained unscathed and he no longer had any of those heavy bills weighing him down. I never questioned it at the time as to why he could all of a sudden turn his life around, but then again it wasn't any of my business.

Darren explained that rather than certifying himself bankrupt, and whilst he still had the chance, a self-certification mortgage was his only remaining option. He also explained the downside and that the mortgage company was a sub-prime lender so interest rates were higher than high street lenders.

I didn't care. If I could do the same as Darren I'd be able to pay off my present mortgage, pay the overdraft, utility bills, credit cards, council tax demands, get my car repaired and even have enough left for a family holiday. Maybe put aside a few months mortgage payments and allow a bit of time to find a proper full time job, rather than apply for anything that came along.

No more worrying about when the next bill will fall on the doormat, no more threatening letters from the gas and electricity suppliers, no more arguing and more importantly no more nagging. Yep, things were looking up – again. Forget about all the mishaps and cock-ups I'd caused trying to rebuild our lives since returning home. Forget about driving for an agency and have some jumped-up twat of a traffic clerk banning me from site.

Darren's idea was brilliant. I felt as if I'd turned yet another corner, overcome yet another huge obstacle standing in my way. I couldn't wait to tell Helen, although I had a feeling Darren would have already explained it all to her earlier.

"Fancy another pint?" he asked.

"Yeah, why not, but make it the last one, I want to go home and have a chat with Helen."

Darren smiled, as if he knew I was going to say that.

He fetched the drinks, leaving me to ponder on what to do in the morning. I was certainly going to be busy. The television in the corner of the pub continued to blurt out situations in Iraq, but I was too engrossed with thoughts of getting my life back on an even keel to notice.

"Here you go," Darren said placing my pint on a beer mat, and started to chuckle.

"What's tickled you?"

"Nothing really. I was waiting to get served and two blokes at the end of the bar were talking about Iraq."

"Oh," I replied, not really taking an interest.

"They said we've made a right mess over there."

I took a sip of my pint, still not interested.

"Does it wind you up, though, hearing people talking about Iraq and not having a clue as to what you lot did out there?"

"Maybe. I try to ignore them."

"But how about when they deliberately blame you, as an individual, for all the carnage and blood spilt, surely that gets on your tits?"

Darren was right, it did, but no matter how many times I tried to explain what we actually achieved and the good we did, my words simply fell on deaf ears, so I gave up explaining.

"Daz, can we change the subject. Tell me more about this re-mortgaging malarkey."

He took the hint and went into more detail as to what to do next. I took it all in: what to say to the mortgage broker; what I needed the money for; explain my employment situation but say that I have a regular wage coming in from a driving agency, albeit slightly exaggerated.

Suddenly my attention was taken away by a lorry rumbling past on the uneven road surface outside, causing the pub to shake and shudder. I was now standing in a small room surrounded by squaddies taking cover from a ballistic missile attack, and the rumbling outside became a distant explosion from a scud missile. We had to find cover, and fast, but what's the best cover from exploding scud missiles? You can't see the buggers and even the Patriot missile batteries designed to intercept attacks couldn't be relied upon, so it was a case of carrying out the IA drill, take cover and pray your hidy-hole wasn't hit.

A brick shed was the best we could find, so at least it gave us some protection should a scud hit one-hundred metres away. Any closer, however, it would be lights out for all of us. Standing squashed with ten other squaddies wearing respirators in a sweltering hot bare brick shed no bigger than three metres square, lit by a dim 40-watt bulb, we looked at each other for some kind of reassurance we were safe. A distinct sound of a siren bellowed, but was it the all-clear or was it a late warning of an impending attack?

"You okay, Kev," one of the soldiers asked.

"How do you know my name? I've never seen you before. You can't see who I am because of this fucking face-welly I'm wearing."

"Kev, it's me, Daz," he said clicking his fingers in front of my glazed eyes.

In an instant I was back in the pub, standing in front of the television.

"You alright?" a voice came from behind.

I ignored it, being more concerened as to why I was standing in the corner of the pub and not sitting with Darren. I then broke out in a cold sweat.

"I was talking when you suddenly got up and walked towards the telly. Was it the news bulletin that grabbed your attention?" Darren asked.

I frowned, confused at Darren's questioning. "What news bulletin?"

"I was only half listening to it, but it showed footage of the time Saddam bombarded you all with scud missiles at the start of the war. That's when you stood up in the middle of me explaining to you about re-mortgaging and walked towards the telly. I told you to sit down, but you totally ignored me, as if the news bulletin pulled you inside the screen."

I tried to think of some rational explanation as to why I did what I did, but couldn't really think of anything, other than I suffered a flashback. And I didn't really want Darren to know I did, but I think he already knew. Thankfully he understood what they were about, and that they can be brought on by the simplest of situations.

"You've just had a flashback, haven't you," he whispered.

I couldn't deny it.

"I must have had, but I can't remember watching telly. You were talking to me about re-mortgaging then I heard a loud noise, some kind of rumble. The next thing I knew I was standing in a small room taking cover from a ballistic attack."

"Was that something you had to do?"

"Yeah, on numerous occasions. Once, Stuart, my crewman, and me ran into a small brick shed for shelter, only to find others had the same idea. Outside, scuds were exploding all around us, sounding as if they were getting closer and closer, like a thunder storm."

"Running into a brick shed is a bit daft, isn't it? If that was hit, it would have wiped you all out."

"We didn't have time to find perfect cover," I sternly replied, "we needed to find something there and then, anything that could give some sort of protection from shrapnel, glass, rubble, and most importantly, a chemical attack."

"But chemical weapons were never found."

"Yeah, but at the time we didn't know that. As far as we were concerened they were there, very real, and Saddam was going to use them on us. During every attack we donned our respirators, and couldn't help but think of those poor sods killed by Saddam using chemical weapons on his own people in 1988. Remember that? In the meantime, we continue the search."

"Sorry, bud, I should have realised."

"Nah, it's ok."

"Do you think NBC weapons will ever be found?"

I let out a laugh. "Well, we found enough tell-tale signs, but the actual weapons were sold to Iran and elsewhere, even Russia, well before the inspections, let alone the liberation."

"Really?"

"Well, I'm not certain, but that was the rumour at the time."

"C'mon, come and sit down, I'll get you another pint," Darran said, taking the hint to change the subject.

I could hear whispers coming from the bloke behind as he muttered something to his mate sitting on a barstool next to him.

"Ere' mate, were you out there then?" he suddenly shouted so everyone else in the pub could hear.

It worked. All the other drinkers stopped in mid-sentence and stared at me, as if I was some kind of freak.

"Did you shit yourself?" he asked, determined to get a response, then started to laugh.

He looked at his mate for some kind of reassurance. Instead his mate stared into his pint, as if to say he had nothing to do with him.

"I bet you shit yourself, didn't ya. Fuck knows why. It wasn't as if you were in a proper war, was it," he added in a drunken state, and continued to laugh.

"Shut the fuck up!" Darren shouted, glaring at him as if he wanted to beat the shit out of the drunk.

"Oh, fancy ya chances, do you? C'mon then, have a go, big man, if you dare," the Pisshead replied standing proudly, showing off his crisp, white England tee-shirt.

He must have been about the same size as Darren, but wouldn't have stood a chance. Apart from the fact Pisshead was swaying from side to side, obviously suffering from a few too many shandies, all that Darren needed to do was flick his nose and he would have tumbled like a stack of dominoes. The pub fell silent and Darren was about to take up Pisshead's offer, but I beat him to it.

Within a split second I'd broken my pint glass on the side of a table, grabbed Pisshead by the throat, slammed him hard against a wall and was about to embed the broken glass into his face. As far as I was concerned he was nothing more than a pathetic, loud mouthed, no-it-all civilian, deserving everything he was about to get, and that was a badly scared face to remind him of this particular moment.

The rest of the pub scattered to all corners of the bar to keep out of the way of the mad man with a broken pint glass. The barman was immediately on the telephone, no doubt calling the police, but I didn't care. Suddenly, instead of a surprised pale-faced westerner looking at me, I was now staring at a Fedayeen militiaman and I wasn't going to let go until he'd drawn his last breath. With a huge smile on my face I pushed the glass deeper and deeper into his face. Blood trickled down the broken glass onto my hand, and I loved every second of it.

My eyes widened with the enjoyment of hearing him whimper and sob. I twisted the glass to hear him whimper some more as it sliced and crunched through the cartilage on the bridge of his nose. His whimpering suddenly turned into a gargled scream, but I didn't want to stop, it felt good.

"Kev, for fuck sake," Darren shouted.

I ignored him.

Darren started to worry. "Kev, c'mon, mate, let him go, I think he's learnt his lesson."

Pisshead's drinking partner stood petrified to the spot, frantically nodding his head with agreement. "Yeah, he was only joking, mate, let him go, yeah?"

"Joking? I can't hear him laughing, can you?" I said, spitting my words into Pisshead's face, "so go on, big man, let me hear you laugh! C'mon, laugh, fucking laugh, big man!"

He squirmed and made squeaking noises as I turned the glass more and more into his face, desperate to obey my command to stop the torture, yet silently begging to scream out in agonising pain. I sniggered through clenched teeth, enjoying every moment, as blood gushed out of his wound. This was fun, fun, fun.

"I'm, I'm sorry," Pisshead attempted to say with a face full of broken glass.

"Not good enough," I snapped, twisting the glass further into his face, "I said laugh, not say you're sorry. C'mon, big man, fucking laugh!"

His squeaks and whimpering gave in to screams of agony; louder and louder he became with every slow turn of the glass. As he screamed I felt a huge surge of adrenaline race through my veins with the added enjoyment of hearing him squirm in so much pain.

"Please, I'm sorry, I'm sorry, I'm sorry," he cried.

"Sorry for what? For being a sissy civilian cry baby who's too scared to fight for his queen and country?"

"Yes," he immediately replied, if only to appease my questioning and let him go.

"Not good enough!"

"Please, please, stop, I'm sorry."

"Er, nah, not yet," I casually replied, "I haven't decided if I'm going to slowly kill you or not. You know, just like we did to innocent civilians back in Iraq."

His eyes widened with fright, and the thought of dying certainly scared the shit out of him. This enthralled me further with utter joy and continued to twist the glass. Decision made, I was going to rid the world of this pathetic piece of shit.

So much blood was now pouring out of the wound and down my hand it completely soaked my arm and his tee-shirt, but I didn't care, I was loving every minute. This is what I needed to relieve the huge pressure of pent-up frustration and anger that had built up deep within since coming home.

"Kev, for fuck sake, let him go!" Darren pleaded.

I looked around the pub, greeted with pairs of wide terrified eyes, full of fear and trepidation as to what I was going to do next. I didn't need this attention so I decided to loosen my grip and pulled the glass out of Pisshead's face, leaving it to bleed profusely over his England tee-shirt. He slid down the wall and collapsed onto the floor trying to stem the bleeding by holding flaps of flesh together whilst screaming in agony.

"Fuck you, fuck you all. You're nothing but arrogant, chicken-shit civilian wankers that haven't a fucking clue," I shouted standing over him, laughing as he desperately held his face together, then smashed what was left of the pint glass over his head.

"Kev, we'd better get the fuck out of here, the police are bound to turn up soon," Darren urged, tugging at my jacket sleeve.

I jumped back to reality, but not through choice. Oddly it was my demon. The very same that taunted me since my return home was now begging me to get out of the pub and go home. It was if it was frightened of my violent outburst; scared that it had pushed me too far, and was actually asking me to stop and get the fuck out of there. For a leaving gesture I knelt down and spat in the face of Pisshead, still screaming in agony as he held onto what was left of his nose, before calmly walking out of the pub.

Darren and I walked through town in silence, and then out of nowhere I started talking about re-mortgages, which troubled Darren a little.

"Kev, do you know what you did back there?" he said pointing his thumb towards the pub, totally bemused as to why I would possibly start talking about re-mortgages.

"Yeah, why?"

"It's just that you don't seemed bothered one tiny bit"

"I'm not. So what do you think is the maximum I can take out on a re-mortgage?"

"Kev, you're not listening to me, you're carrying on as if nothing happened." Darren was worried. He'd never experienced such behaviour from me before. "You do remember what you did with that dickhead's face, don't you?"

"Yes, so what? He deserved it. Never mind that, what about this re-mortgage idea?"

Darren raised his arms in submission. "I can't handle this, I've never seen you behave like that before. I'm leaving you to get on with whatever it is in your head," and he walked off to leave me with my thoughts.

The thing is, I didn't have any thoughts about what I did. All I cared about was to get home and tell Helen about my, or rather Darren's brilliant idea. I virtually skipped home, and noticed the downstairs lights were on. I checked my watch – it was almost ten o'clock – so at least I knew Helen was safely home.

As I turned the key in the lock I could see Helen through the opaque piece of glass running towards the door. She made a grab for the handle and locked the door just as I was about to walk into the house.

"Helen, what ya' doing?"

"You're not coming in!" she shouted, seemingly crying.

"C'mon, luv, what's up now? Let me in, it's bloody freezing out here."

"No, you're not coming in. Just go away and leave us alone."

"Look, if it's about that job last night, I'll soon find something else."

Helen let out a sarcastic bout of laughter. "Darren phoned to tell me what you did in the pub. You're drunk, and I were right, you're mad."

"I'm not drunk, I've only had four pints. As for being mad, that was nothing, really."

"Nothing! Darren said you ripped his bloody face off!"

"No, it sounds worse than it is, I only cut him a little. C'mon, open the door," I said calmly, playing down my outrageous outburst.

The thought occurred to me that although I almost ripped the face of Pisshead without feeling a single ounce of remorse or an impulse to repent my sin, Darren must have thought I'd do the same to Helen or even my children if I was to be antagonised again. The thing is I wasn't upset or even felt threatened. I felt all my pent-up anger and frustration that had built up over eighteen months rush to the surface. It was only a matter of time before I exploded, and unfortunately for Pisshead blurting his bullshit, detonated an unexploded bomb, only to go off in his face, literally.

"How do I know you won't attack me next?" Helen asked.

I wanted to respond by shouting at her for asking such a stupid question, but that would have definitely made matters worse.

"As if," I sniggered, "besides, you're the one that attacks me, remember?"

Which was true, and I have the scars to prove it.

She unlocked the door and slowly opened it, reluctant to let me in.

"Now then, put the kettle on," I said excitedly, clapping my hands together, "and let me tell you all about Darren's brilliant idea."

Helen looked confused, then looked at my hands covered in Pisshead's blood and shrieked.

"It's okay, just a little bit of blood, honest. I'll wash it off."

Standing motionless and frightened at my lack of remorse for what I did, Helen slowly realised I wasn't a threat to her or my children. After

I washed my hands, I calmed her down before we sat talking until the early hours about Darren's brilliant idea. It didn't take long for Helen to forget about my night out, as she was more excited of the fact we could now get out of the huge financial hole we were in.

Incredibly the plan worked.

Time to celebrate and put the past well and truly behind us. The future was now looking great, although there were a few unnerving times I thought it would go tits-up, especially when asked about my income. But as it was, having a mortgage to repay another mortgage wasn't an issue, and within six weeks or so Helen and I had our money in our bank account. It felt fantastic to pay off all the bills, credit cards and overdraft, and to no longer have threatening letters fall on our doorstep. For a moment it was like winning the lottery, although we did still had to pay it back, of course. But as far as we were concerned it was great to enjoy the freedom of having no worries. After all, I thought, we deserved it.

We purchased almost new cars we badly needed, rather than repair the old ones over and over again, replaced furniture and planned to build a kitchen extension. The extension, I thought, was an extravagance we didn't really need, but Helen set her heart on it, and I for one didn't want to upset her dream. The downside, as there always is with any good luck and fortune, is that I still needed to find a job. But that wasn't an immediate problem as I set aside six months mortgage repayments for such an eventuality.

Helen and I eventually grew closer together, mainly due to the fact we no longer had any money worries. Her ultimate dream of the perfect kitchen extension was almost complete, less the actual units and white goods, which she wanted hidden away behind matching unit doors. I also re-decorated the entire house with the colours she wanted, replaced the bathroom with the suite she desired and re-landscaped the front and rear gardens to her personal specifications.

I returned to TA duties where I could finally concentrate on further training. I attended a few weekends after my plastercast was removed, but my heart wasn't in it due to money worries and lack of employment. I was even prepared to leave the TA should my brief driving job turned full time, which undoubtedly would have included weekend work. Thankfully I didn't need to, and was now back on form and couldn't wait to get back to training on a regular basis.

Returning to regular TA weekends, however, became boring after a while.

Thankfully all of the lads from my company that went to Iraq returned in one piece, but they too appeared to be different; their characteristics were alien and they seemed distant, as if they wanted to be somewhere else. I still had that feeling – a longing of returning to my battlegroup in Iraq.

When I joined the TA in 1995 the former Yugoslavia was gripped in the middle of a civil war. We all hoped to be called out to fight alongside our NATO allies, but it never came to any fruition. Instead the MOD called for volunteers only, and even then they were swamped with requests from many TA soldiers from many trades. Only a few were chosen, mainly for their medical skills. I too put in a request, but was bluntly denied, simply because I was nothing more than a fresh recruit with no trade as yet.

I remember drinking with my grandad at his local working men's club talking to him about the war in the Balkans. I said to him that I longed to go out there and prove my worth, fight for Queen and Country. He almost choked on his pint when I told him this and responded by telling me he hoped I would never go to war, because if I did and was lucky enough to return home, I would never be the same again.

My grandad served in the artillery during the 2nd World War. A nine-mile sniper, he was nicknamed, fighting the Japanese in Burma. His trade was that of a signaller and was away from home for three long years. When he returned, as did hundreds of thousands of other Tommies, his and their lives were never the same again. Many were jobless, homeless, suffered flashbacks and combat stress. Often resulting in destroyed families, divorce, debts and suicide. That's what many returned home to. The incredible thing is, it's no different today.

My grandad was right about feeling and being different, but would I listen to him? No, of course not. I just wanted to prove to my battalion I could carry out my trade to the best of my ability. Little did I know that Grandad's words over a pint would echo through my mind eight years later as I fought my war 3,000 miles away. Not for Queen and Country, well, maybe a little. But mainly for my mates fighting alongside me.

CHAPTER 12

COMFORTABLY NUMB

Thursday, February 2nd 2006. As one door closes another one shuts, an old boss of mine used to say. Although seemingly confused with this old saying, he was actually right. How did I end up in a deeper hole than I was in before? It was all going so well, so where did it go wrong? My idea of keeping back six months' worth of mortgage repayments was a tad short. In fact I should have put aside two-years if I had enough to spare, had I known how the future would pan out.

Helen's kitchen was completed, all shiny and new to her specifications, and I slowly grew to accept it. Rachel got her treats and James had all the things a toddler needed. All I wanted was a full time job to pay for it all. It was getting beyond a joke, a joke that Helen and I didn't find remotely funny. Once again agency driving was my best option, but they could only offer a maximum of three days per week; the majority of which included a Friday evening, which meant I was left with no option but to leave the TA. Still, work and family came first and it was better than nothing, although I didn't earn anywhere near enough to sustain a family and a huge mortgage.

Of course the inevitable happened; I'd remarkably created the exact same mess we were in almost two years previous, only this time in considerably worse debt. Red bills turned into threatening letters – once again, council tax and credit card companies threatened court proceedings – once again, and yep, the mortgage company wanted immediate payment or the house will be repossessed.

The telephone rang. I hoped it was good news for a change. Fat chance. It was the agency telling me I wasn't needed for work that evening.

"Who was that on the phone?" Helen shouted from the kitchen.

"Oh, no one, just the agency."

"What time are you working tonight?" I didn't answer, and my silence said it all. "You're not working again, are you. I bloody knew it!"

I remained silent. It wasn't worth responding to her, anyway. As soon as I said anything it ended in some sort of argument.

Helen came storming out of the kitchen baiting for answers. "Well, what's happening, are you working or not?"

"No," I sternly answered.

"No! Is that it, no?"

"What d'ya expect me to say?"

"I was hoping you'd say they have something else for you. Can't you get anything right?" she added.

"I'm trying to find more work, you know that."

"Yeah, of course you are. I've heard it all before..." And there she goes, on one of her rants. I switched off as soon as she started. I'd had enough of hearing the same record play over and over again. "... so you'd better find something quick!"

"Finished?" I sarcastically asked.

"You think it's all a joke, don't you."

"A joke? Can you remember the shit I went through to get us on the straight and narrow?" I replied.

"How could I forget, and how could I forget what I went through."

I could feel my anger grow inside, bringing back memories of the past two-years. "What you went through? I tried anything and everything to find work, and if you took a moment to notice, it hasn't been easy for me either."

Helen huffed at my remark and pushed past heading for the living room, quickly returning with a fist-full of letters and bills.

"Remind you of two-years ago?"

It did, and I was standing in the same spot when she did the same thing before.

"These are down to you to pay, all of them. They need paying now or we're going to lose everything. And if that happens I'm leaving you."

Wow, she'd repeated the same promise as well.

"So you expect me to magic something out of thin air to pay these bills, just like last time? Hey, maybe we could re-mortgage." I sarcastically added.

"Fuck off!" Helen snapped as she walked back into the living room.

I didn't care, and this time my lack of interest was far worse. I'd tried everything to keep afloat, and before Darren's bright idea I thought I'd reached my lowest, until now. I'd come to the end of my tether, with definitely no way out. It was a miracle I'd managed to keep the wolves from the door by fobbing off my creditors with stories the Brothers Grimm would have been proud of. And it was a further miracle I'd actually found another job, albeit agency driving for three evenings a week, which suited me to keep out of the way of Helen. We'd been growing apart again since the money ran out, and the thought of returning home after a night shift just as she left for work tempered the delicate atmosphere.

Weeks turned into months, and then into years. As they passed I simply grew accustomed to the status quo, to the point of expecting it as I knew nothing else, even though I needed a wage to suit my new and extortionate outgoings. In the meantime history repeated itself. I would come home from a shift greeted by the usual bills and threatening letters just like before. And like the previous time I promised to pay a little here and a little there, and it worked for a while, although the interest slammed on top of the original bills meant I'd be paying for forever and a day. My life simulated the film *Groundhog Day* where every day appeared to be the same as the last, and this carried on month after month after month.

I'd come home from a nightshift, have a shower then straight to bed just as Helen got up to start her day. I'd stay in bed until mid-afternoon, make something to eat and get ready for work. After which Helen would then come home after fetching the kids en route from school, as I left for work.

Helen and I would never speak to each other or even pass comment on our day's events. The only time Helen spoke was when she wanted to know how much money I earned that week, or if I had saved from the previous week. Chance would be a fine thing. Nevertheless, Helen was adamant I put a few quid aside, or even had a secret bank account – and she wanted it.

I look back at this particular time and think of it as being some sort of respite, a break from the previous years of constant worrying and nagging from Helen. I suppose I enjoyed it, and didn't want it to end. To me, going to bed as Helen started her day without passing a single comment to each other was living a normal life. But of course, the world continued to turn, as it did when I was in Iraq, and my creditors wanted their money.

The mortgage company demanded immediate payment, gas and electric suppliers hung by a thread and credit card companies already forwarded my details to debt collection agencies – yet again. Yep, I'd been down this road before and as far as I was concerned they could all swivel. On my days off I sat around watching television or sleep the day away. I had no energy and neglected my children. Rachel seemed to distance herself and James looked at me as if I was a total stranger. To make matters worse I didn't care.

It wasn't long before sitting around on my days off became boring. I wanted some excitement, some action, but what? I'd left the TA so I didn't have weekends to look forward to and virtually renounced by my own family, let alone the public. I didn't have any money saved so I couldn't afford to take the family away for a couple of days, so what could I do? After much consideration I thought, what the hell, I'll sit in front of the television and vegetate.

"Surprise!" a little voice shouted in my ear.

"What's this?" I asked Rachel as she passed me a card and present wrapped in DPM camouflaged print wrapping paper.

"Happy birthday Daddy," she added, standing swivelling side to side as cute little daughters do.

Bloody hell, I forgot it was my birthday. In fact I'd lost complete track of time and paid little attention that it was now early June.

"I hope you like it," Helen said.

I unwrapped my present revealing a DVD collection box *Band of Brothers* and a book about the Battle of Britain.

"I love it, thank you darling," and gave Rachel a kiss on the cheek, which I think she took as a cue to bugger off and play with her toys now she'd carried out her duty.

I looked up at Helen, greeted by a smile.

"Fancy a cup of tea?" she asked.

"Er, yes please," I replied, although slightly confused. Maybe she wants to call a truce? I thought. Following her into the kitchen I wrapped my arms around her waist as she filled the kettle.

"Oi, what d'ya think you're doing? Get off!" she shrieked, shrugging off my cuddle.

"I thought that's what you wanted, you know, call a truce and start a fresh start."

"You must be joking. Just because it's your birthday it doesn't change anything."

I didn't see that coming.

"I'm making you a cup of tea, that's it, so don't read anything into it. I'm only being civil in front of the children."

"Oh, I see, so nothing has changed, then."

"No. And it'll be like this until you get us out of the shit you put us in, again!"

"I bloody knew it was too good to be true."

Helen screamed and threw my mug on the floor, smashing it into a thousand pieces. "See that broken mug," she shouted, pointing at the floor, "that's our marriage, and if you think you can repair it, forget it, it's over!"

The brief moment of feelings I thought I had for her were quickly whisked away, replaced with a comfortably numb feeling I'd grown accustomed to over the past couple of years. I should have known; this was my life, and I'd better make the most of it.

Helen stormed out of the house with Rachel and James, no doubt crying all the way to her bloody mother's. I grabbed a fresh cup and made my tea, carefully stepping over the broken mug covering the kitchen floor. Taking advantage of the peace and quiet I thought it a perfect time to watch my new DVD collection box.

As the DVD played the night sky suddenly illuminated with a brilliant bright light, complemented by a loud thundering explosion.

I didn't have any choice about the ditch; instead of avoiding it I dived into it, rolling head-over-heels in the sand. A few seconds later there was another explosion. Instinctively I thrust my face into the sand clasping my hands over my ears, attempting to dampen the effect of the shock wave.

The blast was close enough to feel hot air rush past, and the shock wave made my ears pop. The point of explosion couldn't have been much further away than one- hundred metres. I quickly crawled towards the straight bar of my Foden recovery vehicle that had a Bedford TM truck attached to it, which we had recovered earlier that day, and lay face down on the ridge of the ditch as shrapnel rained down from all around.

"Okay, Kev?" Stuart asked, as he crashed landed beside me.

"Yeah, fine, just taken by surprise, that's all."

A voice shouted from the front of the convoy, "Stand to! Stand to!"

Others quickly followed suit, diving for cover in the ditch. Our immediate problem was none of us had any 'stand to' positions; the whole scenario became improvised. I 'made ready' my rifle and pushed the safety catch to the 'off' position. All around I could hear others doing the same. Something was going to kick off, and we weren't in control. It had all the hallmarks of an ambush, albeit a bad one.

Our positions, including our cover in the ditches, may have been pre-sighted and could well have been a 'killing zone.' No time to think the worst, we had to get out of this situation and it looked like we had only one option – bring the fight to them.

"What's happening, Mike?" Stuart asked.

Stuart, my crewman, talked to Mike, the driver from our vehicle casualty – the Bedford TM – belonging to the Light Infantry.

"It looks like the LI have taken out a T62 but they've compromised our position when they used the 'LAW' (light anti-tank weapon) and a second T62 fired off a round."

Mike was in close contact with his LI mates further up the convoy. They in turn had details relayed to their vehicles from the battlegroup about enemy movements within our area. And the tank the LI guys hit answered the question as to where the shrapnel came from.

Crack, crack, crack! Small arms whizzed over our heads.

"Return fire!" a voice cried out, "my tracers, on bushes dead ahead, rapid!" the voice commanded, and quickly opened fire with his LSW (Light Support weapon) using his tracer rounds to locate the enemy position.

A split second later thirty or so SA80's, LSW's and GPMG's (General Purpose Machine gun) opened fire in the direction of the tracer rounds landing on the enemy position. Bursts of automatic came from the bushes to the left of the convoy, about one-hundred metres ahead of the front vehicle, which was about one-hundred and fifty metres ahead of me. I didn't get a fix on any muzzle flashes but I certainly knew the general direction of the bursts thanks to enemy tracer rounds whizzing overhead.

We trained our weapons on enemy tracers and soon joined the others letting rip into bushes to our left, towards the front of the convoy. Within what seemed only a few seconds I'd emptied my magazine with small bursts of rapid fire, and it soon became apparent I'd have to conserve my rounds as I only had a further three magazines left in my ammunition pouches.

The convoy continued suppressing their fire towards the bushes and I soon emptied my second magazine. I struggled to locate a fresh one from my pouches as half a dozen enemy rounds fell onto my position, kicking up sand and dust. I eventually managed to reload and tucked another full magazine down the front of my CBA (Combat Body Armour) to save time when reloading later, which by the look of things will only be a matter of seconds. I continued to return fire but still couldn't eyeball any targets, so it was a case of giving covering fire to keep the enemy's head down.

Stuart ceased firing and pointed down the dirt track to our left. "Some heavy shit coming up the track, I can hear it in the distance!"

I strained to hear the armoured vehicles in the distance over the noise of Mike's automatic fire coming only inches away from my head, but yes, I could faintly hear something.

I tapped Mike on his shoulder. "What!" he said sharply, whilst firing off a few more rounds.

"Armour, coming up on your left."

Mike shifted back a little to take cover and shouted into his radio whilst the rest of us continued firing. A few seconds later he returned to his position with a huge grin across his face. "Warriors, two of them and a Challenger, coming this way to sort the bastards out!"

"Cease fire, cease fire!" a voice cried from further up the packet.

We ceased fire and within a matter of seconds the cavalry arrived. We stayed under the straight-bar between my recovery vehicle and Mike's Bedford TM, bowing our heads to try and prevent the dust and sand kicked up by the tracked vehicles getting into our eyes. The armour didn't hang about as it thundered past with little room to negotiate between our packet, having no alternative but to drive with one track in the ditch opposite. This particular obstacle didn't seem to hinder their performance, though.

Sporadic bursts of automatic fire from enemy positions suddenly ceased, indicating only two explanations as to why: they either noticed the armour racing towards them and legged it or we finished them off with our blind suppressive firepower. Whichever, the skirmish couldn't have lasted any longer than five or six minutes, but it was too early to get complacent and relax. The only way of being certain was when the Warriors and the Challenger 2 tank did their job securing the area.

BOOM! A huge explosion, quickly followed by another, then a gigantic firework display appeared immediately ahead of us across the dirt track, roughly one-hundred meters away; the Challenger hit the second T62 Iraqi tank.

The gap in the hedgerow revealed a spectacular silhouette of a dying tank, complemented by brilliant white molten metal and an orange flame spitting out of the tank's hull and decking plates. A fireball lit up the night sky allowing us to watch the turret of the T62 blow clean out of its hull then crash down back onto it, coming to rest on its side with the gun barrel pointing towards the front of the hull.

A series of explosions quickly followed as shells inside the tank's magazines exploded. A few seconds later the distinctive sound of a Warrior's 30mm cannon could be heard pounding into other targets; then silence, apart from a burning hull of the T62, sounding as if it was screaming in agony. Or maybe that was the crew.

"Yeah, nice one, cheers Steve," Mike said, speaking into his radio. He then told Stuart and I what had happened. "Both T62's destroyed and the Warrior has just annihilated an Iraqi gun position, eight dead, no survivors. My guys are mopping up the rest of the area, so we're to sit tight."

Captain Schaffer swaggered down the dirt track like 'John Wayne' with a 9mm pistol in one hand whilst holding the barrel of a SA80 in the other, slung over his shoulder.

"Get the fuck up and sweep the area!" he commanded, "and that includes you REME lot, as well!"

"We'd better have a wander then," Stuart said, in a disturbing calm manner.

I changed my magazine for a fresh one and climbed to my feet to join the others. Mike joined his LI guys as they advanced through the enemy positions to 'mop up', whilst Stuart and I searched the immediate area of our Foden and casualty vehicle should there be any further surprises to our rear.

Every few minutes we could hear bursts of automatic from SA80's coming from a few nervous LI guys opening up on anything that moved. After half-an-hour a further four bodies had been recovered from the enemy position armed with AK's. Two of the dead found next to a Russian built 7.62mm chain-fed machine gun, not unlike the GPMG in its performance.

"All clear!" a voice cried out.

I started to feel sweaty and clammy, but couldn't work out why. I desperately looked around to find Mike and Stuart but they were nowhere to be seen. I was now on my own, except for a WW2 Sherman tank and other armoured vehicles from that era chasing retreating Germans so the LI could finish 'moping up' and clear the area. Now I was confused.

As the smoke cleared reality finally kicked in and I realised I'd been watching a scene from my new DVD box set collection triggering my flashback as it bared similarities to the ambush I experienced in Iraq – the time we were followed by a couple of T62 Iraqi tanks as my convoy searched for a harbour area to rest for the night, only to fall into an ambush.

I needed to get out of the house and go for a walk to clear my head. But what if they, the public, are watching me? Instead I grabbed the car keys, filled up with fuel and went for a drive, going nowhere in particular and thinking of nothing but the road ahead. I felt free and didn't want the road to end, but inevitably it did as I reached a car park at Heacham, near Huntstanton on the East Coast.

Why I drove to Heacham I'll never know, but thought it best to turn around and head back home or Helen will kill me for being late. But late for what, and why should I be bothered what Helen thought, and what is home? I had no job to go to, not a real one, anyway. My wage wasn't enough to pay off anything other than slow down the process of having gas and electric cut off and the house repossessed, and I certainly didn't have any money to pay my creditors.

Helen's wage only kept us in food, although most of it went on bloody children's must have gadgets and latest fashions, and she didn't give a shit about me any more, so what was the point of going back? Instead I decided to go for a walk along the beach. After all it was my birthday.

A typical cool breeze from the North Sea swept across the beach picking up loose sand, acting like an abrasive sandblaster against my bare arms and face. In between gusts I looked out to sea, my mind emptying as if the outgoing tide took away my past life, leaving a void to fill with a new one. For those brief moments I no longer had any money worries, flashbacks, not even a wife or any children. It felt great. If only I had a week of this instead of a few hours.

Then it happened. My paranoia returned and started to shout instructions at me: *Run away, go on, do it, never to return,* it said, over and over again. I thought I'd heard the last of David Tennant. After all, it had been a good few months so I thought I was finally free of him. But no, as soon as my growing problems started to stack up and hurtle out of control, he returned to finish what he intended to do in the first place – send me mad. With the little remaining strength of sanity I had I ignored the yelling in my head and walked back to the car, but still my demon shouted the same words: *Run away, go on, do it…*

By the time I walked back to the car park the sun was setting, not realising how long I'd been walking along the beach. I wasn't wearing a watch and the clock in my Vauxhall Vectra wasn't working, but it must have been late considering it was early June. I started the car and drove inland, but the voice in my head continued to taunt me more and more.

I reached a 'T' junction and the signpost opposite giving direction to the nearest towns seemed to suggest I should either turn left if I wish to go home, or turn right if I wanted to start a new life. Tempting as it was to turn right I decided to go home. And as I turned left David Tennant suddenly stopped taunting me.

I crept in the house so not to wake the household, and switched on the kitchen light, noticing the clock on the wall – it was almost two o'clock in the morning. I tried to make a cup of tea without making too much noise, but the kettle seemed to boil the water purposely loud so to wake the whole house. It wasn't long before Helen came thumping down the stairs, seemingly to have a go at me.

"So you decided to come home then?"

Yep, I was right.

"Where did you go?"

I didn't answer.

"Am I going to get the silent treatment now?"

I couldn't help but grin. After all, I thought it was her idea not to talk.

"And now you think this is funny," she said throwing her arms into the air.

"What d'ya expect me to say?" I eventually asked.

"You could have at least phoned and let me know where you were."

"For fuck's sake, I can't even get any peace and quiet on my bloody birthday!"

I finished making my tea and walked in to the front room, quickly followed by Helen who'd obviously hadn't finished ranting and raving. "So where did you go?"

"Heacham."

"Where's that?"

"On the East Coast. I went to the seaside for the day," I replied sitting on the settee and taking a sip of my tea.

"You went to the seaside without thinking of taking me and the kids. You selfish bastard!"

"I didn't know I was going, I just drove and ended up there. I needed to get away for a few hours, clear my head. Besides, you'd gone out and taken the kids with you."

"I don't care, anyway, cos' we're going to Tenerife for a week. Mum has paid for us to go with her and Dad, and guess what? You're not invited!" Helen childishly replied with some sort of satisfaction she'd gone one better and won the argument.

"Suits me," I said taking another sip of my tea, although I didn't expect Helen to come out with that one.

"You really don't care, do you," Helen sobbed with yet more tears.

I looked up at her. "When are you going?"

"Saturday. And I can't wait to take the kids and get away from you!" she snapped walking back upstairs.

I couldn't wait for Saturday to arrive either, and when it did I breathed a sigh of relief. I now had a week to myself. With the house empty I could do what I want, when I wanted. The fact is I didn't want to do anything, apart from sit in front of the box and watch hours of crap television. But first I needed beer, and a copious amount of it. That meant spending money put aside for pacifying creditors, and more importantly, enduring a trip to the shops in the middle of town to mingle amongst Them – the public.

The thought of going into town filled me with dread. The thought of getting pissed made the trip a little easier to execute, although I couldn't help but feel I was being stared at again. Eyes seemed to follow me around the isles of the mini-mart; even the security cameras felt as if they were watching my every move. Doing my best to ignore everyone I filled my basket with cans of beer and made my way to the checkout.

"Oi, you!" a voice cried out from behind.

I ignored it, after all, why would someone be shouting at me?

"You with the basket of beer, I wanna word with you!"

I looked round and noticed a familiar face but couldn't place the name.

"You're the twat that had a go at me in the pub a few years ago!"

Oh boy, I couldn't believe it. Out of all the faces to bump into.

"See what you've done to my face!" he said pointing to it as he walked down the isle towards me.

He wasn't a pretty picture before our altercation, but he did look a tad uglier with a scar across his nose and under his left eye.

I shrugged my shoulders, not really giving a shit about his scars and turned to face the queue, but he wasn't having any of it. He grabbed the back of my shoulders and forced me to turn and face him. Whether he expected to receive an apology for what I'd done or satisfy a deep seated revenge, I wasn't about to give him the opportunity for either.

Still holding onto my basket of beer I reacted by head butting him hard on the bridge of his nose as soon as he got in range. He fell onto his arse with his legs spread, holding his nose as blood poured between his fingers, screaming so loud the entire shop ran to see what the shouting was all about.

I stood over him, not unlike our last brief encounter, laughing at this pathetic excuse of a civvy as he held his nose screaming in pain. Whilst his legs were spread apart I couldn't resist the temptation and kicked him hard square in the bollocks.

I knelt down beside him as he withered around in the fetal position, now holding his bollocks as well as his nose. "If you ever bother me again, civvy, I will kill you, do you understand, kill you," I calmly whispered in his ear.

He didn't say anything but vigorously nodded, which I presumed meant he understood what I said, although his attention was grasped by the sharp, agonising pain from the north and south regions of his body.

Without a care in the world I stood up, took out a twenty-pound note from my wallet and threw the money on the checkout counter. "Ere' luv, keep the change," I said to the petrified checkout girl, still in disbelief to what she'd witnessed.

And just like my last encounter with Pisshead, I simply walked out of the shop and drove home as if nothing had happened.

CHAPTER 13

SHOULD I STAY OR SHOULD I GO

I popped the beers in the fridge to chill for a few hours and put the kettle on. I smiled at the thought of having a whole week to myself, just like my own holiday. It even felt like the first day to a new life, in some respects. Letters and bills on the kitchen table conveniently left by Helen for me to notice every time I walked past, however, were a stark reminder of my real life. So I gathered them together and threw the lot into the bin. As far as I was concerned they no longer existed.

The telephone rang. I thought it might have been Helen telling me they'd arrived at the airport safely. It wasn't, it was the driving agency.

"19:00 hours tonight, Kev, okay?"

"Nah, not tonight, I'm on holiday."

There was a pause. "You never mentioned you were going on holiday."

"Yep, for a week. Not going anywhere, just doing bog all."

"You're at home then?"

"Yep."

"Oh right, so you can at least do tonight," the young girl said, hoping I'd say yes.

"Nope."

I could hear muffled talking as she seemingly cupped the receiver in the palm of her hand.

"If you don't come in tonight you can forget about coming back next week!" one annoyed male voice said. It was the shift manager.

"Suits me, bye," I replied, and cut off the conversation.

180

The telephone immediately rang again. It was bound to be the agency desperately trying to talk me into doing the shift, no doubt because they had no other driver available. I ignored it and went back into the kitchen to make my cup of tea. My mobile now sprung into life. I ignored that too, knowing the agency will try a few more times over the next half-an-hour, leave a few snide comments on voice mail before finally giving up.

Taking my tea into the living room I placed it on the side table, picked a book from my collection about the First World War from the bookshelf, slouched on the settee and started to read. Bliss. Within ten minutes, and as predicted, my mobile ringtone blurted out its merry 'Red Dwarf' theme tune from the kitchen table. Once again I ignored it knowing who it will be and concentrated on reading my book.

The phone calls did stop within half-an-hour and I thought that would be the end of the interruptions, but I forgot about the front door. At first I ignored the doorbell, but the annoying person was very persistent and clearly wasn't going away. I jumped up and answered the door. Standing on the doorstep stood a young gorgeous woman dressed in a flowery summer dress with a huge cleavage tightly packed within. She was holding a few booklets in her hand and without saying a word thrusted one towards me.

"What a beautiful day," she said.

Looking a little perplexed I simply replied, "yes, isn't it," as I automatically reached for the booklet – The Watch Tower – trying my up-most to be a gentleman and divert my gaze from the lady's obvious focal point, which wasn't easy, believe me.

"Er, no thanks, luv, not interested," I said returning her booklet, although I was quite interested in her.

Without persuasion she simply returned a smile and went on her way, but she got me thinking. Not about joining her crazy club, but about starting a relationship with someone else. Nah, stupid idea, I thought. Instead I returned to my book, but the young Jehovah – and her cleavage – kept springing back into my mind, then the thought of starting afresh quickly followed.

I knew of guys that had returned from Iraq only to fall into another women's bed for one reason or another. A friend of mine I served with met a young squaddie girl from the regiment he was attached to. When he returned home he simply had enough of his past life and left his wife and children to set up camp with his squaddie girlfriend. Not for me, though, no matter how difficult life got at home. I just couldn't see myself doing the same. Or could I?

I closed my book and switched on the television with hope of getting these stupid thoughts out of my head, but I picked the wrong moment. An advert inviting you to join their website and find your perfect partner sprung out into the room. I was about to switch to another channel but found myself hypnotised by the advert. It was as if it personally gave me instructions to find my perfect partner. David Tennant decided to make an appearance and agreed: *Run away, go on, do it, never to return*, it said over and over.

Although it was only three o'clock in the afternoon I needed a beer to help get these stupid thoughts out of my head. I managed to pull myself away from the television, grab a can from the fridge and lit a cigarette – inside the house – which was a big no-no usually. My ex-haled smoke quickly filled the downstairs rooms with the stench of cigarette smoke and I begun to feel a tad guilty, half expecting Helen to barge through the front door and catch me in the act, not unlike a naughty school boy being caught by his parents. I opted to go into the garden and finish my cigarette there.

With a can in one hand and a cigarette in the other, I sat on one of the brick pillars either side of my garden wall and enjoyed the warm sunshine as it concentrated on my face. Smoking in my designated area reminded me of the time we landed in Kuwait, staying at camp Cambrai. Even during a conflict, squaddies could only smoke in designated areas. Then again, thousands of smokers in one small area generated a lot of cigarette butts, and the army, even at war and in the middle of a desert, demands a tidy camp.

I finished my cigarette, stubbed it out on one of the concrete paving slabs and threw the butt in the bin, just like a good squaddie should. Time for another beer. As I walked into the kitchen I could hear my mobile playing its 'Red Dwarf' ringtone again. I chose to ignore it, presuming it was the agency having one last ditch attempt to talk me into working my shift. Instead I cracked open another can and slouched on the settee for the rest of the day, deciding to watch the rest of my *Band of Brothers* DVD's.

During a disc change for some reason the player reverted back to whatever is on the television, and found my attention gripped by the same advert I watched earlier. It was if it deliberately picked the right moment to catch my attention and purposely instruct me to join their website. I stepped back from the DVD player finding myself taking a mental note of the website address, but decided not to act upon it and popped in another DVD instead.

I couldn't concentrate. That bloody advert played around my head repeating the website address, convincing me to join and start a new life. It was as if the advert was the key to all my problems. Fuck it. I grabbed another can from the fridge, fired up the laptop and waited for it to logon. I was going to satisfy my curiosity and take a look at this bloody dating site, then maybe I could forget about it and concentrate on my DVD collection.

I typed in the address and within a few seconds the website appeared, showing all its wonderful ways of meeting new people and why it is successful at joining couples far better than any other similar websites. Ignoring all the jargon I clicked on a few of the examples that showed, pretty obviously, the best looking couples that had signed up to their site, or were they models pretending to be couples? Whichever, they continued to brag how blissfully happy they were, thanks to the website.

To see which women were compatible to me I had to click on a form and give a few details: height, weight, eye and hair colour... The usual stuff. I then had to add my status, which I answered as being separated. Well, in a way I felt separated. I was then instructed to click on another page and that's where I lost interest; they wanted to know my credit or debit card details, and I wasn't about to pay for this crap, so I cleared the website from my screen.

As I did, page after page of adverts sprang up from nowhere offering their dating website details. I frantically clicked on the cross at the top, right corner of each page, but more and more took their place. Eventually they subsided and I managed to clear my screen, apart from one advert that caught my eye, telling me that their website was one-hundred percent free to join.

Not convinced it was truly a free website I clicked on it anyway, which led me to a page that needed my details so I could navigate the site and send messages to its members. I was pleasantly surprised to see nothing more than the requirement of my usual statistics, which of course, my status for the sake of this experiment was separated. I then had to write a few lines about myself. The last instruction was to write a few lines about the type of person I wish to meet and click on the appropriate boxes, and that was it, I'm in.

I looked at my immediate geographical area and noticed there were hundreds of women either married, separated, divorced or single. Some obviously seeking nothing more than casual sex – although they didn't say that directly, but you could tell. Some were still married, some wanted to just chat online and some wanted to find that special person. This was a huge eye opener for me; I simply had to delve a little deeper and find out more about these elusive women.

My trips to the fridge, and of course trips to the toilet became more and more frequent as I researched the website. I was having tremendous fun. I checked out various women's profiles and noticed some didn't include a picture – obviously hippos. Some had pictures that were clearly hippos without a conscience, yet others were drop-dead-gorgeous. So why were they advertising themselves?

You could tell by looking at their photographs they wouldn't have any problem pulling in a bar or nightclub, but that was the problem, or so they said in their profiles. Sick and tired of 'that type' of bloke frequenting bars purely to pick up girls for nothing more than sex, or being more interested in themselves, many wrote. In other words, complete tossers, as one woman wrote.

My next giggle was to trawl through the women in my area and see if I recognised any of them. I didn't – damn it. I took the next step and sent a few messages to some of the so-called compatible women on my page to see if I got a response. Time for a smoke, I thought, and headed to the back door, grabbing another can on the way. Five minutes or so later I returned to the laptop – nothing. Not even a nibble.

"What a load of bollocks!" I said out loud, and decided to return to the settee and watch some naff film instead, falling asleep in the process.

I woke up shivering and apart from the flickering light coming from the television I was in total darkness. I switched on the living room lights, closed the curtains and went to investigate where the draft was coming from. It didn't take long to find it. I'd left the back door wide open, and even though it was June, the draft was bloody freezing.

My head was pounding and instinctively knew as to why judging by the empty cans overflowing the kitchen bin. I opted to make a cup of tea. The clock on the kitchen wall said it was two o'clock in the morning, and thanks to my nap I was no longer tired, so what to do? I didn't fancy watching any more DVDs or television, and then remembered the dating site.

I made my tea stood next to the laptop and casually tapped the finger-pad to wake it up, and there it was, still logged into the website. I looked at my inbox message board and it didn't register at first, but yes, I had three messages, one of which was sent by someone I hadn't contacted first. Wow, this was exciting. I sat down, read the messages and opened their profiles to see what they looked like.

Not at all bad, actually. I replied to the messages saying nothing in particular, other than answer their questions, asked how they were and why they signed up to this site? Obvious and pathetic replies, really.

Realising the time I didn't expect a reply – if any – until a more acceptable hour. Ping! Within minutes I had an immediate reply from the one that sent me a message, asking what I was doing on this site and am I a typical player, to which I didn't have a clue as to what a player was or did, so I asked her.

Within seconds she answered, and with some clarity. She then asked if I was on MSN. I didn't know what it was or did, so she gave me instructions on how to download the software. Boy, I was enjoying myself. I downloaded the software and within the hour we were chatting, or rather typing messages to one another. Before I knew it the sun was shining through the curtains. I checked the clock on my laptop and noticed it was gone five o'clock.

You want to call it a night? I typed.

Why, do you want to go? she immediately asked.

No, I didn't want to go – ever, so I simply asked: *I thought you'd want to get some sleep.*

185

Nooooo, she replied, *I like talking to you.*

Bloody hell. Had I pulled? No, I don't think so, after all this was nothing more than chatting over cyberspace. As far as I was concerned there were nothing to read into this. It wasn't exactly having an affair.

The hours flew by, chatting about anything and everything, but I was beginning to feel a little hungry, so we both decided to continue our chat later in the afternoon.

Bye for now, she typed, then added a few kisses underneath.

I didn't know how to reply to that so I typed the same.

I made a bacon sandwich and thought, "What on earth am I doing?" But I loved the attention and couldn't wait to talk to her again. As the hours ticked by she remained on my mind throughout the day. I couldn't think of anything else.

I tried to keep myself busy, to the point of doing some housework. I cleaned the kitchen, did the washing up, vacuumed the house – upstairs and downstairs – cut the lawn, yet only a few hours had past. So I decided to have a shower, shave and spruce myself up a bit before our next chat online. God knows why I did, but wearing fresh clothes and being clean made it feel right.

Finally the time arrived to log onto MSN and continue our chat from earlier. Where was she? I stared at the screen for what seemed an eternity, but no reply. I logged off and on again just in case it was the internet connection, but no, still no reply.

Bollocks to this, I thought, and sat down to watch television.

Every so often I glanced at the laptop sitting on the dining room table mentally debating as to whether I should have a look and see if she tried to contact me. Who was I kidding. I shrugged off this stupid idea of cyber chatting, instead concentrated on crap television had to offer.

Slowly the hours ticked by, yet the temptation was too much to bear, I had to have a peek at the laptop and see if she'd tried to contact me. I jumped up from the settee to satisfy my curiosity. No she hadn't. I was about to log off, but I was glad I didn't, because there she was, sending me a message.

How are you? she asked.

I wasn't too sure if I should reply. After all she'd kept me waiting for bloody hours. But, of course, I did.

Hey, where you been? I asked.

Can I call you?

You mean by telephone?

Lol. Of course by telephone. You do have a phone, don't you?

Yes, I replied, and typed my mobile number.

Without warning she signed off. I thought that was it, never to be heard of again.

A few minutes later my mobile rang. I noticed twelve missed calls on the small screen, which where obviously the driving agency, but this time I answered, having a tingling feeling whom it might be.

"Hello, is that my MSN friend?" I asked.

There was a pause, then, "yes, I suppose I am," a calm female voice replied.

I couldn't think of anything else to say. We'd been chatting on the internet for so long I felt as if we'd exhausted every topic of conversation under the sun.

"Er, so, is Susan your real name or is it Bob?" I asked jokingly, quickly thinking of something to fill the silence, no matter how stupid it sounded.

She laughed at my ridiculous question, which seemed to break the ice.

"Yes, Bob is my real name. So, is Kev your real name, or is it floppy dick?"

We both laughed, then Susan quickly changed the tempo of our silly conversation and came straight out with it, "Wanna meet up?"

Boy, I wasn't expecting that. The situation suddenly jumped from a bit of innocent fun across cyberspace to something more serious, with potential serious consequences. What the hell, I was enjoying this.

"Yeah, I'd love to, but where?"

"I know a nice little pub next to a canal close to where I live. We could meet there if you want."

"Sounds good to me."

"But I can't tonight, I have a few things to do. I can tomorrow evening though."

We arranged a time and she gave me instructions on how to get to the pub, which was about a twenty-minute drive away. I put the address into my SatNav and she abruptly finished the conversation.

Bloody hell, what have I done? I felt a little ambivalent about this somewhat explosive situation, but I couldn't stop myself.

My mobile rang again. I quickly answered it. "Is that you, Bob?"

"Bob, who's Bob?"

Shit, it was Helen. Thankfully I didn't answer it by saying Susan. That would have put the cat amongst the pigeons.

"Sorry, I was expecting a call from someone called Bob from the agency."

And so the lies begin.

"I've been trying to phone you since we got to the airport. Where have you been?" Helen asked.

"Oh, I've either been working or sleeping. So how's Tenerife?" I asked changing the subject, and giving her another lie within a matter of seconds.

Helen was none the wiser and went on to say how the flight was, what the hotel was like and how the kids were loving the holiday. She was chatting away as if we were a happily married couple, and that was hard to understand and accept, because now I felt guilty for what I was doing – or about to do.

I did get a glimmer of relief when she said it didn't change anything and as far as she was concerned our marriage was over if I didn't sort out our financial problems. A feeble excuse, I know, but her last comment, as I saw it, gave me the green light to go ahead and meet Susan with an almost clear conscience.

I couldn't wait for tomorrow. When it finally arrived I must have spent hours getting ready, and still had four hours to go before our meet at seven-thirty. I was a nervous wreck before I'd got in the car, let alone seeing her for the first time.

I followed the instructions given to me by my SatNav, which took me directly to the pub carpark. It was a typical warm summer evening and Susan couldn't have picked a more tranquil place to meet. She said to wait in the carpark and look out for a black 51-plate Peugeot 206. The wait was agonising. It didn't help being half-an-hour early and for Susan to be ten minutes late, but eventually a black Peugeot 206 drove slowly in the carpark and parked near the entrance.

I was parked at the bottom end and my heart was in my mouth. Why I felt like this I don't know, but it felt great, if not a tad nerve wracking. Susan jumped out of her car and clicked the remote on her key fob as she scoured the carpark to see if she could recognise my Vectra.

As she looked around I couldn't help but stare at her 5ft 6-inch tanned, slim body, with long light brown hair and blonde highlights. Her three-quarter length light blue jeans were tight against her sexy legs and her slim fitting yellow top clung to her, revealing a sensible handful only blokes will understand.

Blimey, jackpot. She looked fantastic, and certainly didn't look her age, even though she was eighteen months older than me. I tried to look cool getting out of my car, then realised I was chewing gum to disguise the smell of tobacco. Not good, so I quickly spat it out hoping she didn't notice. Susan waved when she clocked me from the other side of the carpark and I instinctively waved back, still trying to look cool. Bah, who was I fooling, I could never look cool.

It seemed to take an eternity for her to walk over and my heart started to beat harder and harder, but she came across as extremely calm. Then I thought about how do I greet her. Give a hug, a peck on the cheek, bow? No, too obvious and maybe too forward. Too late, she's standing right in front of me.

"Hi, at last we meet," she said and stuck out her hand.

Oh heck, what do I do now, shake it like some long lost friend or kiss it as if I'm meeting the Queen? I opted to softly shake it, remembering not to bow and make a complete arse of myself.

We stood in the carpark for a few awkward seconds before I had a brilliant idea – go into the pub for a drink. Like the perfect gentleman I escorted her to the bar and bought her half a lager and myself a pint of bitter, promising myself I will have only the one then stick to soft drinks afterwards. Susan beckoned me to follow her outside, taking me down some steps to an area with wooden tables and chairs lined neatly to one side of a patio overlooking the canal.

We talked about anything and everything, just as we did on MSN. The scenery was that of a typical idyllic, tranquil evening on the bank of a quiet English river – or canal in this case. I didn't want it to end.

We eventually started to talk about our ex-spouses, where I had to come clean and tell Susan I was still actually living with mine.

She didn't mind. I think she appreciated the truth, well almost. I did add I was in the process of leaving her, although I hadn't really given that eventuality much thought. In Susan's case she had separated from her husband and bought a house of her own from the proceeds of her share of the marital home. In fact she was very open about her marriage; too open for a first date.

She told me what a dickhead her husband was and how he treated her like shit. She went on to explain about his drinking being out of control and that he went to the pub every night, never taking her. His constant affairs, violent mood swings... The list went on and on. He came across as being a complete twat, and what I couldn't understand was how could he have been to this gorgeous creature sitting opposite?

I could see it was upsetting Susan talking about her husband, so I changed the subject, talking about my parents, their divorce and where they now live with second partners. I thought it would prompt Susan to do the same, but no. Instead I made matters worse and Susan now had tears in her eyes. She explained that her parents were also divorced and that her father remarried, but her mother had an accident many years ago that resulted in suffering from dementia and was now in a home.

I was useless at this dating malarkey and thought I'd lost her interest, but as the evening went on and we changed the topic of conversation to a more joyful subject, we got on really well. This time Susan insisted she'd buy the drinks and promptly walked up the steps towards the pub, where I couldn't keep my eyes of her sexy, slim legs.

The evening sadly came to an end so I asked that difficult question, "would you like to do this again?"

"Yes, I'd love to."

Oh boy, she said yes. I couldn't believe it.

"Er, okay, when?"

"Tomorrow, same place, same time?"

"I think I can make it," I replied softly.

Too bloody right I screamed in my head.

I risked a further gamble and leant over the table to kiss her soft warm lips, then anxiously waited for a smack across the chops for being too forward, but it never arrived. I didn't want to spoil the moment, or my luck, and try for a second kiss, so I escorted Susan back to her car and watched her leave before I jumped into mine.

On the way home I was grinning ear to ear and couldn't wait to see her the following day. It was great to go out with a lady that didn't moan, argue, criticise, nag, shout, blame, punch and constantly remind me what a mess I'd made of things. Then again she knew very little about my past, not even Iraq. For now, I thought it best to keep that part of my life hidden from view.

As I threw my car keys on the hallway table my mobile bleeped telling me I had a text message. Without looking I knew who'd sent it. I flipped open the lid and sure enough there was a message from Susan. It simply read: *Thank you for a lovely evening. Can't wait to see you tomorrow… x* .

Those few words made me feel something that I hadn't felt for god knows how long – happy.

The following morning I woke thinking of the brilliant date I had with Susan, and then, as per usual when something good came along, my paranoia decided to raise its ugly head to fill my thoughts with doubts and dread. I shrugged them off. No way was my demon going to put me down when I was feeling so happy.

Ah, I forgot about the post. And there they were, lying on the doormat, a pile of brown envelopes eagerly waiting to greet me with bills, final warnings and threats. So I picked them up and without having any interest in there content threw them on the kitchen table. I was determined to have a worry free day, and nothing was going to spoil it. Of course, it didn't take long for something to try and have a go.

I picked up my mobile. "Yes," I said sharply.

"I have a run for you at 1900 hours."

I couldn't believe it, it was the bloody driving agency. They must have been desperate to call me considering I'd let them down.

"I never expected you to call me again, not after yesterday."

"Sorry, I haven't a clue what you're talking about. 1900 hours tonight."

"No, I'm on holiday."

"What?"

"Like I said yesterday, I'm on holiday this week."

"I didn't know that, nobody told me," the agitated young lady replied, "so can you do the run, cos' we don't have anyone else."

"Put it this way." I then cut her off, placed my mobile onto the hallway table and walked in to the kitchen counting backwards from ten before reaching two – cue 'Red Dwarf' theme tune. "I said I'm not interested!"

There was a pause. "Oh, sorry, I thought we were getting on fine."

Bollocks, it was Susan.

"Sorry, I didn't mean you, I thought it was my boss calling me. He wants me to cover a shift for him tonight but I said no, I'm busy."

"Oh right. But if you have to work we can meet some other time," she replied, seemingly trying to help out and not upset my boss.

"You must be joking. I'll see you at seven-thirty as planned. That's if you still want to see me," I added, then cringed, sounding like a cheesy love-struck teenager. Thankfully she said yes.

We continued to chat for about ten minutes before she had to dash, which left me thinking about the driving agency. Here I was, offered work that may stretch to almost a full week and most probably many more, and I turned it down. That meant I was turning down money to clear debts that were mounting up on the kitchen table. So what on earth was I doing? Throwing my only lifeline away, that's what I was bloody doing. But I didn't care. Seeing Susan was the tonic I badly needed.

As soon as I started to convince myself seeing Susan was better than going to work David Tennant sprang up from nowhere, chanting in my head as it did in Heacham: *Run away, go on, do it, never to return.* Then memories of the past three years ran through my head: when I was sacked for being called out, the lack of interest from my MP when I asked him to help; Miss Smart-Suit at the Jobcentre; the job interviews; many job applications, only to be rejected over and over again because I was in the TA; the youth calling me a murderer... On and on my memories continued to taunt, to the point of screaming at me. I felt angry, confused and numb. I needed an escape, and that was Susan.

Our second date went as good as the first and we certainly liked each other's company. And like the first date, time seemed to rush by. Before we knew it the pub called last orders, but neither of us wanted the date to end.

"If you want we could go back to my place and continue our evening from there," Susan surprisingly said.

I didn't need asking twice, although I thought I'd better play it cool.

"Are you sure?"

"Only if you want to."

"Yeah, okay," I calmly replied, but in my head I was shouting, too bloody right I want to.

I followed Susan home and nervously walked into her house. Why I was nervous I don't know. I suppose some primeval feeling returned from my teenage years, when you don't know what to expect as you walk into your girlfriend's house and meet her parents for the first time.

"I have a bottle of wine, or do you fancy a cup of coffee?" Susan asked walking in to her kitchen.

I immediately thought that if I have a glass or two of wine I'd definitely be over the limit and that would mean I'd have to stay the night, and that would be very awkward considering it was only our second date. But she also asked if I wanted a cup of coffee, so maybe it was a test to see if I only wanted an excuse to stay over and get in her knickers.

Being the gentleman, "do you have any tea?"

"Yes, no problem. Sugar?"

"Two please."

As she made the tea I looked around her living room, noticing a framed photograph on the wall of her two daughters and son, and a few more framed pictures of, I presumed, other family members.

"Are these your children?"

"Yes," she shouted from the kitchen, realising I must be looking at the photograph on the wall, "the two girls are thirteen and fifteen, and my son is nine. The others are of my sister, father and mum. None of the ex-husband, though," she added with a snigger.

Susan gave me my tea and we sat on the cream leather settee talking about nothing in particular. Eventually the conversation reached a point when we talked about our partners again. Over the next few hours we both relived our failed marriages, children growing up and what we wanted from the future. A difficult topic for me, as I no longer knew what I wanted.

At this point I thought it best to mention my tour in Iraq and what had happened since. To get it out into the open, so to speak. Susan could then decide if she wanted to see me again. Complete silence followed.

Shit, why did I mention that, why, why? Susan will be disgusted to think she'd let a child murdering, raping, village burning thug into her house. After all, she's a civilian and that's what civilians think of me, so why should she be any different? Instead, Susan cupped my face in her warm, soft, petite hands and slowly kissed me. This wasn't the reaction I expected. A smack across the face, yes, but not a kiss.

Susan was eager to know more about the war and what I witnessed. I hadn't even told Helen about the horrors of the conflict, and I wasn't about to tell Susan. I thought about this for a second and opted to tell her about the lighter side of the war:

My crewman, Stuart, thought it a brilliant idea to bury deep into the desert sand our cans of cola to keep them cool overnight. Only to have a sandstorm that evening, which blew away any evidence of a freshly dug hole, and Stuart forgot to leave some kind of indication as to where he buried the bloody cans.

Journalists and reporters were a pain in the arse, especially British ones. They had little or no respect for other people's safety, let alone their own, just because they wanted that unique story to thrust them up the career ladder and make a name for themselves. Oh, they made names for themselves, but not the kind you could print.

We'd had enough of their constant interfering so we made up many, many stories to keep them busy, such as: Saddam Hussein was last seen running through the streets of Basrah trying to escape coalition forces dressed as a woman, heading for the Iranian border.

Or the time we told reporters we'd found loads of scorpions with miniature cameras strapped to their backs walking around our camp in Kuwait just before the conflict started. We said that they were trained by the Iraqi army to infiltrate the perimeter and walk around beaming back images of our troop levels, armour and weaponry. This particular story kept them busy for hours.

We even told a few bizarre yet true stories to throw them off the scent including: because the Iraq airforce was all but destroyed, the Iraqi army were using microlite aircraft to spy on our positions. The journalists were now totally confused and unsure whether to believe us or not. They soon realised it wasn't a good idea to interview squaddies – British in particular – because all we did was take the piss out of them.

Susan loved all these silly stories television, print media or radio failed to tell the public back home. All she watched, heard and read about was the incredible and outrageous reports of British soldiers indiscriminately killing innocent women and children or false allegations of torturing Iraqi PW's – thanks to Pierce Morgan. I put her straight on that one, remarking that the press, in particular the BBC, were biased towards Saddam Hussein, against the liberation of Iraq and freeing the Iraqi people from a tyrant, constantly remarking that it was an invasion.

Before I knew it, it was half-past-two in the morning.

"I'd better go and let you get some sleep," I said.

"Christ, is that the time? Okay, so when will I see you next?" she asked, seemingly hoping it was sooner rather than later.

"Tomorrow, or rather later today?"

"Yes, of course. I'm only working in the morning, so come round in the afternoon and we could go out to a park or something. Say around four o'clock?"

"Sounds good to me."

I gave her one last kiss and drove home feeling happy and content I'd told Susan about my past and that she appeared to be okay about my tour in Iraq. It felt great to meet someone that genuinely didn't hold a grudge and listened to what I had to say, instead of switching off, believing their version must be right because the television told them so. The thing is I didn't really know how to accept her sympathetic approach. It felt good but also felt strange and unnerving at the same time. The feeling of ambivalence hitting me once again.

Our afternoon date rolled into the evening, and when it was time to part we instantly made a date for the following day. It was if we couldn't stand the idea of being apart. Eventually the inevitable happened and we slept together. The following afternoon, after she'd come home from work and the kids walked from school, I arrived and we'd spend time together doing what normal families do – make dinner for the kids, go out on bike rides, playing football… I was getting along fine with her children and found myself doing the things I should have been doing with Helen and my children.

In the evening we'd come back from the park and make supper. The kids would then go and visit friends or sleep over at their father's house, leaving Susan and I alone to watch a film on television or a DVD and share a bottle of red. It was bliss. It was also something Helen and I never did, and I now knew what I wanted – a proper family life, which was never going to happen living with Helen. My mind was made up, I wanted to be part of Susan's life, simply because she gave me the comfort of living one day at a time and helped me forget about my past.

On the Friday evening we lay in bed without saying a word, staring at the bright moon shining through the bedroom window, secretly thinking we never wanted this moment to end. It felt good lying in bed holding someone in my arms that had the same feelings as me, rather than lying next to a cold, thoughtless, unloving wife that cared about no one but herself.

"You know you could move in with me." Susan suddenly said.

In reality there was no way I could do that. But in the insane world I was now living I replied, "that sounds like a brilliant idea," whispering quietly, and held her closer.

We didn't say anything else, just slowly drifted off to sleep in each other's arms in our make believe, untouchable, happy bubble. We were blissfully unaware that the sane, real world continued to spin and there was no way I could drop everything and move in with Susan. But at that precise moment it seemed right. We were living our moment, our holiday romance to the full, and I didn't want it to end.

The following day, however, I had to leave early to get back before Helen arrived home from Tenerife. That didn't mean my holiday romance was over, far from it. We both wanted it to continue and Helen was nothing more than a thorn in our side, preventing me from returning to my perfect make-believe world. But do I tell Helen about Susan on the day she arrives home from her holiday?

Before leaving Susan's I promised to tell Helen but not straight away. I needed to pick my moment. When, I didn't know, but I couldn't leave her hanging on too long. I also knew that Helen wasn't happy in our marriage and that she'd made it abundantly clear that if I didn't get a full time job and arrange a proper plan to pay back our creditors she would leave me. That was my perfect excuse to use, albeit a pathetic one.

By the time I arrived home the crazy week had caught up with me and I wanted nothing more than go to bed for a few hours. It felt strange climbing into my own bed, sleeping under my own roof. As I rested my head on the pillow it didn't take long before my demon reminded me I no longer cared about my financial mess and I'd thrown away my only chance of working for the agency by ignoring the calls I received through the week. All because I selfishly wanted to escape my past, Helen, even reality, and live an insane life with Susan.

"Don't block the doorway, Rachel!" Helen shouted.

I woke with the noise of Helen and Rachel returning home.

"Help Mummy with the bags, then. Don't leave me to do it all!"

I contemplated staying in bed and letting Helen get on with it, but thought it best to get up and greet her home.

"Typical," Helen muttered as I walked down the stairs. "Been in bed all day, have you?"

I checked my watch, it was mid-afternoon. Ignoring her comment I climbed over the suitcases left in the hallway and made my way in to the kitchen to make us both a drink, but was stopped in my tracks by Rachel and James desperate for a hug from their dad.

"Been in bed most of the week, I bet!" she sharply added as she emptied the contents of the suitcases over the kitchen floor.

"By the sounds of it you had a wonderful time," I sarcastically muttered whilst being hugged by the children.

"What's that supposed to mean?" Helen asked, sorting the piles of washing, the majority of which seemed to belong to Rachel.

"Bloody 'ell, can't I ask if you've had a good time?"

"We did, Daddy, we did!" Rachel and James shouted and jumping in unison.

"Have you paid the bills I left you?" Helen looked at the letters on the kitchen table, unaware I'd thrown away the ones she left, but quickly noticed a few she'd never seen before. "What's this lot?" she asked flicking through the envelopes.

"More bills. Want a coffee?"

"You haven't even opened them."

"No, I haven't. Do you want a coffee?

Still ignoring me she started to read the letters one by one. I continued to make the drinks as she hastily read one after the other, dropping them on the kitchen floor in between.

"Oh my God, this one is from the mortgage company." She read through the letter like a woman possessed. "We've lost the house, do you know that, we've lost the fucking house, and it's all down to you!" she screamed, waving the letter in my face.

I glanced at it but didn't really pay any attention to its content. Instead, I calmly placed it back on the table. I just wanted a cup of tea.

Helen sneered at me and picked up the letter to read again, then burst into tears. "They want immediate payment or we'll be out."

"We've had letters like that before. They don't mean it."

With her eyes now red and bulging with anger Helen pushed the letter in front of my face. "Read it!" she hissed, spitting in my face in the process.

She was right. Steps were being made to repossess the house, and this time it wasn't a threat.

"We'll just have to sell the house," I calmly said.

"And that's it, the end to all our problems, sell the house! Kids, go and play upstairs, Mummy and Daddy need to talk."

Oh boy, here we go again. Helen had been home two minutes, and as soon as she walked through the door she had to start nagging. No doubt planned to ever since landing at the airport.

"It's our only option," I added, passing her a mug of coffee as I walked towards the back door, leaning on the frame.

I lit a cigarette, contemplating a few thoughts of my own. I had to face the fact it was decision time – should I stay or should I go. I knew we had to sell the house before repossession and I knew moving to another house with Helen, rented or otherwise, my life would remain the same. If I left her, I'd miss the children, naturally, but at least I'd be able to visit them whenever that may be. I also had somewhere to escape this fiasco and leave it all behind, and that somewhere was Susan's, so all should work out for the best. Decision made, I'm moving in with Susan. But how do I tell Helen whilst she's so upset?

"Kev, tell me the truth," a voice said from behind, still clutching the letter from the mortgage company, "do you still love me?"

I thought about it for a few seconds but already knew the answer to that question from years ago. "No," I replied.

"So that's it then, we're finished?"

"We were finished a long time ago, Helen, but you've been so wrapped up in your own little world, you couldn't see what was happening to our marriage."

"So it's all my fault, is it?" Helen snapped, chasing back tears.

"No, no, it's our fault."

"And what about Susan, does she come in to it?"

I snapped my head round to look straight at Helen, suddenly feeling nervous as to how on earth she knew about Susan. But I should have known, Helen was holding my mobile, and in her typical suspicious minded way, looked through it only to find all the text messages I'd saved from her.

"I'm not denying it, I've been seeing someone else, but she isn't the real reason why I no longer love you. I only met her last week, and we've been seeing each other whilst you were on holiday."

There, I came out with it. Not the way I planned, but nevertheless I said it.

Helen stood in total shock, eventually blowing a gasket. "Get out of my house, go on, get out now!" she screamed, throwing my mobile at me.

"Oh, it's your house now, is it?" I replied picking up my mobile and the battery cover off the floor.

"It is now you've thrown away your right to be here."

I laughed. "Just because I met someone else?"

"Yes, now pack your things and get out!"

Wow, easier than I thought. I packed a few clothes and belongings, throwing them into the boot of my car and drove off, leaving Helen to wallow in her failed marriage. But I didn't go running to Susan, not straight away.

After an hour or so driving nowhere in particular I found myself driving up the M1 motorway and, as far as I was concerned, heading for Chilwell. For a fleeting moment I thought I was off to be demobilised. Was I dreaming or was I subconsciously thinking of hoping to go back in time and right the wrongs I'd made over the past three-years? God knows. Coming back to reality I turned off the next junction and headed south towards Susan's.

"Hi honey I'm home," I joked as I made my way in to the back garden.

"I never expected you today," Susan said, hanging out the washing.

I gave her a hug and told her the news that I'd left Helen.

"Oh, so I suppose that means you have nowhere to go now," she said, as if she didn't care.

"I thought you said I could move in with you."

She smiled. "I can't keep a straight face. Of course you can move in. C'mon, I have a bottle of red, so let's celebrate your freedom."

Celebration wasn't a word I'd use to describe how I felt. Empty, numb and confused would have sufficed. Nevertheless, I was free of my marriage and the crap that went with it, for the time being, anyway. In the meantime, the grass definitely appeared greener on the other side.

CHAPTER 14

COMING TO TERMS

I thought it was the answer to all my prayers – move in with Susan and live happily ever after. But it never works out that way, does it? Our holiday romance soon diminished not long after I moved in, with a little contribution from Susan's ex-husband, Lionel, taking a keen interest in our relationship and trying his best to wreck it. When the honeymoon period ended it didn't take long for him to interfere, thinking he was the ultimate hard man amongst men, threatening to either break my legs or give a severe beating.

Yep, I had a giggle at his pathetic threats, and at his bravely making them through Susan because he was too scared to say or do anything directly to my face. I guess he was only trying his best to look tough in front of Susan and save face, maybe it was even a feeble attempt to win her back. It wasn't working. After all he was nothing more than a scrawny, alcoholic, chain-smoking, eleven stone (wet through) civilian sissy, who hadn't the courage or nerve to don a uniform and fight for his country. Looking back I am amazed I kept my cool, considering my instability, and that he was one very lucky individual I left alone, rather than enjoy myself ripping him apart.

Not only did I have a jealous prick of an ex-husband to contend with, like a carefully coordinated pincer movement I also had Helen constantly interfering. She'd make any excuse to call me on my mobile – day or night – reminding me that a bill needed immediate attention or play the guilt trip card by using the children as a weapon against me. She'd also put the house on the market two days after I left, and was on the verge of selling to the first couple that viewed it a week later, but hadn't heard anything for over two months. She then received a call from them with an offer, that Helen stupidy accepted and without consulting me.

In doing so she agreed to an offer well below the market value and we only made around £16,000 from the sale, and Helen pocketed the lot. I couldn't help wonder if she knew exactly what she was doing, planning everything to the last detail, including keeping all of the profit from the sale and leaving all previous household bills for me to deal with. As the old saying goes: There's nothing worse than a woman scorned. And boy, was I being punished.

Sunday 12th November 2006. "Kev, your mobile is ringing," Susan shouted from the kitchen.

It was my brother, Ryan. I hadn't spoken to him for years, and he had no idea about Helen and I splitting up.

"Kev, it's Dad, he's been taken into hospital. Don't worry, he's okay, just needs a few tests. He's been quite ill with flu, but no need for you to rush up."

No need to rush up? As soon as he told me I was in my car driving up the M6 towards Wigan. I quickly walked – to the point of almost tabbing – down the many corridors of the old Victorian hospital, not really knowing where I was going. A porter gave me vague directions but they went in one ear and out the other. The clinical smell of disinfectant followed me as I read the numerous signs hanging from the ceilings desperately searching for the one pointing to my dad's ward.

I approached an operating theatre as the double doors burst open, quickly followed by a bed wheeled out with a patient lying on it, still unconscious from anesthetic. As the bed came closer I couldn't help but look at the patient lying motionless. Blood stained sheets covered his body and his face was charred, resembling injuries from an explosion of some kind – maybe a mortar round. His eyes suddenly opened wide, full of fear and dread, looking directly at me. He let out an ear-piercing scream and raised his hands revealing further burns and strips of skin peeling away from what was left of his fingers.

"We didn't see them coming, the bastards ambushed us!" he shouted.

I stood pinned against the corridor wall, not able to move a muscle. I wanted to look away, but couldn't; totally transfixed, staring at this young, petrified soldier. Forced to look at him and absorb his physical pain to compliment my self-induced psychological torture.

"Move out of the way, there's more of your friends due in any moment," someone shouted, but I couldn't see from where.

I looked around and noticed a nurse wearing a blue plastic apron over her desert CS95 combats wheeling the bed, ignoring my presence as she raced past. I started to shake and feel dizzy. The corridor whizzed round and round as David Tennant decided to make an appearance, repeating over and over: *Run away, go on, do it, never to return.*

"Kev, are you okay?" another voice said. It was my brother.

The corridor stopped spinning and I was back in the Wigan Royal Infirmary.

"Yeah fine," I pretended, "I'm trying to find Dad's ward."

"You looked as if you were a million miles away."

I was actually 3,000 miles away, but I didn't expect Ryan to understand, so I kept quiet.

"You know how hospitals get to me. How's Dad?" I asked, quickly changing the subject.

"He's taken a turn for the worse, and is now in intensive care."

"What? I thought he was in a ward waiting for tests."

"He was, but about an hour ago he slipped into unconsciousness and his breathing became extremely shallow."

I couldn't believe it. "How did this happen?"

"I don't know. C'mon, I'll take you to him."

Ryan ushered me to Dad's bedside, and he looked different. He's supposed to be a big strong bruiser, weighing eighteen-stone at 6ft 2in tall. Nothing frightened this man. In the 1970's he worked at various holiday camps employed as a doorman, and used his bulk participating in wrestling matches to raise a few quid.

Singing was his passion, though, in particularly opera and musicals. When Ryan and I were little, Dad would leave us for months on end to pursue his pipe-dream of becoming a famous singer. When he did return home, he showed little interest, other than looking forward to the next few months away at some run down grotty holiday resort.

He'd always wanted to be a professional singer, but couldn't get that much needed break. He even asked his old school friend, Jim Smith (professional name of Jim Dale) for help. Back in the late 1950s Jim made a name for himself singing, making it on the then called hit parade. Jim's successful singing career catapulted him towards acting, where he starred in many Carry On films. Dad always said he suited the haphazard characters he played, simply because he was naturally funny and clumsy at school. Always breaking things and getting into trouble.

Dad tried to contact Jim for help and guidance to find an agent, but only had Jim's agent as a first point of call. Predictably Dad didn't get a reply to any of his telephone calls and letters, so he took a gamble and auditioned for talent shows on television, such as Opportunity Knocks and New Faces that were as popular as today's X-Factor.

Unfortunately he was pipped at the post by a young 16-year-old up and coming comedian named Lenny Henry, so Dad never became that famous, professional singer he always wanted to be. Instead, Mum divorced him for abandoning his responsibilities at home. In his defence he insisted he tried to make a better life for his wife and family. The result was to lose them both.

I looked down at this unrecognisable, skinny white-haired man, arms covered in bruises caused by the medication he took to thin his blood, and an oxygen mask covering his face. I couldn't understand it. What was up with Dad? Was it his heart, lungs or something else? He'd suffered a heart attack when he was only 48-years-old, then three more attacks in later years. He'd also contracted emphysema in his younger years, and was actually born with pneumonia, so I suppose it was inevitable these ailments would catch up with him in his autumn years.

"What did the doctor say?" I asked Ryan.

"Nothing much, other than they'll keep an eye on him and let us know of any changes to his treatment."

"Changes? He's not gonna come out of this, is he?" I asked, having a sudden feeling of foreboding.

"No, I don't think he is," Ryan replied.

"So, what next?"

"Dunno. I suppose we'll just have to wait and see."

Ryan and I talked for a while; mainly about Dad, his condition, and caught up with what we'd both been up to since we last met. He was shocked to hear about Helen and I splitting up, but wasn't totally surprised. He'd always had a feeling it wouldn't last. As he saw it, we were never compatible, and he was right.

A few hours past with nothing to report. Then suddenly Dad sat bolt upright, stared into one corner of the ward, pulled off his oxygen mask and belted out a loud pitch perfect top 'C' as if he was singing his last breath. Only to collapse back onto his pillow and drift back into unconsciousness.

"What happened there?" Ryan asked.

"God knows. He must be dreaming," I replied.

Nurses ran to his bedside to see what the fuss was all about, checking monitors and replacing the oxygen mask over his face.

"I'm going out for a smoke. I'll be back in a few minutes."

When I returned, Maureen, Dad's second wife – the proverbial wicked stepmother – said that doctors had spoken to her when I went out for a cigarette and gave their verdict of Dad's ailments – he had pneumonia. She added it was pointless hanging around because he was sedated and needed plenty of rest to let the antibiotics take their course, so it was best to leave him alone and return the following afternoon.

I checked my watch, it was close to 10 o'clock in the evening. I had a long drive ahead, unlike my brother and stepmother living only a few miles down the road. I said my goodbyes and told my brother to keep me posted of any improvements, should there be any.

I'd rather my brother telephone me because my stepmother and I never really got on. For some reason she had always resented Ryan and I, and hated the fact that Dad had a previous marriage. My dad nicked-named her 'LF' or Little Fart. She was like one of those yapping Yorkshire terriers, constantly getting on your nerves. I remember questioning Dad as to why he married her. He said he needed someone to iron his socks, but I suppose he loved her, in a way.

The long drive back to Susan's gave ample time for my mind to wander. The flashback I had triggered by searching for Dad's ward reminisced to a memory of a patient in the field hospital at Shaibah airfield. I remember seeing a young lad rushed into theatre screaming from his injuries, hands and face burnt from a mortar round exploding only a few feet away. But why did my demon suddenly spring up to mutter through my head: *Run away, go on, do it, never to return?* I thought I'd obeyed by leaving Helen.

Once again doubts filled my head and paranoia started to argue with my subconscious: Maybe you should have stayed with Helen and made it work. My subconscience would then answer: I'd tried that, but I couldn't make it work no matter what I did. I was simply beat. What about the children, how do they feel losing their dad? My paranoia would ask. But they haven't lost their dad, my subconscience would answer, I'm here and always will be for them. But they don't have a stable home now you've left them, my paranoia would say, and now they've lost their home too because of you. Maybe you should have never gone on that dating website, then you wouldn't have met Susan and you'd have had a full time job with the driving agency. You'd still be married to Helen, the kids would have a dad they could rely upon, you'd have a roof over your head and you could have been well on your way paying off your debts by now, my paranoia added.

Over and over my paranoia battled with my subconscious, bickering and arguing over what I did or didn't do. I tried to ignore it, only for these thoughts to be replaced with scenarios of what ifs. When I tried to beat them off, explosions from the war echoed in the back of my mind, followed by David Tennant whispering: *Run away, go on, do it, never to return.*

I had to pull over. I found a petrol station and bought a coffee, which seemed to offer some relief from the storm raging in my head. By the time I made it back to Susan's it was 3.20am. All the lights were out and the street was silent, apart from the sudden cold, icy wind that seemed to run through my body and chill me to the bone, unnerving me a little as I walked towards Susan's front door. Slowly walking up the stairs I crept in to the bedroom and lay on top of the bedcovers fully clothed so as not to wake Susan.

I stared through the gap in the curtains reflecting upon my life. I'd been living a lie, and it had cost me more than money. For five months I'd used what was left on my credit card and it was only a matter of time before I needed to sell my car so I could continue to sustain my make believe life. I was still in huge debt, had no job, and hadn't even told Susan about my employment and financial situation. All she knew was that I'd left Helen for her and only had the house to sell. I started to nod off but was woken by my mobile springing into life.

"Kev, it's Ryan. Dad died about ten minutes ago at twenty-past-three."

I didn't say anything. Instead I cut Ryan off and continued to stare through the gap in the curtains.

"Who was that?" Susan asked half-asleep, curled up in the quilt.

"Nobody. Go back to sleep," I calmly replied.

Dad's death was a huge kick up the arse for me. Returning from Iraq and the consequences that quickly unfolded created a monster within. Thankfully, I could handle the conflict and the shit it threw at me. In fact, I miss it in some ways. The memories and flashbacks of the conflict, however, stirred a dormant demon within. Unbeknown, my subconscience had not only unlocked Pandora's box, it ripped the lid off it creating a foul and festering soup of cancerous thoughts, only to exacerbate memories hidden since childhood.

My mental attitude towards normal life became surreal, and nothing no longer mattered, not even my own family. I'd become a slave to my inner demon, overreacting to situations I could no longer handle, eventually blowing a gasket and allowing my demon to run amuck. Confusion, paranoia and maybe a touch of schizophrenia quickly followed when I found it hard to try and come to terms with losing my job because I was called-out, not being able to find further employment, the inevitable mounting debts, Helen's constant nagging... So on and so on.

Three-years after returning home and trawling through a world of shit, it took my father's death to bring my real world into focus.. I also realised my paranoia wasn't trying to destroy everything I worked hard for – my house, wife and family, or in its own words: *Run away, go-on, do it, never to return.* It was David Tennant telling my demon in my head to bugger off, leave me alone and allow me to come to terms with the sudden transition between arriving home from war and living a civilian life.

Unfortunately I never did have that precious time to contemplate my transition between war and Civvy Street. Instead my life went full throttle from the moment I set foot on tarmac at Birmingham airport. Not only did the aeroplane's landing legs run as it landed, my life did also.

Slowly but surely Susan and I drifted apart, which came as no surprise, and certainly pleased her jealous, alcoholic ex-husband. Although we lived together we never really shared our lives. Susan and I were attempting nothing more than trying to forget our past by desperately filling a void we both created because of our failed marriages. On the rebound, I think it's termed.

Of the five months we lived together four were endured, with Susan fretting over her two teenage daughters staying out late and getting drunk, not coming home at all and getting drunk, or moaning about her clingy nine year-old son who never left her side. I wanted out, but quickly learnt I no longer had anything to fall back on. With my marital home now sold, Helen moved out as soon as she could and rented a house on the other side of town.

Our family home was now empty until the New Year. This was my get out clause: move out of Susan's and make use of the front door key I still had to my house. I packed the little belongings I had and without even saying good bye I drove away from Susan's house for the last time to basically squat in my own house. Whether that was a good idea at the time considering my mental state of mind, I don't know, but I was now in an empty house, echoing past memories dear to me.

I didn't have time to wallow in memories, sad or otherwise. I was far too busy transfixed on grabbing control of my life. I had only two months to find full-time employment before the new owners moved in, aptly on February 2nd 2007, and it was only three weeks until Christmas. That meant it would be almost impossible to find a full-time job before the New Year.

The telephone line and internet connection were still live, and the water, electric and gas only turned off at the mains. Sitting on the living room floor in my empty house, surrounded by a rucksack and a quilt, I plugged in my laptop and started to surf the internet for a job. I knew my only option was to complete applications online and wait to see if I got any interviews in the New Year. In the meantime I had to find something quick. Agency driving was my only option – again.

I listed a few agency telephone numbers and made inquiries to see if they were hiring over the Christmas period. Thankfully some were. By the afternoon I made appointments to complete their obligatory forms and take a tacho and HGV driving awareness test. One of the questions on their forms was, of course, my home address.

Without thinking I put my old address, maybe subconsciously thinking I still lived with my wife and family. I was also asked which shift patterns I was available for and what type of work would suit my routine. I simply answered available immediately for any shift pattern and didn't mind what type of work offered. Be it trunk, multi-drop, tramping, shunting trailers around the yard... I didn't care. I just wanted a job.

All I could do now was wait for a telephone call, hopefully with good news.

My next task was to telephone my mother and beg to use her car for a few months so I could sell mine. Luckily she said yes. Mum couldn't use it, anyway, because of a speeding conviction, caught twice by the same policeman, both within an hour. She already had six points on her licence and was consequently banned for six months.

On my way home – or to the empty house – I dropped in to a few garages and second-hand car dealers to see what I could get for my 6-year-old Vauxhall Vectra. As usual the excuses came out as to why it wasn't worth much: bad time of the year, not the type of car that would sell, high mileage... But I had to sell it – now – and was at the mercy of second-hand car salesmen.

I knew I was going to be ripped off, but I didn't have any choice. My only option was to accept the best offer of the day, and that was a paltry £1,400. Selling the car, however, would give me a huge boost towards a deposit I quickly needed to rent my own place and set up a new home.

I telephoned Mum and told her I was on my way to collect her car. Not having one made me feel as if I'd sold one of my limbs. It was awful not being able to jump into my own vehicle and drive to a destination whenever I pleased. Instead I was forced to rely upon public transport, taking an eternity to travel only fifteen miles to her house. After I'd explained what I was doing – sort of – and getting a lecture in return, I used some of the cash I made from the sale to buy a few supplies such as food, kettle, saucepan, shower-gel and toothpaste. I thought I might as well make myself as comfortable as possible whilst squatting.

When I returned to my empty house I made myself a bacon sandwich and walked through to the dining room. Looking out of the patio doors into the garden I reflected upon the achievements I made within only one day; then questioned myself as to why I didn't do this three bloody years ago? The fading sunlight cast a long shadow across the lawn, and for a brief moment I felt as if I was back home with my wife and children, half expecting Helen to come running in to the living room clutching a handful of bills.

A shudder shot down my spine. The mere thought of Helen standing behind me nagging about unpaid bills covered me in an ice-cold feeling of dread. To clear my mind I fired up the laptop and browsed through a few estate agent websites to see what they had to offer for rent. One site led to another, eventually linking me to sites purely for house letting. For a split second I was tempted to have a sneaky peek at the website from where I met Susan, but thought better of it, thinking what had happened last time.

I spent hours looking at hundreds of flats and houses. So many, in fact, it was difficult to choose. Some were way out of my price range and others far too cheap – reflecting the kind of areas they were in. I had to narrow it down to a price I could afford yet be in a decent area of town, providing I received continuous agency work to pay for it, alongside the usual bills.

By the end of the week I found somewhere suitable to live and within my price range should I be agency driving. But I still didn't have a job, which was most definitely a minimal requirement for any letting agency. I should have known I wouldn't receive a telephone call from any of the driving agencies I signed up to, but undeterred I continued to feel optimistic, putting it down to being so close to Christmas.

Approaching my old house after a shopping trip and visits to letting agencies I noticed a few plant pots dumped by the front door. At first I thought Helen may have dropped them off for the new owners as some sort of welcoming present, but as I opened the front door and entered the living room a television and bits of furniture also appeared. This wasn't good. Clearly the new owners were moving bits and pieces into the house and could easily return at any moment with more furniture.

I was tempted to telephone Helen and find out if the moving-in date had been brought forward, but she'd only get suspicious about my questioning and want to know why I needed to know. My pots and pans and other bits and pieces in the kitchen were still piled neatly next to the draining board. I only hoped the new owners thought they belonged to Helen, otherwise they will wonder where they appeared from. Luckily I always stowed my quilt, wash kit and other items in the boot of my car – or rather my mother's car – every time I went out. Most probably from an old army habit, and from fearing Helen suddenly turning up unannounced, only to see my gear sprawled across the living room.

I searched the house checking the kitchen, garage and upstairs floor, but no furniture or boxes of precious ornaments had been stored. However, I was left no alternative but assume the new owners would return. Decision made, it was far too risky to stay so I had to leave the house, but where do I go? I had no choice but live in Mum's car for the time being. Not the best option considering it was December and only a few weeks until Christmas, but I had no other options.

I gathered my bits and pieces and took a drive to think things through. My plan, as per usual, was failing, and my only future was in the hands of a few driving agencies. As soon as one telephoned to offer just a few days a week, that will be enough to get me into rented accommodation. Until such time my new address was simply various carparks, Volvo V40 estate, anywhere.

My first night in the Volvo wasn't too bad. I had a quilt and the car's heater, so I didn't freeze. Boredom was the problem. And because it was December nights were long, very long. I couldn't even pass the time by reading a book due to the dim interior lights.

By the third night I was getting a tad fed up. Laying back in the driver's seat eating a Whopper burger I subconsciously weighed up my situation: I was jobless, homeless and effectively a bloody tramp. A tramp with a car, granted, and I may have just over £1,300 left from the sale of my car. Nevertheless, I was still homeless and jobless. My only creature comfort was the radio and cassette player. Unfortunately I only had a few cd's at hand so Radio 4 and The Archers were my evenings entertainment.

I didn't mind. It was a blessed release from being nagged at by Helen, or having to put up with Susan or her clingy son. Not forgetting the alcoholic ex-husband constantly telephoning in the early hours demanding that Susan pick up her thirteen-year-old daughter from the gutter because he was also too drunk to drive her back. Nah, I was rid of that life, so living in a borrowed Volvo wasn't a bad place to be after all.

In the meantime my list of entertainment grew each day, with the added bonus of the launderette. My next port of call was the public swimming baths, becoming my source of exercise as well as having use of the showers. By the beginning of the second week I was getting used to my new routine and a worry free life. I even did some Christmas shopping and thought I'd treat the kids to something nice.

My next hurdle was to visit the kids for the first time since splitting with Helen.

I'd spoken to them occasionally on my mobile, but I was now ready to see them now my mind was well and truly within the land of the living. Visiting the kids, however, also meant facing Helen. I knew we weren't exactly going to make amends – far from it. Even if I wanted to I'd burnt that particular bridge months ago. What I was hoping for was to make things right for the children.

I parked outside Helen's house, took a deep breath and braced myself for the onslaught about to be unleashed.

"Oh, look what the cat dragged in!" Helen greeted me with, leaning on the doorframe with her arms folded.

"I thought I'd bring some Christmas presents round for the kids," I said choosing to ignore her comment.

"I don't suppose you have some maintenance for me as well, do you?" she sarcastically remarked.

Without saying anything I waved an envelope in front of her.

"Oh right," she said surprisingly, "I suppose you'd better come in."

Paying Helen my entrance fee, I stepped over the threshold and walked in to the living room. Rachel and James were in the middle of helping Mummy put up the Christmas tree. Watching them brought back happy memories of the time Rachel used to help me with that particular task. Tears welled up in my eyes. I was feeling a strong emotion that I hadn't felt for years, and it came back with a vengeance, hitting me with the force of a cannon ball, reminding me what a total arse I'd been, and the family life I'd thrown away.

"Daddy!" Rachel shouted when she clocked me standing behind her, "Are you staying here for Christmas?" she asked, flinging her arms around my legs in much the same way she did when I returned home from Iraq.

"Well, Daddy might be working, but I'll see what I can do," I replied combing her long blonde hair with my fingers.

James didn't know what to do. He sat next to the tree looking at his big sister hugging a strange man. Tears welled up in his eyes, setting me off again. I could see he wanted to be hugged just like his sister, but appeared to be a little confused as to who I was. I though, was desperate to hug him. I had a shed-load of making up to do, but right there and then it was James that needed a hug the most, and to say sorry for missing his third birthday. I didn't even send him a card, let alone a present. I was so wrapped up with my make believe life with Susan I selfishly opted to forget about my own children.

I managed to prize off Rachel's arms from around my legs and knelt down.

"James, do you want to give Daddy a hug?" I asked softly.

His eyes lit up not unlike the lights on the Christmas tree and ran towards me at full speed with his arms outstretched ready to hug his estranged father. A father he hadn't bonded with yet he seemingly knew I loved him so much and forgave my stupidity. Rachel quickly joined in and both of them showered me with loads of wet kisses and hugs, knocking me off balance and giving them the advantage to hold me down and continue to kiss and hug me.

"Okay, I surrender, I surrender" I screamed in joy.

"Let Daddy get some air, you two," Helen said, letting out a laugh.

They jumped up, noticing the carrier bag I was holding.

"What's in the bag, Daddy?" Rachel asked.

I sat crossed legged and opened the bag.

"Well, first we have a birthday present for a special little boy who was three last month."

James's eyes lit up with his arms out stretched again, this time to grab his present – a big yellow dump truck.

"The other presents are for both of you, but you can't open them until Christmas."

James was too busy opening his birthday present to notice them, but Rachel had that look only daughters can give their dad when they are disappointed. I took out the presents and placed them under the tree, leaving one small present in the bag. I knew Rachel would be looking at my every move, and no doubt half-expected me to conjure a non-birthday present for her, and she was right.

"Here's a little something for my Princess."

I handed her the carefully wrapped package, but instead of unwrapping it she placed it under the tree.

"No, it wouldn't be right," she said shaking her head. "I'll open it on Christmas morning, then I'll have one more present to open."

Helen and I laughed at her noble gesture. My Princess was growing up.

"Fancy a cup of tea?" Helen asked.

"Yeah, that'll be good."

Helen went into the kitchen whilst I helped Rachel colour in a picture of a jungle and showed James how to use his new dump truck. I was in Heaven, and I didn't want it to end.

"I need to tell you something," Helen said returning from the kitchen.

"Oh, here we go."

"No, it's not money, it's something else." Helen looked a tad sheepish, as if wishing she'd never started to tell me."

"Well, what is it?"

Helen beckoned me to go in to the kitchen with her so not to be heard by little ears.

"Well?"

"Sssh, keep your voice down, it's nothing bad. I've met someone else." Helen quickly blurted out, then looked down at the kitchen floor.

"Is that it?" I said without a care. I was actually surprised, shocked and even relieved at the same time, but didn't want to let on.

214

"You're not bothered, then?"

"No, of course not, why should I be, considering what I did."

"That's what I thought, but you really don't mind? I don't want you to turn out to be one of those, you know, jealous ex-husbands and cause problems."

I let out a laugh, thinking of Susan's ex-husband. No way was I like him.

"I can assure you I have no intention of spoiling anything."

"Good. So I can tell Mark you're okay with it."

"Yes, you can," I replied, emphasising my words.

"So, how's you and Susan?"

I paused before answering, but Helen beat me to it. "You've split up, haven't you?"

"How did you know that?"

"I've known you a long time, Kevin, and I know when you have something on your mind. I could see it a mile off. So where are you now, living at your mother's?"

"Yes," I quickly replied, making sure I didn't pause before answering, otherwise she'd smell a rat and know I was lying. "What's this Mark like?" I asked, changing the subject.

Helen told me all about him, although I didn't really give a damn. She continued to tell me where they met and how good he is with the children. He has two children of his own and was also going through a divorce. Quite messy by all accounts.

"What about our house, have the new owners moved in yet?"

I had to ask, and thought it a casual enough question, hoping Helen didn't become suspicious as to why I wanted to know. She didn't and because she knew the couple that bought our house she actually gave me quite a detailed profile on what they were up to and why they were moving furniture into the house, even though it wasn't strictly theirs yet. No money or contracts had been exchanged, so technically the house still belonged to Helen and me.

Their moving-in date was still planned for February 2nd though, and Helen had no reason to believe otherwise. I was tempted to raise the question again as to why she accepted their offer, but thought it best to stay quiet and enjoy this unusual and somewhat unnerving peace.

We both returned to the living room and I played with the children until it was their bedtime. They didn't want me to go, nor did I want to leave them, but a new chapter was beginning in both our lives and there were some major adjustments to make. Reluctantly I left, promising I would see them the following weekend.

Driving to my adopted car park next to a Travelodge I contemplated Helen's news. It was a bit of a surprise, there was no denying that, and I was left with trying to accept the fact that there was no turning back the clock. Helen planning a new life with someone else certainly emphasised the fact our marriage was well and truly over. I also had to deal with the sudden flood of many emotions I thought I'd lost within the ether of madness, and losing the closeness of something dear to me – my children – certainly woke a few dormant feelings to say the least.

The damage had been done and my immediate priorities remained the same: find a job and somewhere to live. Then and only then could I concentrate on rebuilding my life. I was pleased for Helen, and hoped her boyfriend would be a better partner, or maybe husband, than I ever was. And now Helen had someone else to nag, Mark had taken the heat off me a little, for which I am truly thankful.

CHAPTER 15

SWIMMING AROUND A GOLDFISH BOWL YEAR AFTER YEAR

Yet another Christmas had come and gone. Helen allowed me to visit my children in the morning and watch their faces as they opened Christmas presents. The arrival of Helen's boyfriend a few hours later, however, placed us all in a somewhat awkward position, especially when Rachel asked if Daddy could stay for dinner. I simply made my excuse by saying Daddy had to work. She then asked if I was helping Santa deliver presents to other children, which I thought was an excellent idea to exploit and say my goodbyes.

Leaving the children to spend Christmas at a different house and with someone else cut deep into my all ready mixed-up feelings and emotions. It was only the previous Christmas we were all together in our little family unit, surrounded by our furniture and possessions in our own home. I had no alternative but get used to the idea we were no longer a family.

I parked in the car park next to the Travel Lodge I'd been using as my adopted abode to celebrate my first Christmas as a homeless and jobless person. The deserted spaces surrounding me appeared surreal. Usually the car park was almost full, even at weekends, but predictably Christmas day was bound to be quiet, even from those meeting at the Travelodge to carry out their illicit affairs.

I saw in the New Year from the back of my mother's Volvo, celebrating with a bottle of red wine as I heard Big Ben chime on Radio 4. Although those that worked relished the holidays, I couldn't wait for the festive season to end and the world to get back to normal so I could find work and somewhere to live.

When Tuesday eventually arrived I was overdue a shower and fresh clothes. It's all very well living in a car bill and mortgage free, but basic amenities are few and far between. A simple wash and shave was about my limit. And going cap-in-hand to Helen's and use her bathroom wouldn't have been a good move considering she thought I was living at my mother's, and asking my mother to use her bathroom because I was homeless and living in her car wasn't an option either. All that would have done was give her something new to worry about and ample reason to nag.

Freshly showered and shaved, thanks to the swimming baths re-opening after the Christmas break, and a change into fresh clothes, thanks to the launderette opening too, I sat in the driver's seat and started to make my way through the list of driving agency telephone numbers I'd collected on my mobile. As predicted they all said the same: work has slowed down since the Christmas rush and won't pick up again until Easter. I was back to square one, only this time with nowhere to live.

I slumped back into the driver's seat as a feeling of hopelessness overwhelmed my pathetic expectations of self-recovery, of working towards rebuilding my life. I felt useless, and that my life was going to be nothing more than living in the back of a Volvo, having nothing to look forward to and nothing to offer my children.

Sod this. I picked up my mobile and continued to call the rest of the driving agencies I'd previously signed up to. "Yes, we do have work. Enough to keep you busy for a few months, anyway. When can you start?" the cheery voice said.

Music to my ears, although a slight feeling of doubt entered my thoughts. After all, I'd been down this road time and time again, and as usual, let down time and time again.

"Are you sure you have work. I mean, as from now, tonight?" I asked.

"Yes, that's what I said. So you can start tonight, then, at seven?"

Too right I could. I wrote down the details, half expecting nothing will become of the assignment, but decided it was worth going through the motions. After all, I had nothing to lose. I grabbed a few hours kip and at half-past-six made my way to the distribution centre, which was only a few miles from my adopted car park. My duties were nothing more than a trailer swap from the truck stop at Carnforth, which was the same destination I went to with the last agency.

Walking into the transport office I expected the typical reception agency drivers usually get from distribution centres, and I was right. Only this time I didn't care about the bad feeling or resentment from either the office staff or full time drivers. I was only too pleased I had some work, and knew that as soon as I'm free of the gatehouse I'll be on my own. So putting up with the usual jibes and insults for a few minutes was a small sacrifice to pay. I took my paperwork, hooked up to my trailer and made my way up the M6 hoping I wouldn't have a repeat performance of last time.

When I returned – flashback free – I was given my start times for the rest of the week, and on the Friday I was offered start times for the following week, and so on and so on. I'd made it – albeit agency work – but at least it was continuous. I could now put the money I received from the sale of my car to good use and find somewhere to live.

Within a couple of weeks I found a small one bedroom flat to rent, ironically in the town I was born. Moving in didn't take long. In fact it took all of twenty minutes to move all my possessions into the flat. All I owned was a laptop, a rucksack full of clothes, small collection of army relics and a few other bits and pieces thrown into bin liners.

As I fetched the last of my possessions from the car and piled them on the living room floor, for a brief moment I looked outside the window as the crisp, clear winter sun shined through the dusty glass. I could see my old junior school and the park next to it where we made up games to occupy our young, innocent minds for hours on end on those long, hot summer days in the mid 1970s.

My mind wondered back to being that innocent eight-year-old child playing in the park. I remember thinking, as that child did I ever glance towards the main road, at the petrol station where my flat now stood and imagine in the future that is where I shall live as a grown-up after I've been to war and made a mess of my life?

I lit a cigarette and fast forwarded two-years to the summer of 1976 – the time my childhood memories suddenly changed from playing happy families to playing dungeons and dragons. At the age of ten I suddenly moved away from my childhood home. I didn't have a clue as to what was happening, other than Ryan and I were leaving Daddy behind and we didn't have time to say goodbye. Ryan was only six-years-old and thought it was one big adventure, but I remember something wasn't right. Something had gone drastically wrong between Mum and Dad and this was the outcome.

We ended up living in Grantham, Lincolnshire, above a dark and gloomy, damp antique shop where my mum worked during the day. The three bedroom flat was big, as far as Ryan and I were concerned, and we had great fun playing hide-and-seek amongst the many cubbyholes and musky antique wardrobes stored in the spare bedroom. In the evening Mum worked at a pub around the corner to earn extra money so we could eat, having no alternative but to leave her two sons home alone to watch television. Of course, we promised to be in bed by 8 o'clock.

One evening, whilst working behind the bar, Mum met a guy, Sid. They must have hit it off pretty quick because within a few months we were living in his house. Fantastic, a new house to live in with a huge garden to explore, rather than living in a murky old flat above a crummy antique shop. Sid used to be in the RAF and trained as a pilot in the mid 1950's. After years of training and flying jets such as the Vampire and Buccaneer, he qualified to fly for Bomber Command – Victor bombers (nuclear and conventional) and fuel tanker variants. A few years later, and getting bored of flying slow aeroplanes – as he put it – Sid decided to retrain and have a go at becoming a fast jet pilot, ending his career as a Squadron Leader flying F4 Phantoms in 54 Squadron.

The last two years of his service ended, unfortunately, working from a desk, and not through choice. He trashed a Phantom jet fighter on take-off. Thankfully he and his navigator ejected, ending up with only spinal injuries and a burnt face. His boss, however, decided that he thought it best to keep Sid well away from anything with wings for the foreseeable future. In other words, he didn't want to risk Sid playing with the shiny new Tornado fighter bombers due to be delivered.

He retired in 1975 and must have been forgiven for his little mishap trashing a multi-million pound jet fighter when the RAF presented him with a painting of the aeroplane he crashed, as well as the usual trophies and gold clock. He also left with a shorter spine, losing an inch due to the sudden departure from his F4 Phantom.

Sid was a fantastic sort-of-stepdad. I say sort of because Mum and Sid never married. Of course he continued his interest in aviation when he retired by making many, many flying models, including Spitfires, Hurricanes and WW1 biplanes powered by tiny CO_2 engines. He even taught me how to design and build my own rubber band powered model aeroplane out of balsa wood.

One year passed, then the next, then third and forth. I was finally settled for the first time since the age of ten. I even managed to pass a few CSE's and O'Levels and looked forward to getting a job with a roofing company. But no, by the summer of 1982 the bubble had burst. I was now sixteen and just before leaving school my woodwork teacher asked a group of us if we wanted to go parachuting to celebrate finishing our exams. Of course, being sixteen, we all thought this was a great idea.

My old woodwork teacher, Mr Pratt, was one of those outward-bound types. Always doing something, be it whitewater rafting, mountain climbing or shark wrestling. On one occasion he caught a group of us smoking by abseiling down the side of the gym building. We noticed a rope drop between us and a few seconds later Mr. Pratt came hurtling down. "Aha, caught ya!" he shouted as he landed. Fair play, he caught us red handed.

After our parachuting weekend I couldn't wait to tell Mum and Sid all about it. But as I walked down the cul-de-sac where we lived I noticed a grey Land Rover parked outside the house blocking the driveway. Walking nearer and nearer I could see Mum and a man loading the back of the Land Rover with cardboard boxes and bits of furniture. I then noticed my quilt being thrown in the back. My excitement of telling Mum and Sid about my weekend suddenly flushed away as I ran towards the house.

"Hey, what's going on?" I shouted just as the strange man climbed into the Land Rover and drove past without even looking at me.

"It's okay, nothing to worry about," Mum said standing at the front door. Before I could say anything she added, "get the rest of your stuff from upstairs, he'll be back soon for the last load."

I stood motionless and confused as to why this was happening, yet knew the outcome – we were moving out – and Mum wanted to leave before Sid came home from his usual Sunday afternoon pint. Mum's reasons for leaving Sid were her own, and she obviously had good reason, but I was now experiencing a feeling I first had when Mum left Dad. Before I could grasp what was happening and where we were going, Ryan and I were sitting in the back of an old Land Rover hurtling down the A1. An hour later I was standing outside a dreary council house back in my birthtown, Wellingborough, Northamptonshire.

My mum's new boyfriend, Derek, was now my new sort-of-stepdad, and completely different to Sid. He never became a father figure. In fact, he gave the impression Ryan and I were in the way. Then suddenly Ryan developed mental health issues, and after a series of appointments with a child psychiatrist his state of mind was fragile to say the least, maybe caused by moving to different houses and having another new stepdad. The conclusion was Ryan needed stability and Dad recommended that he should live with him in Wigan. I, however, thought Ryan's mental health issues were a tad easier to fathom and didn't need to look any further than Derek.

In 1982 Derek was a 40-year-old, 6ft 2 tall, 16-stone brute, and used his bulk on numerous occasions against Ryan and me, simply to get his own way. We were even banished to our bedrooms and not allowed out until the following morning, except to go to school and college, in which I enrolled simply to get out of the house. When we came home, and as soon as Derek arrived from work, the vicious circle started again. If we made the slightest sound, even flushing the toilet, Derek would race upstairs and throw a hissy fit. To make matters worse, Mum was none the wiser to Derek's antics.

As soon as Ryan was gone – which tore Mum apart, but she believed in what the child psychiatrist said, and knew, deep down, living with Dad was his best option for a stable environment – Derek and I started to clash. He began to construct any excuse for me to leave home, so at weekends I would stay with friends to keep out of the way, or, if they were out, would rough it on park benches or around the back of shops.

Anywhere was better than staying at home when Derek was mooching around.

Within a few months our clashes became intolerable. I'd had enough and told Mum I wanted to leave home. Mum was still unaware of Derek's behaviour, and I certainly didn't want to tell her that the love of her life was being a twat, so I convinced her, even at the age of seventeen, I was old enough to look after myself. Of course, that was far from the truth, but I made up my mind and even devised a grand plan. By the autumn of 1983 I finished my college course and managed to find a full time job at a shoe factory. And within a few weeks I saved enough money to rent a room in a house share.

Within a couple of months, however, I had to admit to myself that I was far too young to live on my own, but would never admit it to Mum. So I gave her my excuses that I missed my brother and wanted to also live with Dad. Being a little confused, Mum telephoned Dad and asked if I could live with him. Surprisingly he said yes. Maybe he felt a tad guilty for deserting us both in our early years, but he said yes, so Mum drove me up to Wigan.

Three years later, and being a bit more mature, I decided to have another go leaving the nest once again, only this time on my terms rather than feeling I was being bullied into leaving home. So I returned to where I was happiest – Grantham. What I really wanted to do was return to the summer of 1982 and put right where it all went wrong, including living at home with my sort-of-stepdad, Sid, but it wasn't to be. He'd met someone else and sold his house to start a new life managing a pub. Sadly, Sid died of a brain tumour in March 2000.

Looking back on my childhood, and with its trials and tribulations, I have unwittingly learnt to accept the fact nothing good will last. To the extent of always anticipating some kind of upheaval in the future, be it my fault or of others, only to have an impossible compulsion to quantum leap back in time and put right where I perceived it to have gone wrong. Fast forward to staring out of the window of my one bedroom flat, I'm once again enthralled within my forgotten wish. Only this time it is a desire to put right everything I fucked up since landing on tarmac at Birmingham airport 26th April 2003.

Returning home after fighting a war was a major transition I simply couldn't handle, subsequently expecting the worst to happen. It did – big time. Hopefully, now that I have rediscovered the fear created during my childhood, I can finally put the war and my childhood memories, lying deep within my subconscious mind, well and truly behind. Having my own flat and an almost regular income from HGV driving certainly helped towards rebuilding a new life.

Over the following year I concentrated on making a home, having my children stay on a regular basis and starting a repayment plan for the debts I still had hanging around my neck. Flashbacks continue to reoccur from time to time, and that is something I will have to put up with for the rest of my life, apparently. But on the whole my new fresh start didn't look too bad after all.

In June 2009, I was still trying to concentrate on rebuilding a new life when my past decided to raise its ugly head from a dormant snooze, not unlike an alcoholic convinced that his first glass of wine in years wouldn't do any harm, only to drink himself into oblivion.

At the age of twelve my eldest son, Stephen, from my first marriage, couldn't keep his eyes off the television as the war in Iraq unfolded before him, hoping to catch a glimpse of his dad alive and well. Ever since watching those images and knowing his dad was out there, he has wanted to join up. Answering to an advertising campaign he was invited to attend an open day at Wollaton Park, Nottingham.

Stephen wanted me to go with him; of course, I jumped at the chance.

They were all there – Army, Navy, RAF and Marines – all strutting their stuff. Artillery, Engineers, Cavalry and Infantry Regiments, all proudly showing off their weapons and hardware for civvies and ex-servicemen to climb over or play with. I was in squaddie heaven.

As I drooled over the artillery pieces, weapons and armoured vehicles, Stephen and I came across the RAF Regiment tent where I almost drowned drooling over a GPMG set up on the ground for civvies to play with – unloaded, of course. I jumped at the chance and dropped down behind it, picked up the butt and instinctively carried out the weapon's drills accompanying this particular weapon.

"Used one of these before?" a voice asked.

"Just a few times," I replied.

Before I knew it I was swapping stories with a young Lieutenant about our tours in Iraq and how much I missed the TA. Not ten minutes later I'd signed up for a recruit selection weekend at RAF Cottesmore. Stephen, however, decided that a career in the armed forces wasn't for him and wanted to continue with his college studies. I, on the other hand, couldn't wait to start training with the RAF Regiment, which isn't dissimilar to the infantry. Their role being to protect airfields and aircraft installations, which includes patrols covering hundreds of square miles, not just inside a perimeter fence.

When the day arrived for me to start my recruit selection weekend I was as excited as Jeremy Clarkson about to test-drive the latest Aston Martin. My excitement brought with it a flood of memories filling my head with previous training weekends I had with the TA. After I received my instructions from the guardroom at the main entrance I almost skipped through the gates and ran to the Regiment's shed secreted in a corner of the base.

Although it wasn't the army, and certainly not the REME, I still felt at home. As soon as I walked into the building I noticed other candidates sitting around a table in the bar; about half a dozen or so sat in silence, nervous about what to expect. I, on the other hand, knew exactly what to expect and made myself a cup of tea before joining the other candidates to break the ice and put them at ease.

By my third selection weekend it dawned on me that something was wrong. I had simply attempted to create a substitute for the TA, subconsciously desperate to relive the past. I never realised my mindset was still delicate, even after leaving the TA four years earlier, and merely stepping back to a time I was most happy wasn't concentrating on the future. I took this thought as yet another kick up the arse, I had to forget the past. So my career in the RAF Regiment was short-lived.

A few months after moving into my flat I finally found full time employment, and I'm pleased to say it wasn't HGV driving. I was employed as a workshop/parts controller in a garage that repaired and maintained cars and light commercial vehicles. So you could say I had finally settled down and have a happy ending to my story. But no, it's not quite as simple as that.

One of my duties at the garage was to collect and deliver customer vehicles. I even collected them from the same street Helen and I had our marital home. Sometimes a car may need collecting from the other side of town, but I could not help but make a detour and park outside my old house to endure a flood of predictable, yet painful memories. It was if I was addicted to them and needed a fix from time to time to satisfy my craving for the past.

On one occasion, parked outside my old house, a flashback I had before came rushing to the forefront of my mind: I looked up and down the street, as if to remind me that I am actually home from Iraq and it wasn't all a dream. I noticed the bedroom curtains were closed, and walking up my driveway seemed to take an age.

Reaching the doorstep I was greeted with a half-chewed mouse left behind by 'Digby,' our cat. It was if he knew I was arriving and left it as some kind of welcome home present. Careful not to tread on the remains, I could see myself about to ring the doorbell but found I was frozen to the spot. I couldn't do it. For some unknown reason it didn't seem right.

Before further flashbacks decided to jump to the forefront of my mind I would continue my journey to collect the customer's car for service or repair. I continue to make these detours and torture myself by parking outside my old house, even though I no longer work for the garage. After two years working for the most cantankerous, obtrusive, arrogant, obnoxious, selfish, two-faced twat I have ever had the misfortune to work for, I simply had to leave, otherwise I'd have strangled him.

His ignorance knew no bounds. He even interrupted me during the two minute Silence on 11th November – Remembrance Day. Bang on the first gong of Big Ben at 11am on the 11th day of the 11th month, he insisted he wanted to know, at that precise moment, where I had misplaced some paperwork. After ignoring him for two minutes, during which he grew increasingly agitated because I wouldn't answer his questions, I explained the error of his ways. His reply was: "The world continues to turn, and I have a business to run."

Yep, I was speechless too.

He simply had no respect whatsoever for those that had fallen in past and present wars, yet arrogantly enjoyed the freedom they fought and died to protect. Subsequently I left the garage, which placed me once again in a somewhat precarious position, unemployment. I had no alternative but to use my HGV licence and return to agency driving. Within a week I not only returned to driving a truck for a living, ironically I found myself at the same place I worked prior to the collapse of my world with Helen.

Predictably, memories came flooding back. Memories I should have laid to rest a long, long time ago, but they were far too strong to ignore. And there I was, walking around the same yard, bumping into the same staff, even driving the very same bloody trucks I did when I still had a wife and family. It was if my addiction to relive the past hit an all-time high, overdosing upon past memories made physical by my surroundings.

Sunday, February 2nd 2014. Eleven years after I received the news I was about to be called-out to fight in Iraq, here I am sitting in front of my laptop writing down these words. I have had plenty of time to reflect upon the past years, to the point of realising I was completely to blame for the upset I caused and the demise of my marital home. However, in my defence, I was dealing with the sudden and brutal transition from war to home within a few hours, then the relentless scheme of events that quickly unfolded; I questioned my own sanity and the position in which I found myself.

I have since come to terms with memories of Iraq and the influence of the conflict upon my present state of mind. My childhood memories and their influence upon my adult subconscious, however, remain totally alien. They possess a part of me that quietly laid dormant for decades prior to my deployment, and it took surviving a war and returning home to release that demon; when released it became far too strong to simply ignore, let alone destroy.

I have a sneaky feeling some of you may think I'm nothing more than a lunatic swimming around a goldfish bowl, desperate to continue to relive my past over and over again, refusing to believe it no longer exists. Well yes, you'd be right. And yes, maybe I was in need of some kind of psychiatric help. But the damage I caused has been done, and the only way I can live with it is feeling secure knowing I have the past to cling onto. And although I failed to recognise it at the time, David Tennant screaming in my head was actually my saviour, desperate to protect me from my real demon and prevent me from self-destruction.

As for the future, nah, you can keep it. Tried it, didn't like it. Besides, I have the past to look forward to. And although the storm inside my head has subsided a little, I continue to be torn between the present and my urge returning to 26th April 2003. In the meantime I shall continue living comfortably numb.

A MOTHER'S FEAR

(WRITTEN BY JUDITH JACQUES)

Kevin never returned to Iraq, although he suffered continuous flashbacks of his experiences and the abominable sights he witnessed. And I know, as a mother, there is something deep within his subconscious mind that has been damaged beyond repair. Although, on first appearance, he appears to be fine and dandy, peel away a thin veneer and his mind, body and soul are screaming out for answers: Why do I feel like this? Why has my world collapsed? Why does my country hate me so much? Am I being punished? And because he's a typical British soldier, he won't talk about his mental health. 'We simply don't do that', he'd say.

His spirit seems to drift away from time to time, especially towards the anniversary of the conflict and throughout the time of his tour. Maybe he's searching for answers within his subconscious or drifts back to the war simply because he can't stop it happening. Or maybe Kevin is trying to come to terms with the war and the fact he came home alive when many of his comrades didn't.

Whatever the reasons he will now be scarred for life, just like my dad when he returned home from Burma in 1945 after fighting the Japanese, and like his dad when he returned home after fighting the Germans in 1918. Three completely different conflicts, but all carry with them the same premise – death and destruction of human lives. And for those that survive, a lifetime of flashbacks, frustration and anger closely follow each and every day, reminding them the countless horrors of their war.

What I cannot understand, as a mother and a civilian, is that if anyone asked Kevin if he would go to war again, his answer would be, without question or hesitation, yes. After all, once a soldier, always a soldier. And if he did, all I can do as a mother is the same as before – sit at home and worry. But isn't that what mothers do, what all mothers of fighting men have done since the dawn of civilisation? God save us!

THE FALLEN

With proud thanksgiving, a mother for her children,
England mourns for her dead across the sea,
Flesh of her flesh they were, spirit of her spirit,
Fallen in the cause of the free.

Solemn the drums thrill; Death august and royal
Sings sorrow up into immortal spheres,
There is music in the midst of desolation
And a glory that shines upon our tears.

They went with songs to the battle, they were young,
Straight of limb, true of eye, steady and aglow,
They were staunch to the end against all odds uncounted;
They fell with their faces to the foe.

They shall not grow old, as we that are left grow old;
Age shall not weary them, nor the years condemn,
At the going down of the sun and in the morning
We shall remember them.

They mingle not with their laughing comrades again;
They sit no more at familiar tables of home;
They have no lot in our labour of the daytime;
They sleep beyond England's foam.
But where our desires are and our hopes profound,
Felt as a well-spring that is hidden from sight,
To the inner most heart of their own land they are known
As the stars are known to the night;

As the stars that shall be bright when we are dust,
Moving in marches upon the heavenly plain;
As the stars that are starry in the time of our darkness,
To the end, to the end, they remain.

The Fallen: Laurence Binyon (1914)

GLOSSARY
(AND SQUADDIE JARGON)

Abbreviations

AFAB	Army Families Advice Bureau
AFV	Armoured Fighting
AWOL	Absent Without Leave
AWS	Army Welfare Services
BG	Battle Group
BLP	Back Loading Point
BST	British Summer Time Centre
CBA	Combat Body Armour
CO	Commanding Officer
CP	Command Post
Cpl	Corporal
Cpt	Captain
CRARRV	Challenger Armoured Recovery & Repair Vehicle
CS95	Combat Soldier uniform 1995
DIV	Division
DPM	Disruptive Pattern Markings
DSG	Division Support Group
EFI	Expeditionary Forces Institute
GD's	General Duties
GMT	Greenwich Mean Time
GPMG	General Purpose Machine Gun
GPS	Global Positional System
HGV	Heavy Goods Vehicle
HQ	Head Quarters

IA	Immediate Action
IPE	Individual Personal Equipment
ISO	International Shipping Organisation
LAD	Light Aid Detachment
LAW	Light Anti-tank Weapon
L/Cpl	Lance Corporal
LI	Light Infantry
LSW	Light Support Weapon
LSSA	Longer Separated Service Allowances
MOD90	Ministry of Defence 1990s (identification card)
MOD	Ministry of Defence
MP	Member of Parliament
NBC	Nuclear Biological Chemical
OC	Officer Commanding
PW	Prisoner of War
QMS	Quarter Master Sergeant
RAF	Royal Air Force
RDC	Regional Distribution Centre
REME	Royal Electrical & Mechanical Engineers
RLC	Royal Logistic Corps
RPG	Rocket Propelled Grenade
RTMC	Reinforcements Training Military Centre
2RTR	2nd Royal Tank Regiment
SA80A2	Small Arms 1980s MkII personal assault rifle
SAM	Surface to Air Missile
SDG	Scots Dragoon Guards
Sgt	Sergeant
Ssgt	Staff Sergeant
TA	Territorial Army
US	United States
VM	Vehicle Mechanic

GLOSSARY

Terminology

Bergen	Soldiers Rucksack
Bluey(s)	Letters
Casevac	Casualty evacuation
Chogie	Locals / Enemy
Civvy	Civilian
Doss Bag	Sleeping Bag
Fedayeen	Saddam's Militia
Gas Gas Gas	Verbal NBC alarm
MoD Plod	MoD civilian security
Noddy suit	NBC Suit
Rat Pack	Ration Pack
Recy Mech	Recovery Mechanic
Sat	Satellite (telephone)
Snowdrop	RAF Police
Trog	Driver
Zulu	Greenwich Mean Time

www.eleusinianpress.co.uk